Praise for *The Power of*

'A simple yet profound book that helps us understand the world of colors and our ability to better comprehend the world around us, and our inner world. It offers wonderful ways to integrate this knowledge for the benefit of every aspect of our lives.'
Alexandra Madorski, Reiki Master and practitioner in color therapy.

'Noah Goldhirsh's book is full of knowledge. It opened my eyes and helped me discover a magical world of colors around me. This book gave me tools to help myself and my family and to use colors in my daily life.'
Rinat Zelig-Alfia, practitioner in Traditional Chinese Medicine

'This is a fascinating book, rich in knowledge that awakens awareness and teaches many natural treatment methods through the use of colors. I apply everything I have learned from this book, and I see how the conscious use of colors with children gives amazing results. I highly recommend it.'
Liel Zur, color therapist, Reiki Master, specialist in child care, specialist in Bach Flower Remedies.

'I recommend everyone to enjoy the extensive practical knowledge in Noah Goldhirsh's amazing book, which introduces us to the colors in our world, and teaches us to use them for in-depth self-diagnosis as well as for treating a variety of problems with methods that are easy to apply. This is a wonderful book that is a real pleasure to read and use.'
Dina Cohen, holistic therapist, Reiki Master.

'This book provides a great way to learn to diagnose and create new and diverse treatment methods. The book is clear and accessible to everyone and allows a deep understanding of the environment through the different color circles. A wonderful therapeutic tool that helps patients access their emotional world.'
Lena Madorsky, Reiki Master and practitioner in color therapy

I am grateful to all light entities, all my spirit guides.
I am grateful for the enormous world of knowledge
you have opened up for me; for your exquisite help
at all stages of my life; thank you for being with me always –
thank you.

This book is dedicated to those I love,
You are the light of my life, beloved with all my heart.

This book was written by Noah Goldhirsh. The diagnostic methods and treatment explained in the book are the opinions and suggestions of the author, based on her knowledge and many years of experience.

This book constitutes neither a medical nor a therapeutic prescription and does not set out to replace conventional treatments. A qualified doctor and Color Therapy specialist should be consulted for accurate diagnosis, guidelines and treatment.

This book presents descriptions and the effects of Color Therapy treatment under the heading: "Personal Experiences". Clients' details have been completely changed to protect their privacy and the stories have no connection whatsoever to any living person.

The Power of
COLORS

Discover the path to self-healing and personal
transformation through colors

Second Edition

Noah Goldhirsh

Translated from the Hebrew by Noel Canin

Hammersmith Health Books
London, UK

First published in Hebrew in 2019 and in English in 2020 by eBook Pro, Israel
This second edition first published in English in 2023
by Hammersmith Health Books
– an imprint of Hammersmith Books Limited
4/4A Bloomsbury Square, London WC1A 2RP, UK
www.hammersmithbooks.co.uk

British Library Cataloguing in Publication Data: A CIP record of this book is available from the British Library.

Print ISBN 978-1-78161-252-1
Ebook ISBN 978-1-78161-253-8

Commissioning editor: Georgina Bentliff
Translated by: Noel Canin
Designed and typeset by: Julie Bennett of Bespoke Publishing Ltd
Cover design by: Madeline Meckiffe
Cover images by: Miiisha and Mycteria/Shutterstock
Index by: Dr Laurence Errington
Production: Deborah Wehner of Moatvale Press Ltd
Printed and bound by: TJ Books, Cornwall, UK

Contents

INTRODUCTION TO THE SECOND EDITION

It is always exciting to share the knowledge I have acquired over the years with people interested in learning how to change their lives for the better.

Since The Power of Colors was first published, thousands of people around the world have used it, and many people have written to me to say how much they have enjoyed the book and how it has helped them in their daily lives. Now this book is being published in a new and expanded edition, which contains more knowledge about diagnoses through palm paintings and about working with color cards.

Our world is changing rapidly and the most significant things we can do to live well are to get to know ourselves deeply, follow our unique path, realize our abilities and help those around us.

May this book help you to illuminate your inner and outer paths with all the wonderful colors of the universe!

THE BIRTH OF THIS BOOK

Over thirty years of studying and working in the field of complementary medicine have culminated in the writing of this book. Over the course of these years, worldviews on spiritual and material reality have changed and today more and more people acknowledge the importance of spirituality in our lives. Treatments, lectures, courses and workshops on spiritual issues—which used to be considered taboo—have now become public knowledge. The spiritual way of thinking, once considered alien and extraordinary, is now acknowledged and respected, and my personal world and the world around me have changed unrecognizably.

When I was a little girl, I was always asked what I wanted to be when I grew up. Looking back today, I am amazed by that little girl's connection to spiritual and cosmic knowledge; that child who wandered alone among the trees in the woods surrounding the neighborhood houses, gazing at the sky, the earth, plants and trees, talking to animals, and dreaming of healing people. I imagined sick people coming to me to be healed. The journey toward spiritual and practical healing became my way of life and I use many diverse methods of healing, teaching and conveying the knowledge I receive from the Universe. For over 33 years I have researched and specialized in the methods of Healing, Color Therapy, Healing with Crystals, Bioenergy, Reflexology and Bach Flower Remedies, as well as Reiki, Reincarnation, Super Sensory Vision and Communication With Entities, the Teachings of the Native Americans, Grandmother Twylah's Color Circle, Feng Shui and Complementary Veterinary Medicine.

I have researched in depth and developed and used my unique practical and spiritual methods for effective treatments with the healing powers of the colors in our world, and these unique diagnostic and healing methods are detailed in my book. I have focused on creating a handbook that you can use to connect with the theory of light and color, learning new things about yourself and the surrounding world. The Laws of Physics and Spirit show us that the Universe consists of energy and light, and my wish for us all is that we may connect to the light of the universe and live a beneficial life of enlightenment and joy. May this book light the way toward the infinite, colorful light of the cosmos.

THE COLORS OF OUR WORLD IN DAILY LIFE

We are born into a colorful, diverse world where we are surrounded by the hues of plants, trees, earth, water, sky, and the creatures that live around us. The science of physics proves that our world is made of light frequencies and each color has its own wavelength. Our bodies are built to absorb color frequencies and, consequently, we immediately respond to the presence of light and color, which directly affects our physical and mental health.

Throughout history, humanity has used color in varying ways and each culture has techniques for using color according to its beliefs. In ancient techniques of color healing, various colors would be applied to the body; the person's illness would determine the color of the food eaten; materials of various colors would be used for healing; gems and crystals would be placed on the body and mandalas drawn for health and recovery. The indigenous Native Americans would paint their faces and bodies in various colors according to events in their lives, and each color had spiritual, mental and practical meaning. To this day, in India Color Therapy is used by means of gems, and wonderfully colorful clothing and food, emphasizing the third eye with a colorful dot. Tibetans paint amazing mandalas made of colored sand in order to attain healing and spiritual transcendence; doctors of Traditional Chinese Medicine refer to the color of clothing and food; and Judaism refers to the High Priest who wore twelve colorful, precious stones on his tunic. Throughout human history, great significance has been attributed to skin color and the color of eyes and hair. For many years, dark-skinned people were seen as slaves without rights because of the color of their skin and, to this day, a person's skin color often determines how society relates to them.

Humanity's attitude to color has shifted over the years, but color is nonetheless an inseparable part of our personality and culture.

Thanks to the wonders of technology today, an abundance of colors can be produced with ease and speed, and so it is easier and simpler to buy many items in varying colors, but most people are still unaware of the ability of color to bring about physical and mental healing and balance. When people learn to know colors beyond their daily uses and become acquainted with Color Therapy, they discover that healing through color is effective and useful as a therapeutic tool in itself as well as a support for any other kind of treatment. We can enjoy the healing balancing properties of colors in many diverse ways, and the most basic way to use color is by eating healthy natural food of varying colors every day. In order to enjoy the full spectrum of colors, I recommend spending time daily in natural surroundings and taking pleasure in sunlight. We can choose a stone or stones in colors that suit us and keep them in a pocket or wear them on a chain, a bracelet or a ring and, of course, we can wear different colored clothing every day in order to reinforce our immune system. In order to bring the whole color spectrum naturally into the home each day, we can hang crystals at the windows to reflect diffracted sun rays. In order to arrive at the best results and create a harmonious, healthy home, I recommend painting the home in colors that suit us, adding accessories in colors compatible with the different areas of the home, and using the art of Feng Shui and personally harmonious colors. When turning to Color Therapy, there are many ways of using color in the various kinds of therapy available throughout the world. The color spectrum has enormous significance in our world, and we can use it to improve all aspects of our lives. This book is a collection of data I have acquired over a period of thirty years on the subjects of light, color and spirituality in our lives and it provides tools for physical and mental healing through the use of color. I believe that accurate diagnosis is an important and powerful aspect of any treatment. This book details a number of diagnostic methods and treatments developed to help us all get to know ourselves, understand the meaning of our lives, how best to manifest our abilities and use color as a tool for improving physical and mental health. I am certain that in the years to come we will increasingly understand the meaning of colors and will be able to turn the use of Color Therapy into a practical tool for daily use and that is available to everyone. The ability to use colors is inherent in all of us from the moment we come into the world. Over the course of the years as a therapist and teacher, I've realized that the first instinct of any human being, "a gut feeling," is wonderfully precise. When we are attracted to a color, we should relate to it as a mental and physical need. The "accepted fashion," which changes according to designers' whims, tends to disrupt our basic sense of color and our energetic choices, so it is advisable for all of us to listen to our inner voice, integrate our intuitive knowledge and learn how to use colors that best suit us in every situation of our lives, even if they aren't "fashionable."

Over the years I've seen many people heal with the help of color, for example: One of my patients managed to sleep better after years of insomnia, when she made massive use of the color blue. A patient who suffered from terrible back pain at night wrapped his hips in a green, pink and orange scarf and the pain immediately subsided. A patient who suffered from hoarseness put a chain of turquoise stones around her neck and the hoarseness vanished within five minutes.

Animals also respond wonderfully to color. Many years ago, I was visiting a client whose five-year-old dog was restless, angry, couldn't sleep or eat properly, and peed in the house. The dog's collar was red, and she slept on a red and blue blanket in a bad location in terms of Feng Shui. I advised my friend to replace the dog's collar with a pink one, give her a green blanket to sleep on and change her place in the house. Within a day of carrying out the changes, the dog became significantly calmer, stopped peeing in the house and started to eat and sleep better.

Using color is cheap and simple to do and the results are incredible. When you don't know which color to choose, check the books, ask a Color Therapy specialist, and listen to your inner voice. Finally, I wish to clarify the use of the term "Indians": In Hebrew, this term denotes Native Americans. The English term "Indians" was accepted for many years, although its origin was mistaken: When Christopher Columbus arrived in America, he mistakenly thought he'd reached India and so he called the indigenous people "Indios." The label eventually became "Indians" in the American language, later perceived as derogatory. In recent years, they've stopped using the term, among others. First Nation tribes self-identify as Native American Indigenous Peoples or First Nation Peoples.

THE USE OF COLORS IN DAILY LIFE

When wishing to use color in daily life, the simplest way is to wear different colored clothing according to our needs. During my years of teaching Color Therapy, I have developed unique teaching and diagnostic methods. In order to prove the effects of colors on the human body, I choose a particular color each week, during which all my students wear mainly this color. The students are asked to note down their experiences over the course of the week, paying particular attention to their physical and emotional sensations and feelings, the quality of their sleep and their eating habits. When the students convene for their lesson at the end of the week, they discover that they share similar physical and emotional experiences as a result of the consistent use of a particular color during the week. These experiences relate to the classic effect of a color on body and mind and on each one's personal Wheel of Colors. When we wear a particular color, it has direct impact on our body and mind. To a large extent, the fashion industry dictates the colors we choose to wear and combine. When we are freed from the conventions of dress and color common to our environment at a particular time, each one of us tends to choose the color that suits us. When our choice of clothing and color is unlimited, we choose the color our body needs, without taking fashion into account; however, since we are not unaffected by the environment, it is relatively easy to influence our choices. Our body relates to colors as it does to any energetic nourishment, and so we must understand that when we intuitively choose the colors we wear, the color we choose is actually the color we need at that moment in order to function in the best way possible. When we use a particular color over time, the body grows accustomed to it and becomes "addicted" to this color. For example, women who wear primarily black clothing discover after a while that the color they find physically and mentally most comfortable is the color black because the body grows used to wearing clothes in one main color and, in fact, becomes "addicted" to the color black.

It is advisable and advantageous to wear clothes of all colors according to the needs of the body, to avoid excessive use of one color and to frequently change the colors we wear. Each of us has a personal Wheel of Colors that is tailored to our needs and reflects our personality. Later in the book you will discover your own personal Wheel of Colors and learn how to use it in daily life.

People with cancer should avoid wearing green clothes because this color encourages the growth and development of body cells.

People with high blood pressure should avoid wearing clothes in shades of red, because over time this color could raise blood pressure. People with low blood pressure should remember that wearing blue clothes for an extended period could lower blood pressure.

It is desirable and advantageous to wear colors that match the location of the chakras in the body, and to wear colors in a balanced way. Paying daily attention to our choice of color according to our needs yields wonderful results. Make sure you have clothes in all the colors of the rainbow in your closet and allow yourself to intuitively choose the color that will benefit your body. For example, wearing blue pajamas and using blue sheets could help you fall asleep easily and enjoy a sound sleep; wearing a blue scarf or a necklace of turquoise stones could help a sore, hoarse throat. For many women, wearing orange underwear or placing an orange towel on the belly area soothes menstrual pain; and, for many men, wearing orange underwear or trousers and eating orange food helps treat urinary problems or erectile dysfunction. By paying attention to your body's response to each color, you will be able to try various color combinations and improve your physical and mental state by wearing clothes in the appropriate color.

COLORS AND THEIR MEANING

RED

Red is the warmest, most animating color and relates to sexuality, activity and belief. Red is the color of blood and the Root Chakra, helping us to wake up, raise our level of energy and act swiftly because it raises our blood pressure, stimulates and arouses us. The color red frequently signifies danger or emergency and many illnesses are characterized by a redness of the skin. An excess of red in the human aura can indicate anger, danger or acute illness. When someone is angry, thye turn red, their blood pressure rises and they tend to flare up, which is attributed to an excess of the color red in their body at that moment. The color red has a strong effect on our bodies; it relates to fertility, sexual attraction and temptation, signifying sexuality and sexual arousal. Red is a prominent color that attracts attention; we notice anyone in a red hat from a distance, a red cap on a bottle or a red advertisement. Excessive red could cause irritability, high blood pressure, anger and hyperactivity. In certain places in the world, teachers are forbidden to wear red clothes to class because this color apparently makes it hard for students to sit quietly and listen to the teacher and they become irritable and restless. Several years ago, many women in my country (Israel) started to dye their hair various shades of red according to the fashion. Several of my clients who changed the color of their hair to red started to suffer from high blood pressure, although previously their blood pressure had been perfectly normal. Assuming that it was the red color that was causing the high blood pressure, I suggested they return to their original color. When I suggested to a delightful client that she go back to her original color (brown), she resisted at first for reasons of fashion and beauty, but when she finally agreed, her blood pressure immediately dropped to its normal state.

The color red can help those with low blood pressure to raise their blood pressure naturally. It helps people who have difficulty waking and getting up in the morning, giving them a sense of energy and strength. However, excessive use of red over time should be avoided because it can cause irritability and exhaustion. The color red hastens the healing process of the body, helping to improve the blood flow, speed up the closing of sores and their healing process. An easy way to use color after surgery is to wear a necklace or bracelet of red stones like rubies, red coral, garnets and red jasper, etc.

The use of red on the upper body could overstimulate the energy, raising the blood pressure, so it is preferable to wear red mainly on the lower body, using such items as: red underwear, red socks, red shoes, a bracelet with a red stone, keeping a red stone in a pocket, and so on. Red is a warming color and wearing red socks can help those who suffer from cold feet and slow blood flow in the extremities.

Excessive use of the color red should be avoided in cases of high blood pressure, hyperactivity, anger, irritability, and a tendency to outbursts of rage.

YELLOW

The sun appears to be yellow and so we attribute the color yellow to light, openness, warmth and love. This color appears in nature in the feathers of chicks, the fur of kittens and puppies, and some infants and young children have yellow hair. The color yellow reinforces in us the desire to love someone, protect and look after them. Women who dye their hair a yellow-blond color immediately notice a difference in their feelings and in the environment's attitude to them; research shows that blonde women receive preferential treatment and are considered naïve and very attractive, but they're also perceived as childish, dependent and lacking in knowledge or opinions of their own, and they're often regarded as younger than their age.

The color yellow boosts the intellect, and research has found that writing on yellow paper increases concentration and creativity, and that yellow markers help emphasize and remember words and sentences.

The color yellow particularly impacts the nerves, muscles and digestive system, and excessive use of yellow should be avoided by people suffering from nervous and mental complaints.

We attribute happiness to the color yellow and in China it is considered an imperial hue related to cheerfulness and children.

The appropriate use of yellow has a warm and pleasant effect and painting houses a yellowish shade introduces an earth element. It is usually preferable to choose a pale or pastel shade of yellow because these shades transmit the energy of yellow in the pleasantest, most soothing way. When dark buildings are painted a warm yellow, they become light, warm, open and inviting. This color affects our digestive system. In the West, we often consume the color yellow artificially in food, for instance, various kinds of snacks. Excessive consumption of the artificial color yellow could cause problems regarding attention and concentration, hyperactivity, etc.

It is advisable to consume the color yellow in natural, healthy, non-processed foods.

Yellow is the color of the Solar Plexus Chakra and helps us fuel the fire of our inner will, daring, and progress, to create our futures, independently filled with a passion for life.

BLUE

Blue is the most prevalent color in our world. The "Blue Planet" is blessed with blue oceans and most people choose blue as their favorite color.

Blue is the color of intuition and it connects us to our inner voice and channeling capacity. This color is considered cold and it cools and soothes, lowers blood pressure, imbues us with a sense of peace and helps take care of sleep problems. For those suffering from insomnia it is advisable to use blue pyjamas and sheets. People who suffer from ongoing problems with sleep can paint the walls of their bedroom blue and, in certain cases, even use a bluish night light (5 watts) in the bedroom. It is also advisable to wear blue clothing during the day and drink water from bottles made of blue glass.

According to Feng Shui, the color blue stimulates learning in all fields, and learning in an area where the color blue predominates and/or sitting on blue chairs, helps children with attention deficit disorders, enabling them to learn well and calmly. The color blue is advisable in places of learning, conventions, conferences, etc.

The color blue helps lower blood pressure and alleviates stress, encourages emotional release, reinforces intuition, promotes spiritual knowledge and helps cope with difficult situations in a calm and balanced manner.

People with low blood pressure are advised to take care with the color blue; however, blue is considered a true healing color for all people, particularly when it appears in its natural form, blue flowers, natural, blue stones, streams, rivers, sea and sky.

A Personal Experience

Excessive use of one color has a strong impact on a person's body and soul. I was invited for a Feng Shui consultation at the home of

THE POWER OF COLORS | 23

a woman who was worried about her teen-age son's behavior. The mother told me her son comes home from school, goes into his room and immediately falls asleep. She said that he is often asleep in his room and it is hard to wake him; as a result, he doesn't do his homework or spend time with his friends. Upon entering her son's room I was astonished to find that both the walls and the ceiling were painted blue, the closet, desk and chair were blue, as was the bed and as for the bedding—well, you've probably guessed... blue. I stood there and started to yawn...

I advised the mother to change the colors in the room and use the entire color spectrum; the shift in her son was remarkable and instantaneous. The mother called me to say he had completely "come alive."

GREEN

The color green is at the center of the color spectrum and, in Color Therapy, constitutes a balancing hue with wonderful physical and mental healing qualities. We feel the benefits of natural, green surroundings because for hundreds of thousands of years we were accustomed to living in nature, among green plants and trees. Physically and mentally we need them and cannot exist without them. Spending time in nature gives us a direct link to healing through the color of natural green, which reinforces our immune system and strengthens the healing powers of our body and soul. The color green is considered the color of willpower, which reinforces and invigorates us, encouraging us to grow, flourish and develop. Many city-dwellers experience an ongoing lack of the color green because they live far from nature in industrialized cities, amid concrete blocks of homes and offices. When we go out into nature and stand under trees on a soft green lawn, we naturally tend to take a deep breath... and smile. The organic, healing green of trees and plants is ours in abundance when spending time in a natural and green environment, helping us to heal and restore our body to health and balance. The color green can help treat respiratory problems like asthma, pneumonia, etc., and is particularly effective when combined with the color orange.

Many years ago, when people fell ill with lung disease such as tuberculosis, they were sent away to sanatoriums located in forests among trees and plants. Doctors realized that when patients spent many hours outside in sunlight, among green trees—a spontaneous healing process took place and terminally ill patients were cured.

A natural green can help heal any illness, but it is important to pay attention to the amount; for instance, women should be careful not to wear too much green in the first trimester of pregnancy, when the cells of the embryo are forming.

Cancer patients should avoid using artificial instead of natural green because it might increase the uncontrolled growth of cells in the body. Consuming healthy, natural, green, cooked or uncooked foods can help to improve our health.

The color green improves our mental health, activates the will and the use of healing stones and green clothing, house plants, and spending time in a natural, green environment fosters development, activity, flourishing and growth.

A Personal Experience

One of my clients was hospitalized in intensive care with a blocked intestine. In addition to the healing treatment I gave her, I brought her a potted parsley plant and wrapped its base in pink paper.

The parsley plant is very important in the treatment process as it is known for its powerful ability to concentrate energy (bioenergy), and the color green helps to heal disease and balance the human body. The pink color of the wrapping paper was intended to calm the patient and her surroundings. The doctors and nurses were astonished at the sight of a parsley plant but allowed me to put it on the locker beside the patient's bed. From that moment, the recovery of my client was incredibly swift and within a few hours she was transferred from intensive care to the department of internal care. As I picked up the plant, nurses approached me and said that her recovery was a medical miracle.

The nurses asked me if I'd agree to leave the plant in the room so they could put it next to another patient who'd been lying there for two weeks in a critical condition. Naturally I agreed and, to our joy, the patient quickly recovered.

I warmly recommend taking a parsley plant to any hospital patient and wrapping its base in pink or orange paper. It is truly a gift of health that helps recovery and, in my opinion, is infinitely preferable to the flowers most people tend to bring.

PINK

Pink is the most soothing color. The color of the Heart Chakra is an aligned combination of pink and green. Pink is usually defined as a "feminine color." Attributing gender to it is both mistaken and misleading, since the color pink soothes, gladdens and benefits every human being, regardless of religion, gender or race. As a result of this mistaken definition, many men suffer from a lack of the color pink. Pink is a color that enables us to share feelings and many men may have difficulty sharing their feelings also because from a young age they are deliberately prevented from using this color. The color pink is calming and encourages us to be sincere and honest with ourselves, to share our feelings with others and effectively release emotional distress.

The color pink encourages conversation, peace, sharing and understanding, helping us to open our hearts to love.

When we wear something pink or carry a pink stone for a time, this color helps us open our hearts, cry, share our feelings and secret dreams, and let go of emotional distress.

The source of all distress and disease is unresolved emotion and since it is most important to be aware of our feelings and take care of any emotional problem as soon as possible, the color pink, which supports us emotionally, is known for its auxiliary powers in any treatment.

Pink is considered the color of creativity because it is the color of the palm of our hands, which we use to do creative things and express ourselves and our way of life—writing, cooking, painting, sculpting and so on.

The use of the color pink in our daily lives encourages emotional freedom, true creativity that stems from the depths of the soul and the ability to share our emotional life with others.

WHITE

The color white is considered the color of relationships in our lives because it contains all colors. Intrinsic to all relationships is an entire world and the color white signifies the complexity of all relationships and its ability to unite all colors and turn them into a single, clear, clean color. White represents many different things in various cultures. Throughout the Western world, white is used to unite people during times of joy, celebration and weddings, whereas in China, the color white traditionally relates to parting from the world, death and mourning and, in Judaism, we bury our dead in white shrouds.

In the olden days, only the rich and the noble wore fine white clothes as only wealthy people could afford fine white fabric and to keep it clean. Most people in their daily lives wore simple clothing made of dark colored, durable fabric and white clothes became festive garments to be worn on special occasions. People who wear a white shirt to work are known to this day as "white-collar" employees and over the years have come to be considered as having respected work that is clean and easier than that of employees who are known as "blue-collar workers" because they wear simple, blue clothes to work.

To this day, white is considered a respectable color that conveys reliability and research indicates that marketing people sell more when they wear an ironed white shirt. Traditionally, doctors and nurses wear white clothes and we tend to respect them greatly (particularly when we need their help). In Chinese Medicine, white is the color of the metal element and when we exaggerate its use, we tend to argue more and behave aggressively. Its uses in Color Therapy are varied and help people understand and resolve problems in relationships. The color white gives a sense of cleanliness, hygiene, peace and quiet.

PURPLE

Purple is the color of the Third Eye Chakra. It is considered a spiritual color that stimulates inspiration and reinforces our spiritual capacities. The color purple helps us to develop the unconscious, see the spiritual aspect of our lives, and attain self-fulfillment. It is related to spiritual and economic abundance, giving a sense of security to anyone who wears it.

Purple teaches us gratitude for all the good in our lives, enabling us to see things differently, come to terms with our life lessons, to heal and close cycles in our lives. Purple supports people, helping to end relationships that aren't good for us; it encourages healing and change, filling us with a sense of abundance, self-esteem, gratitude and joy.

The color purple can help lower blood pressure and sleeping between purple sheets or wearing purple pyjamas can help people remember and internalize the meaning of night dreams, which are actually messages from the unconscious.

Purple is a color that can help with any treatment and it works wonderfully when combined with the color green. When using the color purple for the treatment of chronic disease, it helps people to understand why they are ill and to change behavior patterns.

The color purple can help develop children's capacity for gratitude and help them to complete tasks and heal physically and mentally.

ORANGE

Orange is the color of the Family Chakra and considered energetic, cheerful, joyful, and anti-depressive. The color orange is recommended for treating a lack of energy and helps improve and balance the flow of energy in the body. The use of orange on various parts of the body significantly affects them: the color orange on the chest area encourages the elimination of phlegm from the lungs; in the area of the urinary tract it encourages good urinary output; and in the genital area it balances hormonal processes. The color orange helps with diarrhea and constipation, as it balances the elimination of substances from the body. For those suffering from prostate problems, it is advisable to wear orange underwear (preferably terry cloth underwear).

To ease menstrual pain, it is advisable to put a heated orange towel on the painful area and, for relief of breastfeeding difficulties, wear an orange bra and an orange stone. Since the color orange drives and stimulates, it is best to avoid excessive use of orange when treating hyperactive children or children suffering from attention deficit disorder. In cases of despondency, depression, and lack of energy it is advisable to eat food that is orange, wear orange clothing and orange stones in order to raise the level of energy in the body.

Orange is considered the color of studying because it combines red (the color of belief) and yellow (the color of love) and, over the course of our lives, it is easier to study things we love and believe in. Orange encourages us to learn and develop different directions in our lives and learning gives us many tools for a happier, healthier life, enabling us to use our energetic abilities to develop physically and spiritually. Orange invigorates, empowers, stimulates, encourages and brings health. It is advisable to introduce the color orange into most treatments, and it works particularly well in combination with the color green.

A Personal Experience

A student of mine had a five-year-old son who'd suffered from a chronic runny nose since the age of two; he had difficulty breathing and snored a lot at night. The doctors said he was very sensitive but that apart from steam inhalations, etc., there wasn't much they could do. I advised my student to dress her son in an orange shirt and give him a green healing stone to wear. A few days later she called to tell me that enormous quantities of mucus had come out. Two weeks later the child was breathing easily for the first time in three years and sleeping soundly all night.

He felt so good in the orange shirt that even when he started first grade, he made sure to wear an orange vest under his school uniform and always kept a green stone in his pocket.

GRAY

Gray has a low energetic vibration and an ongoing use of this color could dramatically lower the energy of the body bringing about physical and mental exhaustion, boredom, sadness, depression and unwillingness to act.

Research shows that when the weather is gray and overcast and the sky gray—heart attacks, disease, depression and suicide become more frequent. The color gray represents being in a rut, behaving conventionally, avoidance of expressing an independent opinion, and lack of daring. "Gray people" is an accepted name for those who lack uniqueness, who don't stand out, whose lives are boring, monotonous, and lacking in excitement.

Among the Native Americans, the color gray signifies respect because it is the color of elders' and scholars' hair, people who have experienced many things in their lives and acquired great knowledge, and whose words should be respected and honored. Many people discover that when they wear gray, they are respected by others around them; however, they also tend to relate to them as conventional and lacking in courage.

Gray is particularly suitable for adolescents as they feel restless and full of outbursts of energy. Wearing a gray garment soothes these unbalanced outbursts, giving adolescents a sense of self-respect and respect for others around them.

Older people who wish to maintain their level of energy need to use the color gray judiciously because their level of energy tends to drop with age and excessive use of the color gray might cause over-tiredness, boredom and depression.

Generally speaking, it is advisable for everyone to avoid excessive use of the color gray in their clothing, the color of internal walls, etc., in order to avoid a chronic lack of energy.

BROWN

Brown signifies earth and is considered the color of stability, practicality and grounding, which connects us to the practical side of life. The color brown is very common in foods, frequently appearing in "comfort food" (chocolate, bread, snacks , etc.) to which we turn when we're distressed. The color brown helps us feel protected; it gives us a sense of security and stability in our lives; enables us to return to our organic nature, to be grounded; it connects us to the fundamental, tangible and practical will to live, to mother earth and health.

Many energetic treatments advise walking barefoot on the earth or sea-sand in order to connect with the healing, concentrated energy of the color brown in all its shades.

Preparing healthy food for ourselves and others is highly recommended as a stabilizing therapy because when we cook or bake we use the color brown in all its shades in a practical, significant way, an activity that connects us to our creativity, encouraging us to connect with our fundamental existence. The color brown is recommended for treating temporary or long-term situations where we lack a firm hold on reality; situations where we are unable to concentrate, where we procrastinate, hesitate; in situations of insecurity and inability to act. The color brown helps connect us with reality and encourages us to take action, create and enjoy a process of activity and its results.

ROSE

Rose, or fuchsia, increases a person's sensory and extrasensory capabilities.

The color rose encourages people to see through their own eyes rather than the eyes of others and respond to every sensation in a way unique to them, while occasionally supporting thoughts that the road they have taken is the only one, which makes it difficult to listen to the opinions of others.

The color rose increases people's spiritual abilities, helping to treat the area of the Heart Chakra (together with the colors green and pink), enabling people to let go and say what is in their hearts, open up, see the situation from another perspective, be honest with themselves and those around them. Rose supports the color pink and encourages creativity, individuality, thinking differently and the ability to see a situation from different perspectives.

The color rose encourages flexibility of thought and encourages us to successfully change routine life patterns.

Rose is the color attributed to uniqueness, encouraging new ideas, inventions, unconventional solutions for various situations and the ability to think outside the box and swim against the current.

BLACK

Native Americans consider the color black to be the most spiritual color of all because when we close our eyes, we disconnect from the external world and look inward—see the color black.

The color black is related to mindfulness, in-depth reflection, meditation and profound spiritual processes. Throughout human history, people have been afraid of the dark color of night; this is the time we close our eyes and sink into a sleep that severs us from daily reality and we temporarily "surrender" our alertness and control over our lives. The dark night is accepted as a time for inward reflection, disconnection from reality, dreaming and a release of urges. When we have difficulty seeing our environment clearly, we turn inward to deal with what is happening inside. *He who looks outside, dreams; he who looks inside, awakes* (Carl Jung).

The color black is considered a protection against unwanted energies and the finest protective stones are black, such as black tourmaline, onyx and obsidian, etc. The color black protects our energetic environment and causes people to maintain a respectful distance from those who wear it; and it has become the accepted dress for people who wish to protect themselves and create a respectful distance from their environment - such as lawyers, judges and religious figures.

We live in a time of new discoveries, technological inventions and swift, extreme changes that situate our daily lives and thoughts at the center of the world picture and encourage intense preoccupation with the needs and desires of the individual. Consequently, the color black has become acceptable and popular. We should remember that excessive use of this color causes undue preoccupation with the inner "self," self-judgment, worrying thoughts, but when we use the color black wisely and judiciously, it encourages us to observe ourselves and reflect on our lives in depth, to appreciate spiritual theories and arrive at significant insights.

CRYSTAL

This color is attributed to the Crown Chakra and since it is transparent and visibly contains all the colors of the rainbow, it is regarded as the color of transparency, clarity and lucidity. Crystal helps us attain physical and mental clarity, enabling us to see the whole picture in varying life situations, understand the different aspects of a situation, think clearly, come to clear conclusions, with the ability to speak and act clearly, honestly and directly. An ideal combination of colors utilizes the healing qualities of all colors and when we use all the colors of the rainbow, we heal body and mind and find the right way to a full and happy life.

Feng Shui specialists recommend hanging crystals at the window of our home in order to balance the flow of energy into the home. The diffraction of sun rays at the corners of the crystal radiate all the colors on the spectrum into our homes, helping the rainbow of colors enter our lives beneficially and pleasantly. The use of the full spectrum of colors is physically and mentally beneficial for us, so it is advisable to wear clothing of all colors, eat a variety of colored foods, wear stones of all colors and be clear and transparent with ourselves and the world around us.

THE ORIGINAL NATIVE AMERICAN WHEEL OF COLORS

The original Native American Wheel of Colors is a powerful, ancient diagnostic tool that accurately reflects a person's qualities, indicating their strengths and weaknesses. The Wheel shows how our aptitudes find expression in daily life, enabling us to understand ourselves and manifest these aptitudes to the best of our ability. By means of the Native American Wheel of Colors, therapist and client are able to see the latter's abilities clearly, understand what stops the client from fully manifesting their abilities and recommend the best way to use those abilities in order to best manifest their calling. The Wheel consists of 13 colors and each person selects their Wheel of Colors independently or with the guidance of a therapist. The process of selecting a Wheel of Colors occurs once in a lifetime and cannot be repeated or changed. It is a one-time, intuitive and energetic choice and we must relate to this process with respect because the Wheel of Colors chosen is a personal, fixed, unchanging Wheel that accompanies the person throughout their life.

The Process of Selecting the Personal Wheel of Colors

The process of selecting the personal Wheel of Colors takes place in a session that usually takes an hour. It is advisable to sit with a client in a quiet, calm room without external interruption. One may light candles and have healing stones and/or a flowering potted plant nearby, which contribute to an atmosphere of good, calm energy, helping the process of selecting colors to take place beneficially and pleasantly. Concentration is important in the selection process; we must devote all our attention to it.

A. Give the client two sheets of A3 or A4 paper, a pastel color kit with 24 or 36 colors to a box and a pencil or a pen.

B. Instruct the client to write down in a vertical column the numbers from 1-13 in the order of their choice. They might not select the acceptable order (1, 2, 3). It is very important the client understands that the numbers should be selected according to their personal preference.

In the process of selecting the numbers for the personal Wheel of Colors, each person chooses the numbers and arranges them as they wish, with no time limit or pressure and with complete awareness. This is a unique process of selection that will not be repeated.

The selection process differs from one person to another and most people tend to arrange the numbers according to their affiliation with particular numbers. Some people select the numbers in an organized fashion, writing and erasing; others select the numbers intuitively and write them down relatively quickly; while others deliberate throughout the selection process and tend to change the numbers again and again. It is best to give the client several sheets of paper so they can choose the numbers freely and calmly.

To make the selection process easier for the client, it is possible to make it completely intuitive using a pack of 13 cards. Take 13 blank cards and write the number clearly on one side of each card. The reverse side of the card is left blank. Spread out the cards with the blank side facing upward and let the client choose card after card. Write down the numbers in the order of their choice.

To help young children choose numbers for their personal Wheel of Colors, one may take 13 small wooden cubes and write a number on each one. Shuffle the cubes, let the child choose the cubes one after another and write down the numbers for them.

You can choose the numbers for the Native American Wheel of Colors any way you wish.

If the client selects the numbers independently, we ask them to note these down in the order of their selection, in a vertical column (from top to bottom), on the right-hand side of the paper.

For example:

9…

6…

8…

4…

and so on.

When all thirteen numbers are listed in order on the paper, we ask the client to write down the names of the colors, which we then read out beside the numbers they have chosen.

We read the client the classic list of colors and the client writes down the first color we read out beside the top number on their list, the next color beside the next number underneath and so on. It is important to adhere to the order and make sure not to skip a number.

The colors are read out in the following order:

Red, yellow, blue, green, pink, white, purple, orange, gray, brown, rose, black, crystal.

For instance:

9… red

6… yellow

8… blue

4… green

and so on.

The Process of Drawing the Wheel

The client now has a list of numbered colors. We instruct them to draw a circle:

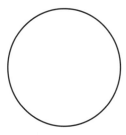

Some people will have difficulty drawing a circle without aid. Be patient, encourage the client and make sure the circle is freely drawn without aid. The client determines the size and shape of the circle. We can allow the client to improve and fix their circle, but we shouldn't devote too much time to this process. There is a direct correlation between the size and form of the circle and the physical and mental state of the client.

We instruct the client to draw another circle inside the one they have just drawn:

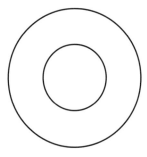

The external Wheel is divided into four segments according to the location of the numbers 3, 6, 9, 12 on the clock:

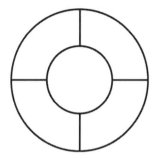

Each quarter is divided into three parts, that is—on each quarter we draw two more lines until the Wheel is divided into 12 segments, like a clock, with the circle in the middle:

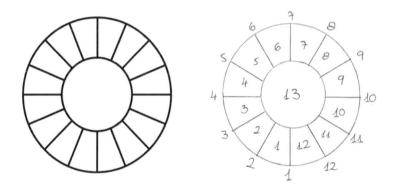

For most people, this drawing looks like the sun.

Each segment is numbered in the following way:

At the center is the number 13; we relate to the Wheel as a clock where we change the location of the numbers.

At the location of the sixth hour, we write the number 1, followed by rising numbers, meaning, 2 appears on the seventh hour, 3 on the eighth, 4 on the ninth, and we continue to write down the numbers in this order until we reach number 12. It is advisable to write down the numbers inside the segments as well as outside the Wheel to ensure accuracy with the colors.

The Process of Painting the Wheel

We place the color kit before the client, asking them to paint the Wheel they have drawn according to the numbers and colors they wrote down at the side of the paper. For example: if red appears beside the number 1, they will paint the segment marked 1 in red. The entire Wheel is painted in order while making sure to paint the colors accurately as listed beside the selected numbers. Many people tend to make mistakes and paint the segment the wrong color, so we must observe the process quietly, avoid disturbing the client and gently draw their attention to any mistake. Most people are greatly affected by the painting experience and some tend to make comments like "we're back in kindergarten".

It is very important to reassure the client during the process, remind them that they can enjoy the coloring and creative process. Finally, the client will have a numbered Wheel painted according to the colors of their personal choice.

DIAGNOSIS ACCORDING TO THE NATIVE AMERICAN WHEEL OF COLORS

A client's personal diagnosis in accordance with the Native American Wheel of Colors is a complex process during which we explain their Wheel of Colors and its meaning in six stages:

1. A detailed explanation of each color's significance;
2. An explanation of each color's location;
3. An explanation of the correlation between the significance of the color and that of its location;
4. An explanation of the significance of the colors according to the order of their appearance on the Wheel;
5. A comprehensive explanation of the client's abilities according to the Wheel, acknowledging their strengths, identifying their weaknesses, and finding ways to address these;
6. A detailed explanation of how the client can use their Wheel of Colors on a daily basis, providing guidelines for the colors we recommend they wear according to their personal Wheel of Colors.

The Wheel of Colors is divided into three principal parts:

1. Our gifts: The Seven Milestones
The numbers 1-7 signify the qualities we receive at birth and are, actually, the gifts with which we are born. Our gifts represent our dominant qualities; indicate our basic, daily behavior and how we think and act; and help us in every situation, guiding us on our way

in life. Discovering our gifts reveals our visible and hidden abilities, enabling us to make conscious use of them. When we use our gifts wisely, they help us progress in life, and if we ignore them, we could encounter many difficulties.

2. Our hidden lessons and skills

The numbers 8-12 represent the life lessons we have to learn. Life lessons tend to repeat themselves and we often say to ourselves: "Why is this happening to me again?"

Over the years we come to realize that our life lessons help us discover hidden skills and use them as best we can; it is only when we manage to understand the meaning of our life lessons that we can change significantly and bring about a beneficial change in our lives. Our life lessons remind us that our life's purpose on earth is to understand ourselves in depth, manifest our skills and learn each lesson.

3. The center - the border

Number 13 is the center of our Wheel and it surrounds and fills our lives, showing us our calling and combining all our gifts and skills in one whole wheel of full life.

The center represents the essence of our personality within which we live, move, act and think. Color number 13 is cardinal to all aspects of our lives since throughout our lives it serves as an axis around which all the other numbers and colors revolve, all of them in relationship: Color No. 13 constitutes the heart that gathers all our qualities and abilities, beneficially empowering and activating them, together with the entire Wheel.

All the 13 colors that appear in our personal Wheel of Colors signify our qualities, and the unique personal order of the colors in our Wheel helps us to know ourselves and identify our inherent potential and the direction of our personal process of growth. The qualities represented in the personal Wheel are fundamental to our personality, constituting the qualities with which we enter and leave this world. Every event in our lives leads us to improve our ability to learn to live in harmony with our qualities, helping us to file down the hard corners of our personality, rather like polishing a diamond.

Our true purpose is to know ourselves, learn to change, improve as much as we can—shine like a polished diamond in the sunlight. Our ability to use our gifts and abilities improves as we learn and progress in our lives and that understanding of our life processes enables us to use our abilities well on earth. Using our qualities to the best of our ability enables us to live our lives fully; learn the lessons of our lives; achieve our goals and complete our calling in this lifetime.

The drawing of the "classic" Wheel according to the order of the colors we call out to our clients is on page 336.

THE COLORS OF THE WHEEL

The Colors 1-7 Represent the Seven Gifts with Which We Come into the World

The First Color: Color of Entry

The first color is that of entry into the Wheel. It is the color of our arrival in this lifetime, the color of all new beginnings, interest, curiosity and daring. The first color is the foundation on which we build the structure of our lives; it reflects the way in which we begin each life process. The first color encourages us to think about new beginnings, helps us plan each new beginning in our lives, spurring us on to action. When we do not make use of the first color, our entire life-wheel stops and we feel "stuck," unable to initiate, create or begin new things. The first color encourages us to leave our comfort zone, open our hearts to new ideas—and implement them.

In conclusion—color No. 1:
- Color of entry
- New beginnings
- The start of any activity
- The color that helps us when we're "stuck" in any sphere of life
- Hope for the future
- The capacity for implementation
- New ideas
- The desire to live
- Inventiveness
- The ability to renew and change

Success is the courage to take the first step

The Second Color: Color of Love and Support

The second color supports the first; it is the color that characterizes the essence of our energy and love and empowers our relationships.

Love is the strongest force in the world and one we all need in our lives. Our supporting color helps us to be happy and act in the best way possible. Support enables us to rise to the heights and create objects that surprise even us. The properties of love, our support and giving are affected by many factors and change according to the people we meet on our path, but the second color always underpins our acts and guides our behavior toward ourselves and others in any type of relationship in life. The second color is extremely important in situations of emotional distress and helps resolve problems in relationships.

In conclusion—color No. 2

- Love and relationships
- A sense of self-esteem
- How we behave in our relationships
- The best color to use when seeking love and good relationships for ourselves
- The physical and emotional color of the heart
- Feelings
- Giving and receiving
- Rejection and attraction
- Collaboration
- Cooperation in every sphere
- A sense of family

The Third Color: Color of Combination

The third color incorporates the first two colors and expands them, characterizing our service. The third color connects the first step we take to every sphere of life with love, in order to create something new, willing and able to act on the subject. We all prefer to do things we love, things that attract and interest us and, therefore, when we're at the beginning (first color) and we add attraction, love and a strong will (second color), it increases the desire to take a step toward what we love. When using the third color, we feel we can do anything we wish to do, in the best way possible, willingly, joyfully and with love.

In conclusion—color No. 3

- The color that expands the abilities of colors 1 and 2
- Connects our beginnings to activity through love and feeling
- The way to listen to what will guide us through any process
- The way in which we serve others
- Cooperation
- Development
- Overcoming obstacles
- Enhancing abilities in all fields

The Fourth Color: Health, Centering and Balance

The fourth color balances and centers us, restoring us to our true essence, the heart of our personality and who we really are; it looks after us physically and mentally, helping us to examine our callings. The fourth color helps us heal and center; it is advisable to use it when treating ourselves and others in a state of imbalance, physical and mental pressure, distress, pain or illness. This color supports the healing of any illness we might have, and we need it in order to live a balanced and healthy life. When we know a client's fourth color, we can use it to treat them, adding our own fourth color to improve and reinforce the recovery process. If we don't know our client's fourth color, we can treat them using our own fourth color.

We use the fourth color to leave this world. If we know the fourth color of someone who is leaving this world, we can send them their own fourth color to facilitate their parting so they can leave the world with ease and grace.

If we don't know the fourth color of someone about to leave this world, we can send them our own fourth color.

In conclusion—color No. 4

- Focus
- Centering
- The way inward, returning to who we really are
- The way to calm ourselves in difficult situations
- The color that heals us
- The color we add when treating others
- The color we send when we don't know someone else's color
- The color with which we leave this world
- The color of our truth
- The color that will extricate us from any physical or mental difficulty
- The color for basic use together with the colors 1, 7, 13.

The Fifth Color: Characterizes and Supports Our Creative Path

The fifth color characterizes our manner of creativeness, supporting it in our center. Each one of us walks the path of this world, creating our life in our own way, a creative act that finds expression in many ways: birthing children, baking cakes, painting and drawing, writing stories, raising dogs, gardening, etc. Anything we create willingly, lovingly, from an inner urge and profound need for self-expression is supported by the fifth color.

This color characterizes our manner of creativity and determination in how we create and supports us so that we may best create the fabric of our lives.

In conclusion—color No. 5:
- The quality of our creativeness
- The way in which we create
- The color that will best help us to create
- The essence of our self-expression
- The creating of fresh awareness within us
- Creativity and the capacity for inventiveness
- Our urge to take action in all spheres
- The ability to create in any field we choose

The Sixth Color: The Gift We Came to Share with Others
The sixth color expands our capacity for centering and creating, collects all our gifts and helps us to share our abilities and creativity with the world around us. The sixth color is that of the gift we came to share with the world, and it characterizes our ability to give and represents the way in which we share our lives and paths with others. The way we live is empowered when we are able to share it with others; our abilities grow, improve and intensify when we share them with the world; out of sharing comes personal flourishing and environmental empowerment.

In conclusion—color No. 6
- The gift we came to share with the world
- The way in which we handle our relationship with the world around us
- Our ability to give to those around us
- It is in the presence of this color that we best interact with our environment

- The willingness for connection and sharing
- Our fundamental need for relationships with those around us

The Seventh Color: Our Color of Protection

The seventh color protects us and our gifts, helps us to protect ourselves in stressful situations and enables us to protect our inner beliefs and actions with a sense of confidence in ourselves, our way of life and our beliefs.

The seventh color enables us to protect ourselves from harm in situations of pressure and stress, encourages us to continue on our path with courage and without fear, protects us physically and mentally and helps us to walk with our heads held high, to feel safe and dare to act with courage—even in the most difficult situations in life, courageously, confidently and with belief in ourselves and our abilities.

In conclusion—color No. 7

- Protection
- Survival
- Defenses, awareness and non-awareness
- Self-confidence
- Treating our fears in the best way possible
- The capacity to feel safe and protected from all harm
- The ability to protect those we love as best we can
- The treatment of trauma
- The treatment of insomnia
- The treatment of anxiety and phobias
- The treatment of obsessions
- A basic color and very important when treating problems together with colors no: 1, 4, 13

The colors 8-12 represent the lessons we have to learn and our hidden skills; once we have learned our lessons well, they become our gifts and skills.
Each of these colors relates to one of our senses.

The Eighth Color: The Color of Our Most Important Lesson

The eighth color is that of the most important and significant lesson for us in this lifetime and we invite various experiences over the course of our lives in order to learn it thoroughly.

We often ask ourselves: "Why am I in this situation again, something similar has already happened in the past... why do I have to go through it again?" The answer is simple: We invite similar lessons into our lives so that we may fully understand the cardinal lesson we have come to learn in the course of this lifetime on earth; for it is only when the lesson is learned and understood that it transforms into a gift we can use. The learning process continues each day of our lives, building our personalities and turning us into who we are striving to become. Sometimes we repeat the same lessons again and again over several lifetimes, until they are thoroughly learned and become part of our gifts, as is the way of every lesson that is well learned and internalized.

The sense that relates to the eighth color is that of touch. Touch is our primary, fundamental way of learning and exploring ourselves and our peers and constitutes the key to physical and mental learning.

In conclusion—color No. 8

- The most important life lesson in this lifetime
- The lesson that will repeat itself again and again in all spheres of life
- Learning in all fields
- Our spiritual task

- The subject that will appear in all our actions and although we are aware of it, will be hard to understand and implement
- Related to the sense of touch: we stumble around in the dark, bumping into the same lessons again and again and, when we learn them, they will illuminate the dark
- This color is excellent when used as a support color in a situation where a person feels they are repeating the same mistake again and again in their life.

The Ninth Color: The Color of the Lesson of Practical and Spiritual Respect

The ninth color represents our principles, our coping mechanisms and the boundaries we build in order to learn our lessons. Our boundaries constitute the principles that define honor in our own eyes and in the eyes of others; developing the ability to respect ourselves and our actions leads us toward a happy, balanced and honorable life. Developing the ability to respect others and those who are different (as we would like others to respect us) enables us to live a life of truth, respecting those around us, avoiding judgment, allowing every human being to be who they really are and honoring their true being with no need for pretense. Respect is the basis of every relationship and true respect begins within. Lack of respect usually causes us to react in anger and even the desire to hurt whoever has hurt us; however, when we respect ourselves and those around us, confident in our actions and knowing our value, no-one can treat us with a lack of honor or respect. Dreadful things are done in this world in the name of honor, all based on the thoughts "I'm right. You aren't..." Only when we learn to respect every living creature on earth will we truly respect ourselves. As long as we think that only we are right and tell ourselves that "it isn't for us to give in"; "it's either us or them"; "it's me against the world"—we wander around in furious, frustrated and painful darkness. When we become part of the world, see that every living creature has a place in our world, and we honor that—then we will be able to put aside war, honor, and live in harmony and joy.

The sense related to the ninth color is that of taste. We have to find the golden path to respecting taste, without fawning or arrogance. Every time we get into a senseless argument on the subject of honor or respect—we must learn to see how pointless it is and stop wasting our time and energy. Will is honor, it is senseless to argue about it. Common sense lies in learning, internalization and true mutual respect.

In conclusion—color No. 9

- Spiritual, practical respect for ourselves and for others
- The capacity for honoring what we have and showing gratitude for what is
- The ability to truly appreciate our skills and talents
- The ability to respect others, anyone different or strange
- The ability to control our anger—toward ourselves and the actions of others
- Patience, forbearance
- Respect for ideas
- Respect for the physical body and the entire world
- Related to the sense of taste, reminding us not to exaggerate respect for ourselves, while not showing exaggerated respect for others or preventing them from respecting us, but to act with taste.

The Tenth Color—The Lesson of Knowing Truth

The tenth color is that of our inner voice, which helps us hear our inner truth and act accordingly. We tend to ignore our inner voice, give up and not follow through with our truth because we're afraid of the external world, of people's reactions. Sometimes, only illness or disaster will wake us up and show us how much we've given up and distanced ourselves from our truth.

The sense that is related to the tenth color is that of smell. We use expressions like: "Something stinks here" or "that smells fishy" whenever we identify a lie, deceit, or lack of truth. Our sense of smell warns us there's a problem from a distance and it is important to know how to "smell" a problem or a lie and choose a life of truth. Life is really good when we learn to listen to our inner truth, do what is truly important to us and live life in a way that is truthful and beneficial.

In conclusion—color No. 10

- Knowing the truth
- Listening to our true inner voice
- The ability to say our truth without fear
- The ability to admit mistakes
- The ability to respect another's truth
- The color that helps people who lie all the time—to themselves and to others
- The color for treating addictions
- Observing ourselves and our truth without fear
- Related to the sense of smell, it is commonly said that lies smell and we can "smell" a lie
- This color teaches us to live a life of truth and avoid telling lies

The Eleventh Color—A Sensory and Extrasensory Perception of the Truth

The eleventh color is that of our sensory and extrasensory perception, reflecting the way in which we perceive things, what particularly affects our perception and how we can improve our ability to see things as they really are. True vision is multidimensional, able to combine external practical vision with seeing things that are hidden from sight, affording us the ability to see things we ignore even when they're in front of our eyes.

When we lack perspective and the balance inherent in seeing from a distance, we tend not to see things that are "under our noses" and frequently have difficulty seeing things in another context or seeing things that people hide from us.

We are all born with a capacity for extrasensory perception, such as: seeing auras, an X-ray vision of the human body, seeing the energy field around a person, etc. When we learn to develop these capacities, we can see better, more clearly and fulfill our purpose of seeing things as they really are, accurately and correctly, combining the capacity for material and spiritual vision.

Think of someone who "seems nice" to you when you first meet them; then think of someone who doesn't "seem nice" the first time you meet them. In both cases your extrasensory ability was activated so you could see the truth regarding the person you met.

This is an ability we all activate intuitively, and it becomes increasingly accurate when used and developed.

The sense related to the eleventh color is that of vision. Each of us develops a personal capacity for vision in the course of our lives, all ultimately hoping to reach a comprehensive capacity for vision that enables us to see all the aspects and diversity of truth in every situation in life.

In conclusion—color No. eleven:
- Sensory and extrasensory perception and receiving messages
- The ability to see the truth
- The ability to see things as they are in ourselves and others
- A capacity for objectivity in every situation
- A capacity for seeing ourselves in a mirror as we see others
- The ability to see that all the world is our mirror
- Inner observation

- Seeing people as they truly are, and not according to what they say
- Related to the sense of sight, reinforcing and clarifying our capacity for sensory and extrasensory perception.

The Twelfth Color—Finding Our Calling

The twelfth color indicates how we safeguard our truth, live a life of truth, connect with our inner quiet and fulfill our calling in life. We must learn many lessons in the course of our lives, and once we have internalized our life lessons, we can find peace and connect to the quiet inside us, where our inner truth can calm us: "Be calm, the purpose of your life lesson is achieved, you have understood where you have succeeded and where you have been mistaken, now you can calm down and be quiet." We must remember to internalize and safeguard the truth we have learned from our life lessons so we won't have to repeat them again and again, and when we are connected to ourselves, we are truly alive and can fulfill our calling.

The twelfth color is that of our calling, and it connects us to our true calling, leading us toward it every moment of our lives and enabling us to live a life of fulfillment and personal satisfaction, truly connected to ourselves and to our eternal souls.

The sense that is related to the twelfth color is that of hearing, which is related to the capacity for really hearing what is said around us as well as our inner voice, although these are often contradictory. The capacity for really listening and hearing—even when we don't like what we hear—leads us to our true inner quiet and the ability to change, grow, live a life of truth quietly and confidently and fulfill our calling.

In conclusion—color No. 12

- The ability to safeguard the truth and not shake it off
- The ability to really listen and internalize what is said
- The ability to listen to ourselves and others without prejudice
- The ability to listen to the inner voice
- The ability to connect with quiet
- The ability to connect with music
- The ability to meditate
- A new ending and beginning
- This color completes the Wheel, showing us our true calling and the way to manifest it
- This color must manifest itself in order for the Wheel to move and start to revolve again from the beginning
- Related to the sense of hearing because we mostly hear what is said selectively, interpreting it as we wish

Our lives depend on listening to our inner voice and only we can hear it.

The Thirteenth Color: Center and Outline

The thirteenth color stands alone at the center of the Wheel, constituting the axis around which the entire Wheel revolves. This is the most important of the colors; it relates to each of the colors and turns the entire Wheel. The thirteenth color represents us more than any other, because it is the organic color of the soul.

The thirteenth color shows who we truly are, the color that surrounds and protects us.

The thirteenth color is simultaneously within and around us. When we work with it, we grow and develop, but when we don't use it, all the colors of the Wheel and their qualities cannot find expression, and we feel "stuck." Whenever we are stuck and not progressing in our lives, we must activate the thirteenth color. This color vigorously activates the other colors, always leading us onward—to learn, improve, grow and develop.

The thirteenth color is the first we relate to in the diagnosis according to the Native American Wheel of Colors; it is the most meaningful color for each of us and the entire diagnosis focuses on it.

In conclusion—color No. 13

- Centers and focuses us
- Relates to every aspect of our lives
- The higher self
- A primary way of activity in every situation
- The main significance of each activity
- Growth and development
- The heart of every subject and process
- Reinforces us in every situation
- The color we always need and seek out in every situation
- The color of our lives that leads us everywhere we wish to go
- The heart of us, physically and mentally
- This is the color on which we base every treatment because it is the most important color for every client; the color that helps every therapeutic process to progress well
- The fundamental color used in every situation, excellent for treatment together with: 1, 4, 7

THE WHEEL OF COLORS—ITS QUALITIES, ABILITIES AND GIFTS

Diagnosis based on the Wheel of Colors refers to a human being's positive and strong aspects as well as their negative and weak aspects. The diagnosis shows us how to change through in-depth work on ourselves in order to facilitate optimal activity in all spheres of our lives.

In my sessions with clients I try to emphasize and reinforce the good and the positive aspects of a color and its location on the segments of the Wheel, showing the client the positive direction of the color. However, we must remember that sometimes a client is in a difficult place in some aspect of their life and they could utilize the negative aspect of a color's qualities. We sometimes have difficult experiences in our lives, so the negative tends to take control of us… happily, when we make use of a positive approach, we can improve a situation. I encourage people to use the positive aspect of the colors, as our progress in all areas of life depends on our capacity for enhancing and using the good in us instead of focusing on the bad, choosing a positive way of action so that we can successfully fulfill our gifts.

Following are details of the qualities, gifts and abilities of each color according to the Wheel of Colors chosen by the client.

THE MEANING OF THE VARIOUS COLORS ACCORDING TO THEIR LOCATION ON THE WHEEL

The Meaning of the Centers

1. Red Center: Belief

Belief is the central issue in the lives of people with a red center. Everything they do is based on some belief, and when they don't believe in something they have to do, they just won't do it.

For people with a red center it is particularly important to build fully credible relationships with people around them; damage to this belief will hurt them to the depths of their soul. They tend to sever a relationship with someone who has hurt, betrayed or deceived them. It is essential that they believe in themselves because they operate from passion and belief in the issue or purpose and should they lose belief in the righteousness of their path, they will no longer wish to do anything. A lack of belief in any sphere paralyzes them, preventing them from action and, for them, a loss of belief in someone else is the hardest thing of all.

It is advisable for those with a red center to practice and learn a balanced way of believing in the various aspects of their life, in order to develop their belief in themselves and those around them, whereupon their belief will become a more conscious part of their life.

2. Yellow Center: Love

For people with a yellow center, *feeling* is at the center of their lives, and their feelings will lead them in all spheres of life.

People with a yellow center tend to be very vulnerable and frequently learn to hide the vulnerability behind a stony-faced façade, avoiding any reaction to difficult situations; they will develop cynical, sophisticated ways of coping with pain caused them, or simply blatantly disregard the feelings of others. The yellow center is the center of those who, for better or worse, cope with the world through feeling and who have a need to feel loved and reinforced in any way possible. They'll do things they like and try to avoid doing things they don't like. Some of them might be very gentle and sensitive, crying easily, while others might be quiet to their "bursting point," ultimately reacting with violence and outbursts of anger. People with a yellow center who did not experience loving support in their childhood might develop emotional rigidity.

It is advisable for those with a yellow center to practice and learn unconditional giving and receiving so that the foundation of their lives becomes based on a sense of love for themselves and those around them.

3. Blue Center: Intuition

People with blue centers enjoy very strong *intuition* and clear, accurate "gut feelings." They have a strong predictive ability and are frequently able to understand people without speaking a word and know the hidden truth in situations. Once they recognize this ability, connect with and use it, they will be able to progress, manifest their calling and take the path that most suits them. In the course of their lives they will experience their intuitive abilities on different occasions but might fear the "illogical" aspects of their sensations and ignore them. When they don't believe in themselves, they tend to "toe the line," do things contrary to inner sensations and consciously avoid using their spiritual abilities.

In time they will learn it is preferable to listen to their intuition and when they acknowledge their abilities, they will learn how best to use their spirituality.

It is advisable for those with a blue center to develop their intuitive ability, practice meditation, learn channeling and fully develop their spiritual abilities in order to live full, channeled lives.

4. Green Center: Will

People with a green center have a particularly strong *will* that finds expression in all spheres of life. Their strong will could lead to clashes with parents, teachers, partners and friends. A green center indicates the need for control, a strong desire that things be done in a certain way; they tend to be stubborn and find compromise difficult. People with a green center are able to withstand difficult situations and when they believe they are in the right they stick to their goal despite the difficulties along the way. If their will is broken at a young age—they could lose it, give up their individuality and become the servant of others.

Parallel to other daily activities, it is advisable for those with a green center to care for a garden or for potted plants, to grow things and allow their personal ability to flourish and develop simultaneously with the growth of plants they seed and put in the earth, taking joy in the process.

5. Pink Center: Creativity

People with a pink center are very *creative* in all spheres of life, and their creativity will promote any subject or project. They might encounter resistance to their innovative ideas or their different way of doing things, but when they give flight to their inner creativity—those around them will enjoy both their original, creative way of doing things and their unique and different way of thinking, which creates a new reality.

Their creativity will manifest in any field that interests them, from cooking the noon meal, to playing the piano, painting or sculpting, or teaching a lesson in an interesting and special way that will stimulate students to want to study the subject. People with a pink center need constant interest in their lives and they will immediately be attracted to any creative activity. It is advisable for them to develop their creativity in any way, learn and practice diverse fields of creativity and do their own artwork in any field they choose.

6. White Center: Relationships

The lives of people with white centers revolve around *relationships* in their lives and they place great emphasis on the significance of people and connections. People with white centers will have many acquaintances and friends or, alternatively, they will be hermits who abstain from closeness with people. Many will want to spend time with people and are reluctant to be alone, but occasionally they will need peace and quiet, away from the "madding crowd." The hermit and the society person can both have a white center, for both are immoderate in relationships, emphasizing their need for them in different ways. The words "all or nothing" represent their feelings on the subject of relationships. People with white centers may find they swing between these two polarities, sometimes feeling the need for many people around them, while at other times they strive to disconnect from the world.

Those with a white center feel they "magnetize" people into their lives without understanding how they do this. Most of them will choose a profession related to relationships with people (teachers, therapists, sales-people, etc.) or they might prefer to disconnect from the world around them and become hermits.

People with white centers are advised to learn and develop in the field of interpersonal communication, in order to do their best in whatever path they choose.

7. Purple Center: Ending, Healing and Gratitude

Purple centers are rather rare, and those who have these could be people who have lived many lifetimes, learned a lot about life and whose souls are highly developed. If they wish, this could be their last lifetime on earth.

A purple center indicates a soul that is willing to heal and bring good into the world. People with purple centers tend toward mysticism and spirituality, closing karmic cycles and debts from previous lifetimes, in this lifetime.

People with purple centers have strong "gut feelings"; they know many things intuitively and are inherently capable of healing and being healed and are grateful for what they have, rather than focusing on what they don't have.

When people with purple centers are encouraged to develop their virtues from childhood; their spiritual abilities are prodigious.

It is advisable for those with purple centers to learn therapeutic, people-related professions, enjoy every moment of their lives and develop their mystic skills in the knowledge that the most important lesson is to show gratitude for what exists and for what they have.

8. Orange Center: Learning

People with orange centers come into this world to *learn* and to teach and in this lifetime, they have chosen to learn all spheres of life and share their accumulated knowledge and experience with others. In most cases they are exemplary students in fields they love and as teachers they impart their knowledge in an unusual way, gaining the love of their students. By virtue of their ability to learn, their abilities in every sphere are innovative and inventive. They have a tendency to learn any subject first-hand and choose to experience intense emotional lessons. People with orange centers will jump into a pool before making sure it is full, and they tend to get involved in unhealthy relationships and learn things the hard way.

They will study in depth any subject in their lives and sometimes tend to despair at the excess of subjects and the intensity of studying in their lives. They should make an effort to learn each subject in its entirety the first time around in order to avoid learning it again. People with orange centers are advised to learn, teach and take an interest in all fields, as studying develops all their spiritual virtues and when they generously share their knowledge with others, additional knowledge will always flow toward them and their spiritual abilities will increase and grow.

9. Gray Center: Honor and Respect

People with gray centers are preoccupied all their lives with the issue of *honor and respect* in terms of themselves and others. The gray center might be hard to live with because honor and respect are complex issues in any relationship. Those with a gray center tend to be insistent, demanding that people behave respectfully toward them, and they maintain respectfulness at all costs. They tend to think that because they treat people with respect and behave well toward them that others should be the same and they're insulted when this doesn't happen. They believe that the whole world should maintain respectful rules of etiquette that match this way of thinking. Any deviation from what they consider respectful is interpreted as a disaster and reason for battle. When they feel their cause is justified, they tend to get aggressive and sharply insult their opponents, and when they are angry with themselves, or when things aren't done according to the way they see things, they tend to become depressed. At their best, they are very pleasant, courteous, respected and respectful people.

People with gray centers are advised to learn meditation and methods of relaxation; and to develop forgiveness and a capacity for accepting the other peacefully and without judgment.

10. Brown Center: Practicality

People with a brown center are characterized by always being active and are full of vitality, energy and the constant will to act; however, in times of stress they are likely to become apathetic and inactive.

When those with a brown center are at their best, they are constantly active in their own interests and the interests of others. Activity calms and balances them as, without action, they feel lost, useless and depressed. They will carry out any task effectively and devotedly in the most practical way. Activity makes them happy and, after completing a number of tasks, they feel calm. Bureaucratic delay, people's laziness and inaction could anger them. They have a wonderful capacity for recruiting others to action or simply getting up and taking action themselves. They are extremely practical people and even when busy planning skyscrapers, they will think of the most practical way of implementing their dreams.

When they're ill or very tired, they tend to go to the other extreme, when they might give up what they're doing and suffer from various pains, which tend to disappear the moment they get up and do something.

These people are advised to keep planning new projects, act in all spheres, and learn various practical techniques in fields that interest them.

11. Rose Center: Sensory and Extrasensory Perception

Those with a rose center see things that other people don't pay attention to and they notice every detail, facial expressions, a hair on a garment or a sense they should be cautious with someone they've just met because something doesn't "feel right." People with a rose center have a unique and different way of seeing things. They see the world mainly through their own perspective and, thanks to their excellent extrasensory ability, they are able to see things people try to hide from them.

People with a rose center "know" things without knowing how they know them, and they have an excellent capacity for seeing, showing and explaining things. They are universally useful thanks to their ability to see "outside the box," invent things and solve problems in an original way, but they tend to get angry when people don't see things their way, and in stressful situations might disrupt things and imagine the worst.

People with a rose center are advised to develop their extrasensory perception in various ways, to practice guided visualization, invent their own ways of doing creative things in fields where their capacity for vision allows them to make their unique voice heard.

12. Black center: Meditation and Mindfulness

People with a black center transmit what happens to them through the inner filter of their thoughts. They are constantly preoccupied with thinking about what happens and reflecting inward on their state of being, so they mostly appear to be deep in thought. People with a black center tend mainly to trust themselves and their own conclusions after deep thought, preferring not to give an immediate "casual" answer but to take their time and think about the subject at hand and they will try to give well founded, serious and well considered answers. Their inner life is extremely rich, and their inner world constantly preoccupies them, but they will not easily share their reflections with others and the world of their thoughts will mostly remain private and secret. They are serious and devoted, work in depth, and can always be relied upon to listen to their inner voice and act accordingly.

Some of them tend to be silent, maintaining a distance from others and having a different perspective on life.

Most of them have an innate capacity for writing and will surprise you with the depth of their ideas. People with a black center are advised to develop their ability to meditate, write, work with people and show others the way to mindfulness and a connection to quiet.

13. Crystal Center: Transparency and Clarity (classic)

People with a crystal center possess many talents and like to be active in several fields simultaneously. The center is the classic location of the color crystal on the Wheel of Colors and it's important for people with a crystal center to allow themselves to work in as many fields as possible and not limit themselves, as the crystal center indicates a capacity and a need for change and changing. The crystal center relates to clarity and transparency, seeing the picture from all sides, understanding all aspects of a situation and acting clearly and transparently in every possible field. When the crystal center is not clear and shining with all its colors it is faded and halts the movement of other colors on the Wheel. People with crystal centers tend to act with clarity and transparency and engage comprehensively and meticulously with their chosen field.

People with crystal centers are advised to develop all their abilities and engage in multiple fields in their lives, otherwise they will feel they're "stuck" and standing still. Their clarity and comprehensive worldview will help them gain considerable success in any field they choose and engaging in many diverse fields will expand their spiritual and practical world.

A Personal Experience

A 30-year-old woman came to me for therapy. She was suffering from head and back pain, a sense of confusion and felt without direction. For most people this sounds like the "usual story" of an inability to choose an appropriate direction, but the story is more complex. The young woman who came to me was successful, particularly smart with a winning personality—and her state of mind brought about depression and physical pain in various parts of her body. In the diagnosis according to the Wheel of Colors we saw that her center, No. 13, was the color crystal. I advised her to wear especially colorful clothing, an *Optical Calcite* stone (so she could examine her path), carry in her pocket a transparent quartz crystal (to receive a transmission of the color crystal to her entire body), while simultaneously engaging in several fields that she enjoyed but hadn't dared engage in because society regarded them as "inferior." Within a short time, she improved significantly, recovered, and found her way in life.

THE MEANINGS OF THE WHEEL OF COLORS IN ORDER OF THE SEGMENTS

THE FIRST COLOR—COLOR OF ENTRY

1. Red (classic)

It is important for people whose entry color is red to believe in every new project or new beginning in their lives in order to engage with it. When they believe in something, they will work and do everything with all their hearts, but if they don't believe in an issue, they won't engage at all. When a person wins their trust, they will gladly connect with them and stay the journey with them but if, for some reason, they don't believe in a person, they won't want anything to do with them. Only when they believe in themselves and/or another, and/or an issue or goal, will they cooperate and begin to engage.

2. Yellow

People whose entry color is yellow begin any process in an emotional way. When they love the subject or the new goal, they will start to work energetically and gladly, but if they don't like the subject or the goal, they won't want to engage with it. When they like someone they'll make contact, but if for some reason they don't like them, they won't even look in their direction or desire any contact whatsoever.

People whose entry color is yellow frequently appear inconsistent and illogical because their heart controls them with every new beginning. They can be appealed to, but not pressured with regard to feeling, because pressure makes them stubborn and persistent in their stand.

3. Blue

People whose entry color is blue will begin everything in life intuitively and they'll listen to their "gut feelings" in relation to any new person they encounter and any new beginning. When they learn to listen to their inner voice and intuition and act accordingly, they will probably choose what is right for them. It is difficult to describe an intuitive way of choosing because everyone listens to their inner voice in their own way. People whose entry color is blue will know where to turn, with whom to speak and what to do so that things turn out well when they listen to their hearts and inner voices. They should, first and foremost, act according to their intuition, even if it contradicts reason.

4. Green

People whose entry color is green primarily rely on their will in every new beginning and any encounter with a new person. When they want to, they'll engage enthusiastically and energetically in any issue, but if they don't want to, it is impossible to persuade them to do something against their will.

Stubborn insistence on what they want characterizes them in any new beginning or with new acquaintances, thus most beginnings are likely to be difficult for them and their surroundings, because they depend solely on their will, despite the fact that later on they are probably calm and pleasant and may even learn to compromise.

5. Pink

People whose entry color is pink start everything in a creative and unique way. They want to do things that are original and behave in a way that is unconventional, creative and interesting; they mainly want to connect with new people who seem interesting and have an innovative and creative approach. Whenever it is difficult for them to start a new project in life, they should look for its creative side and they'll immediately want to try it out, willing to start to create something new. Creativity will draw them to unconventional, innovative and groundbreaking projects.

6. White

People whose entry color is white place great importance on relationships in every sphere of life; when a new project is offered to them, they will first find out who they will be working with. At the beginning of a new project they need people around them and they may need reinforcement from the people they trust in order to begin a new project. They very much enjoy meeting new people and expanding their circle of friends; they are likely to make friends quickly with most people and enjoy many circles of friends; multiple relationships encourage them to act, raise morale and motivation. When working with people who are important to them, they start new projects easily, feeling supported on their path, which enables them to interact well with others.

7. Purple

The entry color purple teaches us about people who come into the world to close cycles in this lifetime and any new projects in their lives are probably connected with closing Karmic cycles. When the color purple appears in the first place, it shows a tendency to pedantry, over-meticulousness (for example, excessive cleanliness), and attentiveness to small details. The color purple at the beginning of the Wheel is an indication of people who "finish" a project in their minds long before it has actually begun, people who have a need to complete and end things "yesterday."

They tend to drive themselves and others to gain swift results and it is difficult for them to settle for results that don't appear to be as good as those imagined when planning the project. They tend to view new friendships as if they had known people forever, but also to get angry with them when they can't meet impossible expectations. In the course of their lives they have to learn and understand that every person has their own pace and way of doing things.

8. Orange

People whose entry color is orange, have a strong desire to learn and will make an effort to learn in detail from the beginning, since for them learning is the first step in any process, encouraging them to progress in life.

They tend to be curious and wish to learn and experience many fields.

Although they will often feel that they are experiencing too many lessons in life, they tend to experiment and will try new and challenging beginnings in multiple fields in the course of their lives.

Learning will enable them to begin any new project in life, spread their wings and utilize their abilities.

9. Gray

For people whose entry color is gray, the issue of honor and respect comes first and nothing in life can start without this. They must respect any subject or project offered them, otherwise they won't even glance at it. In order to connect with new people, they have to feel these people are honorable and worthy of their respect and that they in turn unequivocally and wholly respect them. Honor and respect might become an obstacle in life because they often appear to demand respect and attention to trivialities, and they tend to be angry. New beginnings in life will be easier when they develop their capacity for self-respect and respect for others, for starting new things calmly, respecting the world around them and improve their way of handling life.

10. Brown

People whose entry color is brown feel a strong need to "do something" in any new situation; they like implementing things and practicality opens the wheel of life, helping them to begin and progress in any field. When they are in a situation of inactivity, they tend to feel bored, "stuck" and despairing.

In general, people with the color brown in one of the first six places tend to feel "guilty" when resting; they have a constant need to feel efficient and effective. Implementing a task well makes them very happy and even if they don't succeed with their task—the fact that they tried will calm them down.

11. Rose

People whose entry color is rose have a capacity for particularly sharp initial observation and will activate their extrasensory perception at any first meeting or start of a project, observing the situation carefully before they act. Their excellent extrasensory perception enables them to see details invisible to others, helping them to start projects based on profound insight. They must be careful not to rely only on first impressions, but to continue to observe what is happening around them all the time, in case they have missed details. They are superb observers but tend to see things emotionally rather than objectively. They have to learn to combine their capacity for vision with all aspects of life in a way that is practical, to observe situations over time, able to see each aspect clearly and distinctly on a daily basis, without prior prejudice.

12. Black

People whose entry color is black tend to be quiet, closed and reflective; it takes them time to open up and make contact with people. They constantly think about each project and each encounter, acting on something only after examining it repeatedly to make sure they're doing the right thing.

They will sometimes appear to be hesitant, inattentive, even suffering from perceptual difficulties because each new beginning requires time for them to think, check, and work things through with themselves.

13. Crystal

People whose entry color is crystal have a need to relate to all possible spheres of life, comprehend all the implications of a situation and not live in uncertainty. Their capacity for seeing a situation clearly from all perspectives at the beginning of each project or relationship makes them keen discerners, which means that if they manage to maintain clarity over time, they and those around them will profit.

If information is withheld from them, they will refuse to cooperate until they know the situation inside out.

At their best, they will examine all aspects of every new beginning, enable the project to begin from the best starting point and what they have to say will be clear, direct, distinct and practical.

A Personal Experience

The mother of a seven-year-old boy approached me in relation to her son. The child had great difficulty with transitions; he missed the kindergarten he'd left and found it hard to create new relationships with the children in his class and with the teachers at his school. Upon doing his Wheel of Colors, we realized that his entry color was red. We understood that since he wasn't able to trust the new teachers and children, he had difficulty integrating into the new surroundings and missed the kindergarten he knew and the teacher he trusted. We worked with the aid of nutrition, clothing, healing stones and three colors: The first color (red) for a new beginning; we added color No. 7 (so he'd feel protected); and color No. 13 (for general balance).

I added a Bach Flower Remedy to the treatment to support new beginnings and reinforce self-confidence.

The change was extraordinary, surprising his parents, teachers and even the child himself.

THE SECOND COLOR—COLOR OF LOVE AND SUPPORT

1. Red

People whose support color is red are characterized by relationships influenced mainly by the issue of trust, and they tend to ask themselves: "Am I really loved?" "Should I believe what people say to me?" etc. When they believe in the people around them and receive their support, love and encouragement, they thrive, flourish and feel that the relationship benefits them. When their trust is betrayed, or they discover they've put their trust in something that is unworthy of it, their emotional world collapses and they could react harshly. They believe in ideal relationships, which are difficult to maintain on a daily basis. When they believe in a particular person, they'll follow them come hell or high water, and when they don't believe in someone—they tend to ignore that person completely and won't want to have anything to do with them.

2. Yellow (classic)

This is the classic position of the color yellow on the Wheel and people whose support color is yellow are able to love easily and wholeheartedly, giving their hearts to those they love. Every sphere of their lives is affected by their feelings for it and they might love purely or hate loudly, for their feelings of love and hatred tend to lead them in life, erupting very quickly. When doing something they love, they'll do it wholeheartedly.

Their tendency to pass all their actions through an emotional filter makes them do what they love and enjoy, unless they consciously decide to give this up, diminish themselves, do things the way someone they love does them, manifesting that person's will.

3. Blue

People whose support color is blue tend to rely on their intuition and gut feeling in relationships although they don't always trust their sensations. They're sensitive partners and parents and frequently complete the sentences of people with whom they are close. They tend to know what the people they love want and need even without asking them and often manage to resolve difficult emotional situations with intuitive wisdom.

When they connect their capacity for listening to others with inner sensations, they can act with sensitivity, wisdom and logic.

4. Green

Relationships in the lives of people whose support color is green depend on their will rather than the will of their partner or fellow employees. They tend to be stubborn, aggressive and certain they are right in every argument, and they will try to change the nature and behavior of those they love and influence them to behave in a way they feel is right. Their strong will might cause difficulty in relationships but, if they are inherently gentle, they tend to avoid arguments and quietly and simply insist on having their way. In cases where their will is "broken," they tend to give in within relationships and their tendency to stubbornness will seldom appear.

5. Pink

People whose support color is pink tend to be highly creative in their relationships and the projects they love. When they cannot act creatively as they see fit, they tend to change the way they have acted and/or change the system in order to achieve their desired objective. They are the breakers of myths and builders of new ways and this quality is reinforced when the color red is in a close or significant position in their Wheel of Colors.

They know how to renew and create new ways of engagement in every sphere they love, and in relationships they tend to be original, interesting and creative, always wanting to change, renew and be renewed.

6. White

For people whose support color is white it is very important to have as many friends as possible and they feel at their best among people they love. They tend to work in an environment with many employees and maintain connections with a lot of people; they often need to be reminded how important it is to maintain the quality of relationships to ensure deep and meaningful relations with people. They tend to make friends swiftly, creating a large circle of friends, but it is wise to remember that their friendship isn't particularly selective and might not stand the test of time. Some of the time they need a great many people around them, but in certain circumstances they might want to disconnect from their social circle and abstain from society.

7. Purple

Spirituality and a capacity for understanding their fellow man characterizes the relationships of people whose support color is purple, and they tend to quickly end relationships that don't suit them. Their tendency for perfectionism, resolute wisdom and the desire to perfect any issue that comes to mind might be interpreted by their surroundings as excessively pedantic and might occasionally even anger people. They need to be grateful for what exists in their life, maintain and appreciate everything they have; people they hurt tend to distance themselves and leave them alone.

Their tendency to take care of others mainly finds expression in the devoted, consistent care of those they love.

8. Orange

Profound emotional learning characterizes the relationships of people whose color of support is orange and they are attracted to people and projects that will enrich and teach them. They tend to be in relationships where they need to learn to know their feelings and those of their fellow man and live cooperatively. They will sometimes despair and want only peace and quiet. Their tendency to study makes them attentive, curious and adventurous; they have to learn not to take unnecessary risks and jump into hazardous relationships that attract them because they offer a challenge.

9. Gray

Respect in their private relationships and places of employment is most important of all to people whose support color is gray, and they might confuse respect and love. They tend to be stubborn, rigid and easily hurt in their relationships, hindering the people around them because any resistance to their words or actions is perceived as unloving and a blow to their self-esteem. They need to learn to respect and love themselves and others in a balanced way in order to avoid quarreling in all areas, because it is difficult for them to yield. When they are loved and respected they are delightful and generous, but when they are resisted, or not sufficiently respected, they can be cruel to those around them, angry at the world, suffering from futility and devastation that lead to depression and loneliness.

10. Brown

Practicality characterizes the relationships of those whose support color is brown, and they will act practically and energetically for the people they love. They never sit still, always want to be active, and will act quickly for a person or animal they care about or an idea they believe in. Inactivity frustrates and tires them and if they despair, they tend to stop everything and sit around doing nothing.

The minute they decide to leave despair behind them, they become energetic, taking on many tasks without worrying about the extent or the results of the task and will succeed in doing whatever they wish.

The people they care about will always enjoy their wholehearted love and real emotional support. They frequently like to give of themselves as a way of expressing their warm feelings and love, yet they have to learn to moderate their generosity and channel it appropriately.

11. Rose

People whose support color is rose see relationships in their lives mainly through their own eyes and will tend to give others what they think they need and not what they might like to receive. They tend to be very critical in their work and relationships. Having sensory and extrasensory perception, their criticism might be painful, very scathing and hurt the people they care about or work with and, consequently, they will find it difficult to sustain good relationships over time. It is hard for them to find partners that completely satisfy them, and they tend to "roam" in their search for the perfection they imagine.

12. Black

The love of people whose support color is black is deep, spiritual and hidden. They find it difficult to reveal their love, but they feel it with all their heart. In their relationships at home and at work they tend to listen quietly to the needs of others and act only after deep thought. They will only open their hearts to people they utterly trust. They will frequently be a listening ear for people who need someone to talk to as they have a capacity for empathic listening and wholehearted support, a quality that is enhanced by additional therapeutic colors in their Wheel. It is advisable to listen to their advice, which is given after much thought and profound understanding of an issue.

13. Crystal

Love enhances the clarity and transparency of people whose support color is crystal. In a job they love and in loving and supportive relationships, they will find a capacity for clarity, transparency and eloquence. Love enables them to be at their best and they are able to do everything in the most beneficial way.

It is important to them to be both loving and loved so they can expand their horizons, and improve and balance aspects of their personality. Real love allows them to experience any field they wish and enjoy diverse and interesting relationships. A supportive workplace enables them to relate to several fields simultaneously and enjoy employees whose capacity for thinking and implementing appears to be limitless.

A Personal Experience

A 30-year-old man came to me for therapy because he couldn't find the right partner. We did his Wheel of Colors and saw that his color of support and love was brown. He was astonished, turned to me and said: "I feel I always give with all my heart and will do anything for someone I love, but don't get enough in return."

I advised him to use the color brown in his food, clothing and shoes and to carry a Tiger's Eye stone for the courage to ask his partner to show him her love in practical ways. After a while, he called me to tell me that he'd found the love of his life and they were getting married.

THE THIRD COLOR—COLOR OF COMBINATION

This is the color that expands color No. 1 and color No. 2, combining them, giving us the feeling that we can do anything

1. Red

People whose expanding color is red need some sort of trigger or activity for the start of a relationship and/or support from the people they love in order to believe in and continue their path. Belief enhances their abilities and defines their goals and when they believe in something and/or someone, they are able to continue to implement anything in their lives out of belief and adherence to the goal.

2. Yellow

People whose expanding color is yellow need to combine their tasks and missions with their emotional life in order to best conduct themselves. Self-love and love for others will expand their action-boundaries, enabling them to progress in any relationship and project they choose. They need a clear beginning and a sense of emotional support from their environment, their workplace and relationships in order to implement things well and wholeheartedly.

3. Blue (classic)

People whose expanding color is blue tend to listen to their intuition when starting a project or when a relationship starts to take shape.

They activate their intuition in order to examine if what they are about to do is right for them and, in most cases, they are helped by something concrete and/or practical thinking about a subject in order to activate their intuition and show them the way. Since this is the classic location of the color blue, they tend to be intuitive and spiritual in all spheres of life. However, they must rely on facts in order to progress and develop their vision and spiritual abilities.

4. Green

People whose expanding color is green have very strong willpower and, from the moment a project or a relationship starts, they tend to be consistent and continue even when encountering difficulties. Their stubbornness will help them progress with any project—but will also present a problem because they insist on doing things their way and according to their perspective. It is difficult for them to stop or change a project they've begun if they feel they should continue. They need to learn to stop occasionally to re-examine their path in order to avoid falling into a project or relationship that is not beneficial for them.

5. Pink

People whose expanding color is pink have an artistic approach and, once they've begun a project, they expand the boundaries of their imagination to see possibilities others haven't considered. A new relationship or project will encourage their creativity and unconventional behavior, and they are able to do whatever they want, always finding creative solutions to any problem, a creativity that enables them to expand all spheres of life.

6. White

People whose expanding color is white have a capacity for creating special connections with people and their relationships greatly affect the way they act in life. They have a natural charm that attracts people of all kinds and their lesson in life is to learn to balance power and the effect they have on the people in their lives for better or for worse, so that they can balance themselves and live their lives to the best of their ability. The more balanced their relationships, the greater their abilities, and the ways in which they act are enhanced and thus improve.

7. Purple

People whose expanding color is purple have a deep connection to spirituality and mysticism. They frequently know in advance what is about to happen in their lives, and they are attracted to people and projects that will help them close karmic cycles. They tend to want to end things their way, seeing their plan complete, before others even understand there is a plan. They need to acknowledge the mystical aspect of their abilities since ignoring them might cause them to doubt themselves, fear these hidden abilities and the unknown. They frequently feel a profound need to take care of others and, when at their best, they constitute a true healing power in any chosen field.

8. Orange

People whose expanding color is orange have a powerful passion for learning and their natural curiosity and desire to study will inform all fields of their activity and be reflected in their relationships and places of work.

Their learning capacity relates to any field that emotionally and practically attracts them. They need to be cautious regarding feelings of boredom and lack of interest that might be destructive for them; they should allow themselves to learn and teach while taking into account emotions around them.

9. Gray

People whose expanding color is gray need to feel that they and their actions are respected in all relationships both at home and at work. They have a deep sense of self-respect and don't like feeling that they or their actions are not accepted by those around them. They have to learn to respect themselves, others and the environment in which they live in order to achieve their goals with ease, overcome their tendency to be offended by trifles and avoid arguing with those around them.

10. Brown

People whose expanding color is brown are passionately active and, in their relationships, are characterized by considerable activity and restlessness because activity gladdens and stimulates them. They are highly effective when they believe in what they are doing. They need to take care not to jump into projects for emotional reasons and try to avoid situations of self-exhaustion and a sense of burnout from excessive work. Balanced activity is the solution to their physical and mental problems.

11. Rose

People whose expanding color is rose have sensory and extrasensory perception that allows them to see things mainly through their eyes and not as things appear through the eyes of others. They are very aware of themselves and their desires both in their actions and in their relationships and tend to believe that their way of doing things is the best way.

Their ability to see what is hidden can help them reach higher spiritual insights, but they must beware of their tendency for criticism that could harm relationships with people they love and those around them.

Improving their mystical abilities will help them refine this quality, enabling them to take action in a better way.

12. Black

People whose expanding color is black are deep thinkers; their inner discourse profoundly controls their lives and relationships, which are different from how they appear on the surface. They might be outwardly silent but inside they are constantly examining and deeply debating things. When they have the time, they require to plan and consider in depth, they will implement projects wisely, based on profound thoughtfulness.

13. Crystal

People whose expanding color is crystal have a capacity for seeing their abilities clearly and examining their surroundings pragmatically in order to act at the right moment and with clarity. They are people who are profound, articulate and have a capacity for seeing the whole picture and are transparent in all their actions and relationships. They tend to multi-task in several areas simultaneously and exhaust themselves. They need to remember that they are at their best when healthy, calm and able to connect all the spheres in their lives in a good and balanced way.

A Personal Experience

A 45-year-old director came to me for therapy with a strong sense of frustration at work. On the one hand, he loved his place of work and enjoyed a high salary but, on the other hand, he felt "it wasn't good enough." We did the Wheel of Colors and realized that his expanding color was pink. I asked him if the problem stemmed from his having to act in ways determined by others. Yes. He told me he didn't have a great deal of freedom to act and didn't feel he brought anything personal to the job. I advised him to use the color pink in his food and clothing and to carry a pink quartz stone in his pocket. After a few sessions, he joyfully told me about several creative projects at work and, thanks to a particularly creative idea, he was promoted to a role that he'd wanted.

THE FOURTH COLOR—COLOR OF HEALTH, CENTERING AND BALANCE

This is the color that centers us, helping us to heal physically and mentally

1. Red

People whose centering color is red need to believe in themselves and in others in order to be at their best. Believing in people, an idea, or a project centers and draws out the best in them. Believing with all their hearts in an issue both centers and balances them and they are capable of thinking, feeling and behaving in the most beneficial way. When belief is undermined, they are out of balance and feel as if their world has collapsed.

Someone who undermines belief, particularly when their belief in themselves has been damaged for whatever reason, might bring about severe emotional reactions or even illness, which begins as a result of mental harm. They need to believe in themselves and their ability to heal, and in a difficult situation, they need to learn to restore their belief in order to recover and continue their path. They tend to swing between two extremes, filled with belief on the one hand and lacking in belief on the other, while seeking the golden mean. In every case of imbalance in their lives, belief and the color red will restore balance, helping them to center and resolve their issues.

2. Yellow

People whose centering color is yellow are constantly in need of love, for love of themselves and others constitutes the solid foundation of their lives. If their lives are lacking in love, they tend to feel aimless, without a clear path, even feeling they lack willpower. They need to remember to love themselves unconditionally and avoid situations of self-hatred and/or self-denial, which are often the source of their problems.

When in love, they are at their best, and when they are both loving and beloved, they feel their world is in a state of balance. They need to feel they have someone to rely on, that they are loved and needed. Raising animals they love is beneficial for them, enabling them to feel loved, which balances their emotional state.

They need a great deal of demonstrative love while growing up in order to believe in themselves, and a teacher who doesn't like them might undermine and destroy their self-esteem and harm their studies. In situations of stress, they are likely to grow a "shield" around themselves and shut out the world to protect themselves.

Their emotional isolation harms them as their physical and mental health depends to a large extent on the answer to the question "am I loved?" Emotional learning, the practice of emotional openness, unconditional love, and the color yellow will grant them peace, balance and self-esteem.

3. Blue

People whose centering color is blue are highly intuitive and must learn to listen to their "gut feelings" in any situation. When intuition constitutes an inseparable part of their lives they feel whole and serene; but when they don't listen to their inner voice they could become unbalanced, feel something is missing in their lives and suffer from various illnesses and mood swings for no perceptible reason. Listening to their inner voice enables them to be in good relationship with themselves and those around them, to best walk their path, know a lot intuitively and behave beneficially in any situation.

When suffering from some problem, the solution always lies within. They need to activate their intuition, listen to their inner voice and act accordingly. Seas, oceans, rivers and lakes will attract them and greatly affect their moods. Hydrotherapy will help improve their state of mind.

4. Green (classic)

Most people whose centering color is green will have particularly strong willpower, unless they are confronted at a very young age and their spirit and willpower are "broken." They are capable of emerging from severe emotional and physical states by virtue of willpower alone and they tend to be stubborn and act according to what they want and how they perceive a given situation. For better or for worse, the combination "I want" controls their lives, and even the toughest tasks are not impossible if they wish to carry them out. No mountain is too high to climb for someone whose centering color is green! They will frequently attempt to bend others to their will, mainly because they believe they know best. As children, they tend to be willful and might run the risk of being broken, because the adults around them (parents, teachers) frequently decide to force them to change, and this is by no means the appropriate way to behave toward those with such willpower… they need to be respected to a certain extent; their willpower needs to be constructively guided, for then they will be at their best, doing all they can to succeed.

5. Pink

Those whose centering color is pink are particularly creative in all fields of life; they will strive to do things differently from others and see new possibilities for creativity in every situation. Originality and creativity are *a lantern unto their feet* and they especially appreciate creative people and objects, and creativity in general.

When disoriented, creative activity is the best way for them to return to themselves, get centered, calm down and recover. A simple activity like cooking, stringing beads, raking garden beds or any other creative activity will help them balance and heal. They are at their best when creating, mainly attentive to their inner voice and focused on what they're doing.

They encourage creativity in those around them, mainly in their children and those they love, and those they're close to know that when depressed, an invitation to some creative activity will immediately improve their mood.

They need to remember that constant creativity and originality prevent them from falling into a space of fatigue and spiritual boredom. New, creative and challenging projects are the perfect solution to any situation of depression, sadness or desolation.

6. White

Those whose centering color is white need people in their lives in order to achieve personal balance and their relationships with people can either cause their bleakest moods or, alternatively, encourage their spirit and remove them from confusion and distress. They are likely to be unsettled and in a sea of extreme emotions, the driving wheel of their behavior and balance often held in the hands of others. In moments of distress they are likely to dissociate completely from people around them in order to attempt to listen to their inner voice and find a balance or, alternatively, be totally dependent on the opinion of others without being able to listen to their inner voice.

The color white, color of relationships, shifts from one extreme to another. On the one hand, they are sociable and need society for interaction all the time; they make friends easily, "magnetizing" people, having a strong effect on them; occasionally they may tend to participate in some sort of political activity. On the other hand, they will feel a strong need to disconnect completely, "become a hermit," close the door against the world and be alone with themselves, and some people whose centering color is white will become monks, nuns or hermits. They might be perceived as inconsistent because their balance and centeredness depend on other people and their relationships with them. They need to learn to listen to their inner voice, maintain a sense of proportion, calmly examine their relationships with others, be able to accept help during difficult moments and learn how to extricate themselves from difficult situations on their own, without depending on others. In a difficult situation, a good, balanced, healthy relationship with themselves and with others will restore them to their center.

7. Purple

Those whose centering color is purple are spiritual people with the ability to care for others and heal them physically and mentally. They are able to understand the person in front of them and see things through their eyes, although they occasionally tend to "drift."

Healing, closing a cycle and the capacity for gratitude for the good things in their lives help them center themselves whenever they are disoriented. They're excellent therapists and, in the course of their lives, will probably look after those close to them very well, or turn this quality into a profession and treat people or animals devotedly and affectionately. They tend to mysticism and have an emotional way of thinking that is different and special, since they've come to this world to complete cycles with people from other lifetimes.

They commit to any issue they decide to adhere to; it is important to them to complete things and they are excellent mediators because of their capacity for seeing both sides emotionally and practically.

In times of stress, when they lose their center, they need to complete cycles, know how to say thank you for the good things in their lives, heal and be healed and, what centers them best, is their ability to see things in their lives through a spiritual lens.

8. Orange

People whose centering color is orange are inherently "seekers"; they always seek knowledge, an interesting path to take, or something new to engage with. Their curiosity will lead them to practical and spiritual studies, and they can apply their fresh and curious spirit to any subject they study. They tend to engage with several fields simultaneously because everything interests them and their tendency to learn everything first-hand might cause them to experience difficult and extreme situations in life. They will always seek new lessons because studying each field balances them and restores them to their center.

They can be excellent teachers if in their Wheel of Colors additional colors support their ability to learn and teach others with wisdom and compassion.

Their adventurous tendency propels them into many extreme experiences as they find it difficult to learn from the experience of others and want to try everything for themselves. They need to pay attention to their inner voice and make sure they haven't taken on too many tasks and lessons and make sure that the lesson they are jumping into so happily is really necessary.

In times of difficulty and stress they will find balance and recover by learning a new subject and taking an interest in something fresh in their lives and, if they're shown something that interests them, they will willingly make the effort to engage with new studies.

9. Gray

People whose centering color is gray are deeply conscious of honor and respect and, when they're at their best, they respect themselves and others. When they are not well mentally and physically, they tend to be constantly preoccupied with self-esteem, disparage others and get upset by trifles. They're sensitive and jealous of their self-esteem and the subject of esteem in general, and for them, the words "lack of respect" are derogatory. When they feel someone is treating them disrespectfully, they might become disoriented and react severely, only regaining balance when they are shown respect in a way that suits them. Proper clothing and behavior according to accepted rules are very important in their eyes and they are very sensitive to words, gestures and/or acts that relate to them. Most tend to be tough and judgmental toward themselves and people around them; they tend to get easily irritated and, when angry, are sometimes blunt and harsh. When in trouble or when they feel despised, they might hurt and attack, but if they break down, they could give up, absorb everything, surrender their self-esteem completely and follow others. A respected occupation, an external, respected appearance, and people who respect and support them, help them to return to their center, enabling them to feel better about themselves.

10. Brown

People whose centering color is brown are people of action, which is the centering factor in their lives.

Their thoughts and actions are devoted to intense activity in every chosen sphere and they're mostly unceasingly active but, occasionally, they simply "drop everything" and completely stop all action. When at their best, they find the golden path between intense action and necessary rest. They are extremely good executives with practical and effective ideas in any field they choose; it is important to them to execute tasks in their own way and they tend to feel "guilty" when taking a break and doing nothing because something inside them spurs them on to constant action. They will find a practical solution to any problem and will frequently prefer to act rather than talk. Activity calms and heals them and when they are inactive, they feel physically and mentally ill. They can be trusted with any task and mostly need to be reminded to take a break every now and then to replenish their energy. When they are out of balance, a new activity or task will quickly restore their balance.

11. Rose

People whose centering color is rose have excellent sensory and extrasensory perception and can see things others try to hide from them. They tend to be particular about trifles and pay attention to small visual details, and everything in their lives is passed through the filter of sight, differing from other people's way of seeing. They are capable of seeing "outside the box" with ease and need to remember that this gift also has drawbacks, for when they see things through their own eyes and not through the eyes of someone else, they might distort reality beyond recognition. They're stubborn and likely to stick firmly to an opinion even when they are mistaken, until proved wrong.

When out of balance, they tend to see things pessimistically, negatively and depressingly, frequently needing to listen to the way in which others perceive the situation, combining their perception with others' way of seeing in order to re-balance and achieve a more balanced way of perceiving things. When they see their way with clarity, they are balanced, happy, optimistic and convinced they will succeed.

12. Black

People whose centering color is black think a lot and tend to spirituality, needing to learn to achieve a balance between excessive thinking and dreaming, disconnecting from their surroundings and withdrawing.

Many thoughts constantly scuttle through their minds and it is hard to control this. They can be relied upon to carry out their tasks with wisdom and planning and will give reliable results; but, when they are "dreaming" inside themselves for any length of time, thinking and reflecting on everything on the face of the earth, they are likely to drift into a period of inactivity, which will distress them and result in a lack of balance.

They will be drawn to any kind of philosophy and when they find a practical spiritual ideal that is important to them, such as veganism or Earth conservation, they will adhere to it at all costs. They will stick to their beliefs and ethical values in any field, knowing that if they lie to themselves it will constantly trouble them.

They are conceptual, good meditators and excellent therapists who are always willing to go into the soul in depth. When they are out of balance and their thoughts overwhelm them, the best way for them to achieve balance is to examine an idea that appeals to them, bring it to fruition and gladly implementing it.

13. Crystal

People whose centering color is crystal are clear and succinct in speech and action and tend to be firm and determined in their speech. Their soul is multicolored and strives for constant interest and they are fascinated by combinations of any kind.

They can see any issue from all possible perspectives and can clarify any situation, illuminating hidden aspects and combining them with a general view for the good of the entire project. They need clarity and transparency in every subject in their lives and, when they can't see things clearly, they are likely to make mistakes they will later regret. When things are not clear they are advised to stop, rest, look inward and act only after they have scanned all possibilities of action and all implications.

They have gifts in many areas and should manifest all their potential to the best of their ability and make sure to speak out clearly and distinctly. They are capable of understanding and perceiving the position of others and combining it with general considerations but should prefer their perception over any narrow perception of others.

A Personal Experience

I came to give Feng Shui counseling to someone who suffered from mild depression and an eating disorder. The house was beautifully designed in shades of gray (the color gray has become fashionable in recent years) with multiple glass windows. We did the Wheel of Colors together and realized that his centering color was orange. I advised him to incorporate items like a sofa, pictures, a tablecloth, and so forth, in shades of orange and place a large bowl of oranges on the coffee table. We hung crystals over the windows to bring all the colors of the rainbow into the house and balance the flow of energy. In addition, I advised him to choose a field on the subject of nutrition that interested him and to study and implement it.

Later, he was happy to tell me that his home was pleasant and balanced, and he felt good there. His depressed thoughts had significantly diminished, and he was specializing in a particular aspect of nutrition that made him happy.

THE FIFTH COLOR—CHARACTERIZES AND SUPPORTS OUR CREATIVE PATH

1. Red

It is important for people whose fifth color is red to believe in themselves and their creativity. Belief enhances their creativity, and, in addition, they need to feel the belief of others, which enables them to persevere in their creative work.

When they don't believe in themselves, they become inactive. Encouragement and belief in their ability, both in their own eyes and in the eyes of others, is very important to them.

2. Yellow

People whose fifth color is yellow will create out of love and their creativity depends on their love for the person for whom they are creating or for the subject they are working on. Since creativity depends on their emotions, they don't create anything if they don't "feel like it," or if they feel people don't love them enough, or if they dislike their creative work or the person for whom they create. Their sensitivity regarding the issue of creativity in their lives is great and they need constant love and encouragement in order to be truly creative.

3. Blue

People whose fifth color is blue create intuitively and, since their manner of creativity is impulsive and intuitive, they sometimes find it hard to explain how or why they do something. They "sense" what or when they need to do something and, as long as they pay attention to their intuition, they are creative and act in the best, most successful way. Their intuitive way of knowing what to do increases, particularly when they feel "connected" to a person or subject.

They need to listen to their inner voice and create accordingly, because it is the finest guide for them and for their creativity.

4. Green

People whose fifth color is green will only be productive if they want to be; thus they won't produce anything unless they want to; and if they are creating something it is difficult for them to stop midway; they feel they have to continue to produce. Because their creative work is connected to their will, they tend to experience periods when they're bursting with creativity and others when it's dormant. When they are curious and want to produce things, they immediately leap into action and won't let anything get in their way. When they want to do something, they will carry it out in any way they can, and when they want to create something to make someone else happy or to please, they will make every effort to do so. Their creative power is enormous, and they need to learn to balance creative power and not despise things they don't want to do.

5. Pink (classic)

People whose fifth color is pink are naturally, inherently artistic and will therefore wish to be creative in all fields of life. Their creative minds will make any boring issue interesting and they have the capacity for making the most mundane and ordinary things creative and fascinating. They tend to get bored when doing and creating things similar to others' and need to create things in their own way and not try to imitate others. A creative life with space for their ideas and creativeness will turn them into special people, full of interest and joy.

6. White

People whose fifth color is white are affected by their actions and the relationships they form at a given time.

Their creativity reaches new peaks when in the company of creative people who encourage them to act and to create but will fade when in the company of people who are narrow-minded and don't encourage their creativity or their creative path.

All their actions are dictated by "what will they say" and/or "what will they do," and they need to learn to manage their relationships without limiting their creativity.

They are likely to be particularly creative in the management of their relationships and surprise people in their ability to extricate themselves from any predicament.

7. Purple

People whose fifth color is purple will create from a desire to understand and heal themselves and their environment, completing processes and cycles. They will create mainly when "the muse is upon them" and their creative works are characterized by their spiritual and emotional depth. It is very important to them to complete and see a finished work and they always try not to get "stuck" in the middle of an unfinished project.

They will sometimes hurry a project from a desire to see it completed, but there will always be an aspect of perfectionism in the way they do things and in the finished product.

8. Orange

People whose fifth color is orange produce and experience various techniques in order to learn and teach the best way for action and creativity; they will teach how to create and produce in order to progress, and their creativity is characterized by originality and innovation. At the first stage they tend to observe their creativity and the activities of others in order to learn from them and create accurately, like the students of the past who would copy teachers' creative work until they themselves became proficient. It is important to them to learn new things and experiment with various ways and types of creativity and there is always an experimental aspect to their creativity.

9. Gray

Those whose fifth color is gray create from a sense of respect and, when balanced, they greatly respect creativity in all fields. When not in a state of balance, they might decide that it is only possible to act or create in a way that is acceptable to them or respected by them. They need to feel respected and so it is difficult for them to hear criticism of their artwork or their actions. In their eyes, real respect implies being creative in a way that inspires respect; their need for respect from those around them can lead them to act conventionally so as not to deviate from the norm or, alternatively, to act differently so as to break through conventions.

10. Brown

Those whose fifth color is brown are creative in a practical way and good craftsmen in any field. Sometimes they have difficulty doing things the way they wish and then there's a risk they will take an "all or nothing" approach, saying: "If I can't create as I wish, I'll drop everything and do nothing..."

Their main motivation for creative work is feeling a real desire to do something, which stems from the practical need to manifest things. They will actively make, generating new ideas of how to do things better and how to improve their activity and creativity in additional ways, which enhances their creativity.

11. Rose

People, whose fifth color is rose, create from the perspective of their own vision and, since they are intuitive, creative and imaginative, they will create objects differently from others.

Their artwork stands out in its originality and different perspective on things. They are at their best when creating and expressing their worldview freely, creating differently from other people, inventing various objects and acting in a way that is original and unusual.

12. Black

People whose fifth color is black think about things before taking action, and their creativity expresses the ability to reach the very depths of things. They take time to contemplate creativity and the need to create and act out of deep awareness and understanding of the process of implementation. They will go over and over the idea that occurs to them until they find the best way to manifest it. Their creativity is primarily connected to deep, inner processes and their ability to understand the depth of their feelings, and those of others, is recognizable in everything they do.

13. Crystal

People whose fifth color is crystal are active in many creative fields and integrate a great deal into their artwork in an interesting and unique manner. They are flexible in their creativity and require clarity on this subject. They need to see and hear everything clearly, and if things are vague or unclear, or if the person facing them isn't sufficiently clear, they won't act until things are clarified because they wish to act and create in the best, most comprehensive way.

A personal story

A talented young woman trained with me but had difficulty implementing the things she'd learned in her life. Although she realized that in order to achieve her goal she had to change and re-create her life, she tended to stand still, not believing in herself or her abilities.

When we saw that her fifth color in her Color Wheel was green, she turned to me and said: "It's all clear now! I live in a gray concrete building in the middle of a busy city when I need to live in open, green surroundings in order to re-create myself." She moved to a green environment and, within an amazingly short time, established her dream business that is flourishing to this day.

THE SIXTH COLOR—THE GIFT WE CAME TO SHARE WITH OTHERS

This is our sharing color; it expands the fourth and fifth colors, collects our current gifts and shares them.

1. Red

People whose sixth color is red have come to share the power of belief in our lives with the world, a belief that profoundly affects the people around them in any field in which they choose to be active. Their belief in any issue is an important and primary motivation in their lives, helping them to do things in a wonderful and extraordinary way. If they don't believe in themselves, others, or a particular project, they discover that things in their life come to a standstill and don't develop. In contrast, if they believe in something with all their hearts, everything flows quite wonderfully, manifesting in their life.

2. Yellow

People whose sixth color is yellow have come to share the feeling of love with the world. If they do things with love and from the heart, they carry out incredible projects, but if they don't love what they do it is difficult for them to function or to find joy in life in any subject at all. They come to share their capacity for love in all fields of life and greatly need a sense of being loved and respected in return. Everything they do is "from the heart" or they don't do it at all, and they are primarily known for being influenced by emotion in all their activities.

3. Blue

People whose sixth color is blue have come to share their capacity for intuition with the world. In any situation where their help or advice is required, they will express strong intuition and a capacity for channeling. They will frequently find themselves doing things without exactly knowing why and that will later be revealed as most accurate under the circumstances. When people listen to their advice, they discover that it is excellent because it is channeled and precise, in terms of how they feel about themselves and those around them.

4. Green

People whose sixth color is green have come to share their willpower with the world as well as their profound understanding that willpower can help you do anything. They manage to implement their tasks even in difficult situations and will often draw others after them.

When their willpower is strong, they teach others how to use it, but if their willpower is weak, they will exploit and manipulate them.

People whose sixth color is green need to learn to use the power of thought and feeling in addition to willpower in order to balance their lives and improve their actions.

5. Pink

People whose sixth color is pink come into the world to share their creativity. They are original and creative in how they think and act, tending to do things differently and uniquely. Their need for creativity might easily bring about boredom and they could lose interest in what is happening if they are not allowed to create in their own unique way. They enable people around them to be creative and original as they acknowledge uniqueness and creativity in everyone. When at their best, they encourage every kind of creativity.

6. White (classic)

People whose sixth color is white engage in the field of relationships in this lifetime. They come to share the complexity of most people's relationships with the world and have a capacity for coping with relational problems in the best, most effective way.

The capacity for giving in relationships enables them to learn and teach others the nature of a relationship in all its facets and how to get the best out of the relationships in our lives, improve the level of communication among people and achieve good and empowering relationships.

7. Purple

People whose sixth color is purple have come to share with the world their spirituality and capacity to complete things well, to heal and be healed with true gratitude.

In many cases they will engage in a profession that affects the physical and mental health of people. They will profoundly affect anyone who comes in contact with them, guiding and helping people to learn the meaning of spirituality, gratitude, physical and mental healing both spiritually and practically, as well as the completing of life cycles.

8. Orange

Those whose sixth color is orange have come into the world to learn and to teach. They share with the world and people around them an understanding of the power and significance of physical, verbal, spiritual and practical knowledge because they have the capacity to guide others along paths of cosmic knowledge, while they themselves constantly continue to learn. Their profound understanding of the scholarly nature of the world enables anyone they meet to see learning in their lives in a different light, understanding that this is the nature of the universe: consistent learning in all fields in order to improve ourselves and the state of the world.

9. Gray

People whose sixth color is gray have come into the world to share the importance of mutual respect and, frequently, their ability to respect everything, each living creature, any idea or act. They are able to see the good and the unique in any human being and will occasionally fight for justice and equality because they believe that everyone deserves respect.

Some will fiercely support animal rights; some will support the rights of suffering minorities; or resist nuclear testing; but everyone strives for a world in which there is mutual respect, and they'll very often fail to understand why it isn't possible to respect all human beings just as they are, without judgment. In their eyes, the importance of respect for every living creature in the world is supreme, and they will attempt to implement this in every field of life.

10. Brown

People whose sixth color is brown come into the world in order to share their pragmatism and operational ability. They greatly respect practicality and their ability to teach others its real meaning in all fields of life. In most cases they prefer doing to talking and are known as excellent professionals and operators who can give advice and show others how to carry out tasks to the best of their ability. In many cases they are untiring in their work, with a wonderful ability to carry out a plan that is ostensibly impossible.

11. Rose

Those whose sixth color is rose have come into the world to share their extraordinary perspective. They see every situation from a unique viewpoint and are able to share their ability to think outside the box and see things differently in each field.

They are frequently able to see a solution even in a situation that is ostensibly stuck and cannot be resolved, or see the flaws in a plan that appears perfect. Thanks to their ability to see things differently from anyone else, they offer perspective, "to open the mind" and become open to change and being changed.

12. Black

People whose sixth color is black have come into the world to share their complex inner life and ability to think and enter deeply into things—to meditate and enter the depths of the soul.

They can understand others in depth and, at their best, they contain the people around them, understand their difficulties, help them and guide them to look inward, change and develop to the best of their ability.

Meditation and deep thinking are their tools in every relationship they have with their environment and they know how to say the right word at the right moment, to listen to others and guide them in the enormous complexity of the soul.

13. Crystal

People whose sixth color is crystal have come into the world to share the gift of their clarity and lucidity. They see things very clearly, tell the truth about a situation as they see it and express themselves lucidly and eloquently even when those around them prefer to hear polite statements rather than a clear and truthful one. They need things to be clear or they feel confused and cheated. They find it hard to accept evasion, the withholding of information, and situations in which things are left unsaid, because for them, things have to be "on the table", and a situation must be clear to all sides. They comprehend any problem and can find suitable solutions, thanks to their ability to see any situation clearly and transparently.

A Personal Experience

A delightful woman I knew devoted her life to taking in abandoned animals. Over the years she helped thousands of animals, finding homes for most of them, but the animals that were ill and wretched remained with her, filling her tiny apartment. In a private conversation with me she admitted that she no longer had the energy for this work, that it had taken over her life, but she couldn't ignore the suffering and distress of animals. When we did her Wheel of Colors, we realized that her sharing color was gray, meaning that she honored and took care of every living creature, even when it was too much for her. I advised her to wear a bracelet with gray stones, such as Snowflake Obsidian and Tourmaline Quartz, and try to honor herself too, not only the wretched she encountered in her life. This wonderful woman's home is still filled with animals, but she says she feels she has balanced herself, and occasionally she even goes on holiday.

THE SEVENTH COLOR—OUR COLOR OF PROTECTION

The final color of the Seven Milestones, the seventh color protects us and our gifts.

1. Red

Those whose seventh color is red are protected by their belief. They are really protected if they believe with all their hearts that they are looked after and protected, but if they feel exposed and vulnerable, they could be severely hurt. People whose seventh color is red must believe in themselves and passionately protect their belief in order to progress in life, and it is particularly important they trust and believe in people, because when they experience disappointment and betrayal they feel exposed, fragile and defenseless. They'll find relief when they learn to believe in and trust themselves, for then they will be able to take risks and act according to the belief in their success. They need to conserve their energy and protect themselves energetically in ways they believe in—for instance, protection by light entities, described later in the book (page 305).

2. Yellow

Protection for those whose seventh color is yellow depends on their feelings. When they feel loved, they'll feel protected, safe and courageous, able to manage their lives well, but when they feel unloved, they could become vulnerable, bitter and wretched. Some tend to lack self-love and, in extreme cases, might even harm themselves. Some tend to love themselves excessively and could become tyrants who believe only in themselves.

People around them sometimes find this difficult to understand but they especially need love in order to feel protected and balanced.

3. Blue

Those whose seventh color is blue protect themselves with the help of strong intuition; they intuitively feel the energy of the people they meet and know of whom to be careful. In most cases they have a particularly strong "gut feeling" that will forewarn them of a situation that could put them physically or mentally at risk and they need to learn to wholeheartedly trust these sensations.

They should pay attention to their intuition and allow their inner sense to guide them in protecting themselves and getting the best out of their lives. Utilizing their abilities gives them very powerful, energetic and verbal protection, enabling them to see someone else's weakness and protect themselves in any way they see fit.

4. Green

Those whose seventh color is green protect themselves and their beliefs by means of strong willpower, and they tend to be stubborn and insist on what they want in any situation. Their protection is extremely strong, and they tend to demean others, adhere to their personal opinions and achieve what they want while ignoring the reactions of their environment.

Complacency or misjudgment of a situation might lead them to take a risk but, when at risk, they use all their strength to extricate themselves from the predicament. They can be very rigid, conservative, aggressive and predatory when they feel someone is threatening to hurt them, and they need to learn to utilize their willpower in a way that is balanced and avoid hurting those close to them in a moment of anger and crisis.

5. Pink

Those whose seventh color is pink protect themselves in many creative ways, and are capable of taking any action they can to protect themselves. If one protective measure fails, they'll immediately find three other successful ones and, in order to feel protected, will undertake several actions simultaneously.

They'll often find various, strange ways of "confusing the enemy," enabling themselves to escape and protect themselves. In most cases, their verbal defense skills are excellent; they're flexible, creative and quick-thinking. They always find various, innovative ways to protect themselves in any situation.

It is said about them: "Need is the mother of all invention," and they frequently behave very well in situations of pressure or emergency.

6. White

People whose seventh color is white depend on others for their protection and on their relationships with them. When afraid, they turn to people they rely on for comfort and protection and when the people who are perceived as their protectors leave their lives, they are frightened and suffer greatly.

Because their protection depends on their relationships, they sometimes avoid behaving openly and sincerely with people around them in order to safeguard themselves from harm. They frequently feel empowered by being part of a group or a gang and take strength from the power inherent in "togetherness." When in some predicament or distress they tend to rely more on others than on themselves, frequently starting relationships based on expedience and a long-term perspective so that people will protect them when the need arises. When in trouble, they sometimes completely disconnect and withdraw from people around them, along the lines of "everything or nothing," but most of them need family and good friends who will always come to their aid and they will do anything to create a protective and supportive social network.

7. Purple (classic)

Those whose seventh color is purple, the classic color of protection on the Wheel, will protect themselves in spiritual ways and by mindful observation of what is happening to them. If someone hurts them, they are able to "get inside that person's head" and try to understand why this happened, and will mostly defend themselves gently, striving for understanding and mediation. Once they realize that the situation is a bad one and decide they have no desire to suffer further, they simply sever the relationship with those who are hurting them. They experience this as completing a cycle. They have no desire to suffer or cause suffering, so they choose the most humane solution, even if this requires them to sever relations and end a harmful relationship. When at their best, they know how to be grateful for their life lessons and to view quarrels and conflicts from the perspective of profound Karmic and spiritual observation. They need to distinguish between temporary hurt and long-term hurt, to respond in time, protect themselves and act wisely from a place of mindful observation of a situation in general.

8. Orange

Those whose seventh color is orange will learn to understand their enemies, learn of whom or what to be careful, and will act accordingly. They learn to adapt their responses to a given situation and their defense is based on knowledge acquired, their ability to be flexible and learn a subject in order to extract the best from it. In any confrontation they will devote time to learning the problem, so they are likely to act appropriately in any situation in which they find themselves. It is easy for them to act when they feel that people's behavior and responses in a particular situation are familiar to them. When they don't know what to do, they will attempt to find out and their ability to learn and change is their best protection.

9. Gray

Those whose seventh color is gray tend to be easily hurt by what appears to them to be disrespectful. They could either become angry, shamelessly disrespecting others in order to protect themselves, or cold and alienated, protecting their honor at all costs, careful about the society they keep, avoiding close, intimate contact with their surroundings for fear of being deeply hurt. At their best, they respect all people and will protect those who suffer and hurt with profound empathy, but when they themselves are in a predicament they tend to be hurtful, scornful and disrespectful toward their surroundings, while demanding full respect for themselves. They need to learn to balance their fears, respect themselves and others, honor their life lessons and protect themselves with true nobility and honor.

10. Brown

Those whose seventh color is brown protect themselves in practical ways and it is very difficult to penetrate their armor. They will defend themselves at all costs, using any means at their disposal to do so, protecting themselves from anyone who appears to be an aggressor. They might raise their voices and get angry quickly in order to avoid any trouble and will, on occasion, descend to physical confrontation. They will defend themselves as best they can even if it means "distorting the truth." They have the capacity for practical defense in any situation and must learn to be truthful and sincere, avoid blaming others for their problems and fears and take responsibility for their feelings.

11. Rose

Those whose seventh color is rose protect themselves with the aid of sensory and extrasensory powers that enable them to identify danger in advance; they are also inventive, which enables them to surprise and confuse their enemies and evade difficult situations with unanticipated originality. They protect themselves, profoundly confident in their capacity for seeing the problem while certain their path is the right one. They're experts at finding surprising solutions for predicaments and distress through a capacity for evasion and staying out of sight. They need to learn to avoid angering people deliberately; to understand that a situation is different for someone else, and to try and extricate themselves from any predicament elegantly and wisely.

12. Black

Those whose seventh color is black tend to withdraw and disconnect from their surroundings when feeling threatened or afraid.

They close themselves off, sink into thought and usually act in defense only after reflection and planning. They tend to be quiet and "invisible" when needing to protect themselves in new or difficult situations and, when hurt, they tend to withdraw completely into their shells and refuse any connection with the external world. It is advisable for them to try martial arts combined with spirituality, as well as meditation in order to learn to respond well in moments of crisis.

13. Crystal

Those whose seventh color is crystal are able to defend themselves effectively and their strength lies in their clarity and ability to see all facets of a situation and resolve it. Vague, blurred or unclear situations are stressful for them and they feel most vulnerable when things are concealed from them, preventing them from seeing the whole picture. They are at their best when the situation is clear, and their strength lies in their capacity for clearly articulating the problem and how they think it could be resolved. They often see quarreling as a failure of clarity and an unnecessary "mess." When at their best, they are transparent, clear and stand up for themselves;

they "blur the picture" only when it is to their advantage.

They need to learn to be clear and transparent with themselves as well, ask themselves what they're afraid of, and what would help them to protect themselves and act accordingly.

A Personal Experience

Many years ago, I was heavily pregnant and out walking with my beloved dog, Dana, a German shepherd who was old and sick. As we slowly walked along, a man with an enormous Rottweiler appeared at the end of the street.

I turned down a side path to finish our walk, thinking they'd go on their way. As we started to go in the direction of our home, I saw the man and his dog waiting for us at the end of the path, and heard the man tell the dog: "get them!"

I was in a lonely spot, on my own, and very frightened. I created a circle of protective gold bubbles around me and my dog, Dana, and wrapped each bubble in shining red, the perfect, effective defense color (instructions for this defense are in the chapter on defense). We continued walking, well protected. The man released his dog, but the dog stood frozen, rooted to the spot, looking at us, motionless, despite his owner's shouts to attack. We walked quietly along... although it was only a hundred meters, it was one of the longest, most frightening walks of my life. When we reached the apartment building where I lived, I removed the red protective layer. At that moment, the Rottweiler was released from its frozen state and quickly leaped in our direction with blood curdling barks. We flew home and I slammed the door behind us. I learned an important lesson: dissolve the protection only when in a safe place and not a moment before!

THE EIGHTH COLOR—THE COLOR OF OUR MOST IMPORTANT LESSON

We experience this lesson repeatedly in all fields of life because we promised ourselves to learn it thoroughly, internalizing and acting in accordance with it in every situation and at any point in time.

The eighth color opens up the life lesson series and our hidden gifts on the Wheel of Colors. Once we learn and internalize all the lessons, we turn them into part of our behavior, and they become our true gifts in life. Each difficult life lesson constitutes a true gift with the power of beneficially guiding and balancing us.

1. Red

People whose eighth color is red have come into the world in order to learn the lesson of trust and belief in themselves and others.

They need to learn to trust that they are good and successful, to know that they can do anything they wish, and to learn to trust others. They need to learn that there is good in the world, that they can be trusted, and to trust others—in thought, word and deed.

In the course of their lives they need to learn about spiritual faith, such as religion or mysticism in all its forms, as well as practical belief—who to trust and who not to trust, what is trustworthy and what isn't and, primarily, to learn to believe that they can achieve and implement anything they wish and believe in. Throughout their lives they will encounter belief in all fields, learning about it comprehensively until they know how to consolidate their beliefs and use them beneficially, both for themselves and those around them.

2. Yellow

People whose eighth color is yellow have come into the world in order to learn to love themselves and others. The hardest lesson for most people is that of love and people whose eighth color is yellow in this lifetime have come to learn how to give and receive love in all areas.

Their lives revolve around the question: "Do I love?/Am I loved?" When they learn to love and accept themselves, they will be able to improve their relationships with those around them. They need to learn to accept with love what they cannot change, and lovingly change what can be changed. Love is the force that drives the world and every day they deal with the most powerful explosive of all—emotions. Theirs is no simple task, but when they learn to internalize the lesson and implement it, their way lies clearly and lovingly before them.

3. Blue

People whose eighth color is blue have come into the world to learn the subject of intuition in depth and to develop their ability to channel as much as possible. Once they learn to overcome conventions and listen to their inner voices, they discover that everything flows in life and their path is successful. If they ignore their intuition, they are hurt and repeatedly fail, discovering the hard way that their gut feelings are wonderfully precise, and they should listen to them. When they use their intuition wisely, they can trust it to guide them through life and they will succeed in all areas. It is advisable to learn and specialize in various spiritual fields, gain practical tools, improve their capacity for channeling and use it as a daily tool in all fields of life.

4. Green

People whose eighth color is green have come into the world to learn the subject of willpower in depth and, since their willpower and their stubbornness are tested from the day they are born, they need multiple lessons in order to succeed in merging their will with that of others. They are frequently capable of having their way in something, insisting and getting angry, later to discover that their stubbornness was unnecessary, and they pay a heavy price for mistakes they've made because of their stubbornness. On the other hand, they sometimes relinquish their desire in advance to avoid arguments, later discovering that they were wrong to do so. They learn to use their willpower to manifest their dreams, but also respect their environment and the wishes of others. This is not a simple lesson and they'd be wise to learn when to give in, when there is no reason to insist, and when to insist, knowing they need to keep going in order to achieve the best results.

5. Pink

Those whose eighth color is pink have come into the world in order to express their creativity and they must learn to allow themselves the courage to follow their own unique path and not one determined by others. Creativity is intrinsic to them and, in every sphere of life, they will have original ideas of how best to implement things. They need to learn to integrate their original and creative activity into daily life; allow their creativity to find expression in every field, surprising themselves and others; and act in their own new, special way in every possible sphere. They're advised to learn any form of art that attracts them, as artwork will help them to open up, develop and be creative in all fields of life as well as their attitude to other people.

6. White

People whose eighth color is white have come into the world to learn the subject of relationships with those around them. Their ability to cope with and form good relationships with the people they meet over the course of their life will lead to their ability to succeed in life and fulfill their wishes and desires. Their relationships affect every step they take in life and since they will encounter people of all kinds, they need to learn the art of compromise in their relationships, while maintaining their inner identity and ideals. They act best in a supportive, social environment and, in the main, won't like to be active in an environment in which relationships are formal, difficult or suffocating.

They sometimes become monks, nuns or, alternatively, great leaders, but they need to have good relationships with people around them in order to fulfill themselves and manifest their visions.

7. Purple

People whose eighth color is purple have come into the world to learn the subject of spirituality in depth and they need to learn gratitude for what they have in life and give up the sense of "entitlement." They need to learn to share with others, to heal and be healed, and close their life cycles. Every sphere of their life relates to spirituality and they will have profound spiritual insights at a young age and know things intuitively that others only learn when they're older. Their learning requires them to view every issue through a spiritual lens and adopt a spiritual worldview that is generous, therapeutic and supportive—toward both themselves and those around them. They need to learn to utilize spirituality as well as they can and they're advised to learn various treatment methods, understanding and spirituality in order to promote all fields in their lives; to live in harmony with the universe while using their spiritual abilities; and to close old life cycles, manifesting their path and calling to the best of their ability.

8. Orange (classic)

People whose eighth color is orange have come into the world to learn all fields and to experience all possible paths. This is the color's "classic" location on the Wheel and indicates the soul's clear choice of intensive study in this lifetime.

People whose eighth color is orange need to learn every field in life, internalize their learning and manifest it in their relationships, work and, primarily, their inner work with themselves. Unceasing learning is their deepest need and constitutes the foundation of their life. They will often feel that a particular lesson reappears because they haven't fully understood and internalized it. They feel that their life is a never-ending lesson and sometimes become tired of an excess of lessons in their life, but once something new and interesting appears that makes them curious to learn, they are quick to do so. Their true desire is to experience, learn and develop, so study of all kinds benefits them, helping their life to flow beneficially. Once they have learned and internalized a particular lesson, they will be able to be good teachers for others and share their insights and abilities effectively with the world.

9. Gray

People whose eighth color is gray have come into the world to learn the subject of honor and respect—for themselves and for those around them—and balanced respect and honor are highly significant in every chosen sphere in their life. They tend to be in one of two situations: demanding respect for themselves while ignoring their environment or, respecting everybody while ignoring themselves.

Self-respect is the foundation of learning in their life and they need to learn to respect others and the world around them, while standing up for themselves without humiliating others. When choosing to help animals, people less fortunate than themselves, or anyone whose dignity is undermined, they will see and learn their lesson well, balance and improve themselves, which has Karmic value.

10. Brown

People whose eighth color is brown have come into the world to learn practicality and connection to the earth. They have many practical abilities and need to learn to adapt their dreams to reality, see their vision clearly and focus on it. They tend to make detailed, fantastic plans that don't come to fruition or, alternatively, find themselves in a whirlpool of never-ending action and exhaust themselves. People whose eighth color is brown can take action in any situation if they are able to think about the current state of their life, practically integrate their dreams and ideas with the tools at their disposal and turn them into reality. Their operational abilities improve when they learn a profession or a subject that interests them in depth and in detail. In order to attain maximum results, they are advised to act, combining idea, action and study throughout any process.

11. Rose

People whose eighth color is rose have come into the world to learn to observe things through their own eyes and not the eyes of others around them. They need to learn to see things in their own way, since their capacity for vision is unique and extraordinary and they have the ability to see things beyond, know the truth about other people even if they try to hide it from them, and observe what is happening around them from a different perspective, which enables them to act in a way that is original in all spheres of their life. They need to learn to activate these abilities as well as they can in all areas, allow themselves to see different things and act "outside the box" and, in many situations, they should learn to trust what they themselves see in a situation, rather than what others see. They will benefit from learning spiritual techniques that address extrasensory perception, such as seeing the aura, diagnosis through photographs, etc., in order to utilize their gift to the full and manifest their learning.

12. Black

People whose eighth color is black have come into the world to learn to listen to their inner voice and think before they act. Spirituality and meditation constitute the foundation of their actions and their unconscious is active and affects every sphere of life. People tend to confide personal matters to them, and they know how to listen and respond warmly and supportively.

They will benefit from stopping to think before taking action in any aspect of their life, for their way of thinking is brilliant and they need to learn to use their thoughts more effectively and in a more balanced way. They often tend to vacillate between a quick, spontaneous reaction to a situation and an indefinite delay before deciding what to do, and they need to learn to balance and combine life skills and action in all spheres of life.

It would be advisable for them to learn in depth a spiritual or therapeutic profession. Spiritual and philosophical studies would suit them, enabling them to utilize their mental abilities and original thinking.

Meditation would ease the burden of thoughts scurrying about their heads, and the ability to bring their ideas down to earth and reality would benefit them and those around them, as their ideas are frequently ahead of the rest of the world and they should learn how to carry them out effectively.

13. Crystal

People whose eighth color is crystal have come into the world to learn all lessons in all areas and they will feel this throughout their entire life.

They need to learn to be articulate and distinct, say what is in their hearts clearly, be precise with themselves, find their inner path and manifest their external path accordingly.

They need to be transparent in all fields of their life, and to set and manifest their goal. It is particularly important for them to combine all their abilities as best they can, and it would benefit them to study as many fields as possible because, like the eighth color orange, the more they learn, the more they'll be able to act comprehensively and effectively.

They need to learn to see the big picture, study a wide range of subjects and be able to combine all their abilities in order to resolve any problem.

Studying things in depth will enable them to profoundly develop their multiple abilities, feel more lucid and clearer, and, consequently, their actions will also be comprehensive and clear.

A personal experience

A 39-year-old woman came to me for therapy because she was greatly disappointed in her attempts to find a partner who would offer her marriage. We saw that in her Wheel of Colors her eighth and most important lesson was yellow. She burst into tears, asking me: "So this means I'll have to spend the rest of my life learning and re-learning that the person I want doesn't want me?" I responded that her eighth and most important lesson is to learn to love herself. I recommended she wear yellow, eat yellow foods and wear a mixture of yellow and pink healing stones, such as amber and rose quartz. I advised her to adopt a dog so she could learn to receive and give love with all her heart. I prepared a Bach Flower remedy for her; and taught her several techniques to invite a suitable and loving partner into her life.

After a period of therapy, positive thinking exercises, and focusing her intention on a partner, she found someone who suited her.

THE NINTH COLOR—THE COLOR OF THE LESSON OF PRACTICAL AND SPIRITUAL RESPECT

This color teaches us to honor and respect our skills; live kindly and act patiently and tolerantly; honor our physical body; control our anger toward ourselves and the actions of others; and honor the people around us, even if they're different from us.

The ninth color relates to the sense of taste and the ability to act proportionately and reasonably. We should not exaggerate our demand for respect or the offer of respect to others; we should not look down on ourselves or others.

1. Red

Those whose ninth color is red have great respect for belief and faith in their life; they believe that a life either filled with or lacking in belief is connected to fundamental respect. Whoever they respect, they believe in, but if they don't respect someone, they will not believe either in that person or anything related to them. If they believe in themselves, they are full of self-esteem and confidence but, if they don't believe in themselves, or their dignity is trampled on, they will have a very bad feeling about themselves and their environment.

If they discover that someone they respect and trust has betrayed their trust and disappointed them, they experience an enormous rupture which brings about a lack of self-esteem and belief in the world, as well as a lack of belief in any subject related to the person who has disappointed them. They wholly believe in anything secure and stable but sometimes put their trust in unworthy ideas or people and are hurt, therefore deciding not to trust anyone in the world at all.

They need to trust their inner belief, which will always lead them toward places of dignity and worth, and to take care not to become too dependent on others or their beliefs.

2. Yellow

People whose ninth color is yellow respect those they love and look down on those they don't love. They see love and dignity as interwoven. They need to learn caution, how to distinguish between genuine love, honor and pretense, to maintain their dignity, even when they greatly love someone, and not to idealize or allow others to humiliate or bully them.

Over the years I've realized that the ninth color, yellow, frequently appears on the Wheel of Colors of women or men who are in an exploitive or physically and mentally abusive relationship. The ninth color yellow also appears among people who are physically or mentally abused in childhood. People whose ninth color is yellow are frequently willing to do anything for love, including real, heroic sacrifice, because their dignity and sense of self-worth depend on feeling loved. For them, dignity is an emotional issue and they take devoted care of those they love, inundating them with affection, even overly so at times, even if these people exploit them or are cruelly abusive to them. They need to learn to love and respect themselves, avoid becoming dependent on the love of others and not allow people to exploit their love or confuse honor with love in their life.

3. Blue

Those whose ninth color is blue are supposed to learn to honor their spirituality and intuition and that of those around them, and to understand that spirituality enables them to connect to universal wisdom, allowing their intuition and "gut feeling" to be a significant part of life.

They frequently feel that people despise their sensations and, in order to safeguard their dignity, they will sometimes give up any direct connection with their intuition. They need to know how to respect and integrate intuition into all fields of their life, because intuition is an important part of life and must be honored and used beneficially. They must learn to avoid listening to those who don't respect their spirituality or their capacity for channeling, to act in accordance with their gut feelings and honor their virtues and spirituality in any given situation.

4. Green

Those whose ninth color is green have come into the world to learn to honor their will and the desires of others. If they want something and don't receive it, they become insistent, appearing to their surroundings to be spoiled or stubborn; but if they don't become insistent, they might seem to be undignified. When things don't go the way they want, they tend to feel mocked and disrespected.

They must learn to respect their personal wishes and those of others because excessive stubbornness and a fundamental need to do things their way, as they see fit, might involve them in difficult situations that make them rigid and angry. It is advisable for them to learn to use their strong willpower to achieve sublime and just goals for the benefit of the entire world. Many people I've met who fight for justice have green as the ninth color on their Wheel of Colors and when at their best, they succeed in changing our world for the better.

5. Pink

Those whose ninth color is pink have come into the world to learn to respect the creativity in their life and the lives of others.

If they feel disrespected in any way, they could break with

convention through provocative creativity, or decide to diminish themselves, creating only according to accepted norms. They need respect and appreciation for their work in order to go on creating, and they need to learn to respect their abilities without being dependent on peoples' responses to their actions.

They are extremely creative in their actions when having to defend their dignity, sometimes inventing things to avoid feeling inferior or demeaned in comparison with others. Their self-esteem depends on their creativity and they respect creative thinking just as they respect a unique sculpture or painting. They need to learn to keep creating unhampered by thoughts of their dignity or the way others receive their creative work. Learning various creative techniques will help them to improve their work. They are attracted to any situation with an opening for creativity and doing things differently and are able to introduce creativity and innovation into the world when they respect their own creativity and that of others, enabling themselves to fly on the wings of imagination and create new worlds.

6. White

Those whose ninth color is white are particularly respectful of people and relationships in their life. They attribute special importance to certain people, expecting in return to receive acknowledgment and respect from those around them, particularly those close to them. Respectful relationships are important to them and their self-esteem frequently depends on the question "what will they say about me?" The closer friends and people they have around them, the more respected and loved they feel.

When at their best, they tend to be respectful toward people, making sure there is mutual respect in all their relationships; they will sometimes become fighters for justice and dignity for the weak and the oppressed in the world, fighting for respect for every living creature on earth.

Those whose ninth color is white tend to be extreme and judgmental and are meant to learn to balance their relationships with those around them and act from a place of mutual respect in all relationships in their lives.

7. Purple

Those whose ninth color is purple are meant to learn to honor the spirituality and mysticism in their life and the world around them; to understand that the universe is guiding them toward profound spiritual insights. They surprise themselves with their spiritual abilities, but it is difficult for them to be different and appear "weird" and unusual in the eyes of those around them. Those whose ninth color is purple will, in the course of their life, learn to honor and appreciate the spiritual and mystical realm. They will learn how to heal and be healed, end relationships that aren't good for them and show gratitude for what they have. If their spiritual abilities are belittled, they are likely to diminish their own value, feel deprived, thinking that neither they nor their needs are respected. They frequently feel that their dignity depends on their health, their ability to see things through to the end, and their capacity for helping others.

When at their best, they are able to respect their own spirituality and that of others, whereupon they will complete projects and end relationships capably, in a way that arouses respect; they will feel respected; understand that they have sufficient abundance for all their needs and know how to show heartfelt gratitude.

8. Orange

For people whose ninth color is orange, the issue of respect is connected to their ability to learn and, over the years, I have found that in many cases orange appears in position nine in the Wheels of people who have learning disabilities. Nine orange indicates the possibility of organic learning difficulties and we need to remember to relate respectfully to this person's difficulty and support them when necessary. Students in school are frequently humiliated by a teacher who thinks they are "stupid" or "lazy" and who also spoils the student's parents' perception of them, the usual sentence being: "the child is not fulfilling their potential." Real respect for a child's difficulties and practical support will always yield results, because teaching in a way that respects a person will help them achieve excellent results.

I've encountered professors whose ninth color on the Wheel was orange (dignity = study!) who had overcome many obstacles in their youth, made an effort and learned to "invent" ways of circumventing their learning difficulties and ultimately had become world renowned educators. Hard and humiliating learning difficulties are likely to suppress any desire to learn, but those whose ninth color is orange will learn wonderfully when they discover a particular way of helping themselves to learn or when they encounter a teacher they love and who encourages them, believing in their abilities. Those whose ninth color is orange are naturally curious and love learning anything that interests them, even if it is different and unusual, and it is learning that will become a means to self-esteem.

9. Gray (classic)

Those whose ninth color is gray need to learn a most important lesson on the subject of honor, for this is the classic place for the color gray on the Wheel of Colors. The issue of honor is very important to them in every sphere and they come to realize that this lesson constantly repeats itself in the course of their life. The expression "wish equals honor" suits those whose ninth color is gray, and since they have a highly developed sense of honor, the question "what will they say about me?" affects everything they do. They greatly respect the opinion of others concerning their own actions and life; alternatively, they will ignore the world and do things only in accordance with how they themselves see things, mocking the opinion of others. When out of balance, they tend to be stubborn, hot-headed, impatient and constantly preoccupied with their own self-esteem. When balanced and at their best, they respect themselves and those around them, sometimes even overdoing this. They need to learn to respect themselves and the world they inhabit in a balanced, more beneficial way.

10. Brown

Those whose ninth color is brown connect action with respect, respecting people who take action.

Their self-esteem depends on their actions, and with every project they undertake it is important to them that their ability is acknowledged, and their words and actions respected. They are able to respect the actions of others but if they believe that the way in which others take action is wrong, they are likely to reprove them bluntly, undermining their dignity. They demand that work be undertaken according to their standards, and it is difficult for them to forgive work they consider shoddy, disrespectful or "slapdash," viewing it as a personal blow to their dignity. They are likely to vacillate between overdoing things and laziness or idleness, needing to be encouraged to undertake practical activity through respect for what they do. When they learn to create out of self-respect and respect for others around them, they will be able to balance the lesson of honor and practicality in their lives.

11. Rose

Those whose ninth color is rose have been blessed with sensory and extrasensory perception. It is important to them that things be done their way because they believe that how they themselves perceive things is the best, most accurate way. They are able to respect both sensory and extrasensory perception if they feel it matches their assessment of the truth, but they are also likely to disparage others' way of seeing things and undermine their dignity. Their capacity for seeing things differently from others allows them to reach a place of honoring what is different and an ability to see and respect different things.

They need to remember that their way of seeing things is not the only way and to respect others' way of seeing things. When balanced and respectful of their sensory and extrasensory perception, they are sharply observant and able to see a situation "out of the box."

12. Black

Those whose ninth color is black, honor thinking in every life situation, and for them the greatest honor of all is to possess a profound capacity for thinking. Spontaneous physical actions unaccompanied by thought usually appear to them to be disrespectful, shallow and insignificant. They may delay decisions, primarily out of an honest desire to do the "right and honorable" thing. When their backs are to the wall, they are likely to make a hasty decision (often a mistaken one), getting angry with themselves and/or the environment that made them decide hastily and thoughtlessly.

Some of them will enjoy meditation and various types of yoga, perceiving these as respectable activities. They tend to honor any profession that deals with profound observation of the human psyche and they mostly enjoy fields such as psychology and philosophy.

They need to learn to honor the depths of their fellow man's psyche just as they honor the depths of their own psyche, as well as the thoughts and opinions of others, even if they are different from their own personal way of thinking.

13. Crystal

Those whose ninth color is crystal are blessed with a capacity for honoring the smallest detail but, in difficult situations, they are likely to find themselves in the reverse situation—honoring nothing.

The color crystal facilitates transparency and clarity. These people will mainly enjoy clarity of thought and transparency in relation to honor because they can see all aspects of an issue.

This capacity enables them to fight for true honor and liberty, act for others, animals or the globe. The power of their fighting spirit depends on the other colors on their personal Wheel. Their ability to see honor-related issues clearly usually enables them to avoid quarrels and wars, since they are capable of simultaneously seeing the positions of all participants in a conflict. If they lose clarity, they are likely to arrive at the opposite pole, a state of disrespect and/or reluctance to deal with any honor-related issue. They need to learn to use their abilities, see all the possibilities inherent in the situation in which they find themselves and think clearly during an argument or fight, so that they can be good mediators and bring about real, respectful and respected peace.

A Personal Experience

A five-year-old child was brought to me for therapy as a result of violent behavior toward children in his kindergarten, the teacher, and the afternoon teaching aide. We did his Wheel of Colors and realized that his ninth color was rose. I spoke to the child, asking him when he felt like hitting someone. The child gazed at me and said: "When someone is stupid and doesn't see that I'm the one who's right"…

I advised using the color rose in food and clothing and wearing a Rhodonite or Rhodochrosite stone. I prepared a Bach Flower remedy and suggested to his mother to send him to enrichment classes where his way of seeing the world would be respected and he could develop his unique capacity for vision. Once the child joined classes that were right for him, he succeeded and flourished, came up with wonderful inventions, and had no further need for violence.

COLORS 10-12 ON THE WHEEL OF COLORS— THE COLORS OF TRUTH IN OUR LIVES

Colors 10-12 on the Wheel of Colors are very difficult to comprehend because we live in a world that to a large extent is one of illusion and pretense. Think about all the "white" lies we tell on a daily basis…

Native Americans relate to the issue of truth differently from the way we do; in their eyes it is impossible to live a life that is not one of truth. The tribes of my spiritual mentors adhere to an iron rule: It is forbidden to lie to the members of your tribe. Each person trusts their fellow because, if you can't completely trust each other, the tribe will disintegrate. It is only when you are at war that you are allowed to trick your enemy as part of a survival tactic.

When we comprehend the deep meaning inherent in the word "truth," we realize how hard it is to understand the segments dealing with the knowledge of truth, seeing and preserving it.

In order to live a life of truth in every sense of the word, we must learn to listen to our inner voice and hear our truth, see the truth before our eyes and maintain true and honest conduct in all areas and at every moment of our lives.

THE TENTH COLOR—THE LESSON OF KNOWING TRUTH

The color that helps us to listen to our inner truth and act accordingly.

Each of us must ask ourselves several meaningful and important questions:

Am I truthful and honest with myself?

Am I doing things only because they're expected of me?

What do I really want to do?

Who am I really?

The important lesson of the tenth color is to learn to listen to our inner truth and act accordingly.

The sense attributed to the tenth color is that of smell. People always say "a lie smells," that "you can smell lies" and untruthfulness and, actually, animals such as dogs are known to accurately identify a person's feelings and sensations (fear, lies, etc.) by their smell.

Pregnant women have a sharpened sense of smell because during pregnancy they tend to be honest with themselves and their environment, listen mainly to their inner truth and, accordingly, tend to be extremely sensitive.

We must allow ourselves to live in truth: it saves time, avoids having to remember the lies we've told and, ultimately, truth affords us true peace and a real connection with ourselves and the universe.

1. Red

Those whose tenth color is red need to learn to have faith in their inner truth and completely trust it. When their inner truth is apparent to them, they totally believe in it and act accordingly to the best of their ability, but when their inner truth is not clear, it is difficult for them to believe in themselves or in anything at all. Their deep inner truth depends on the belief they have in themselves and others.

When they know with certainty what constitutes their truth, they are at their best, filled with belief and faith in their actions. When they aren't sure, they tend to doubt everything and trust no-one. They should be encouraged to listen to their inner voice, so they know in whom to believe and trust, enabling them to walk their path, trusting the knowledge of their own truth.

2. Yellow

Those whose tenth color is yellow like to know and live the truth. The lesson of love might be difficult if it appears together with the lesson of truth because unpleasant things might be discovered about the love of their life, such as a truth that has been hidden from them, and they might feel their love is flawed. Any lie revealed in their life will make them feel they "don't really love…"—people, groups, tasks, etc. When they do love something or someone, their ability to love knows no bounds, but if they discover they've been lied to, or that the truth has been hidden from them, their love could turn to hatred.

When they listen to their inner truth, they will love who is truly worthy of being loved.

3. Blue

Those whose tenth color is blue will know their truth intuitively and from a "gut feeling," an instinct, regardless of any rational information. If they listen to their inner voice, even if it contradicts the voice of reason, they are able to live a life of truth, satisfied by their actions, but if they ignore the messages they receive, they will have to "bend" the truth and get into trouble with lies and a life of dissatisfaction. They need to pay attention to every message they receive, relate to it and use it, because these messages allow them to safeguard their truth and live a life of truth.

4. Green

Those whose tenth color is green are connected to their truth through willpower. When they wish to listen to their truth, they adhere to it and live a life of truth and inner listening, but if they are reluctant to listen to their inner voice they are likely to live a life of denial and suppression while persuading themselves that they are living truthfully. Their willpower shows them the right direction and they must relate with intention to their truth and insist on living in accordance with it, even if others try to persuade them to behave differently. Their life lesson is to learn to safeguard their truth and live a true life in harmony with their will and their faith. If they live according to their truth, their willpower will be balanced, helping them to maintain an ongoing life of truth.

5. Pink

Those whose tenth color is pink safeguard their truth through creativity. They love all fields of creativity and since they tend to be very creative in how they perceive, interpret and live their truth, it will, in many cases, be different from that of most other people.

Should they allow themselves to be creative in all aspects of their life, their truth will be alive, growing and developing, but if they suffocate their creativity and attempt to ignore it, they will suffocate their truth and themselves. If they lose their way and live drearily and without inspiration, creativity will restore them to themselves and their truth, helping them to marshal their strength and live in a way that is truly creative and interesting.

6. White

Those whose tenth color is white discover the truth through their relationships. Relationships with people in their lives can remind them of their truth, reinforcing it, but could also divert them from their truth. Any relationship has the power to affect them and significantly change their truth. It is important for them to be honest with themselves and the people in their life, but sometimes it is difficult to safeguard their truth if they are strongly influenced by people. In most cases, it will take them time to allow someone to become a true friend because once they believe in and trust someone they will do anything for them, and if both sides are honest the friendship will be deep and long-lasting.

Sometimes they arrive at the other pole of the color white, which is characterized by a tendency to solitude and a desire to disconnect from people. They then tend to stop, go inward and see their truth in a way that is most beneficial.

7. Purple

Those whose tenth color is purple enjoy inner spiritual consciousness and for them truth constitutes a way of understanding, forgiveness, healing and gratitude. They know that closing cycles is crucial for them and the preservation of their truth and they try to live a balanced spiritual life with themselves and those around them. The lesson of spirituality is not always a simple one for them because it lies close to the end of their Wheel, but they know that if they adhere to their truth, they will ultimately attain spiritual insights.

They are attracted to mysticism in all its forms and should stick only to people who tell the truth, beware of being deceived by charlatans and fakes, and always remember that the key to their true spirituality lies only within the depths of the soul.

8. Orange

Those whose tenth color is orange learn their truth in the course of their life and all life experience helps them learn, understand and discover further aspects of truth and live in a way that is honest and balanced.

They spend their life on a journey of discovery, learning and searching for their truth and it isn't always easy for them to learn, just as it isn't always easy to see oneself in a mirror and understand the nature of one's truth.

They need to allow themselves to learn constantly, without getting caught up in a show of "I know," which serves them when surprised by something unexpected or that they haven't previously encountered, and they're afraid of being perceived as ignorant. Intense, honest learning is vital for them so that they can be honest with themselves and those around them and really live the best life possible.

9. Gray

Those whose tenth color is gray need to honor their truth and that of others. They perceive things as truth mainly when the environment respects them, and they must realize that there are multiple truths that are not respected, despite being completely true. They need to understand that every human being should respect their own truth in any situation, even if it is perceived by others to be mistaken or unworthy of respect. If you respect your truth and adhere to it unreservedly, others will also learn to respect it.

If they learn to respect the world around them, their own truth and that of others, they will be able to live a life of truth, dignity and balance.

10. Brown (classic)

Those whose tenth color is brown know the truth through doing and are apt to act in a way that is practical and true in any field because for them the issue of truth is a concrete one.

If they believe in something or someone, their belief finds expression in a practical way because their slogan is: "If something is true, and you feel it is really good for you, ACT! DO something!" Sometimes it takes time for them to start doing things because they first have to make sure that what they are about to do is really good for them, but when they do take action, they feel obligated to do things in the best way they can.

If they take action regarding something they believe in, they tend to be incredibly practical and can be trusted to implement things honestly and loyally.

11. Rose

People whose tenth color is rose have a unique perception of the truth and in any given situation their truth is revealed to them differently from how the rest of the world perceives it. "The truth is in the eyes of the beholder" is the expression most suited to them. They tend to see their truth as absolute and must learn that others have a different way of seeing things, understand that not everyone sees things from their perspective and avoid self-righteous preaching as much as possible.

They can see the hidden truth of others even if it is well hidden and their extrasensory perception leads them to truths that differ from most people's way of thinking. When they adhere to their truth in a good and balanced way, they are able to be spiritual mentors, teach people to see truth from different perspectives and think "outside the box."

12. Black

People whose tenth color is black need plenty of time for thinking, peace, and quiet away from the world in order to access their deep inner truth. When they reflect on their truth, they refine their ability to live in truth. The truth always stems from their deepest, most secret thoughts and so they usually need a great deal of time and profound thought in order to know their truth and what is really beneficial for them.

Techniques such as meditation and yoga will allow them to discover their truth, reflect deeply upon it and live accordingly.

13. Crystal

Those whose tenth color is crystal arrive at their truth when they are clear-headed and able to see all facets of their situation. For them, transparency, clarity, sincere and direct speech and candid information are basic conditions for truth and an honest life, whereas vague or obscure situations, implicit or devious speech relate to lying and insincerity.

When their truth is completely clear to them, they are clear and transparent and conduct themselves accordingly; when they are unclear, they are vague and evasive, obscuring things as they wish. They need to learn to be transparent and clear with themselves and their environment all the time, so that they speak openly and live a life of truth in every sense of the word.

A Personal Experience

The mother of a 17-year-old young man invited me to do Feng Shui in their home. His mother told me that he spent all his time in his room, in the dark, at his computer. He wore only black clothing, didn't want to meet up with his friends and barely emerged from his room for a meal. She invited me because he'd informed her that he wanted to paint all the walls of his room black.

I asked the young man to sit down with me for a talk and do the Wheel of Colors.

I discovered a brilliant human being, who suffered from troubling thoughts that were constantly revolving in his mind. We saw that his tenth color on the Wheel was the color black.

I told him it was great to seek profound truth but that an excess of the color black in his life made him over-think and disconnect from the world around him. We came to several realizations and insights; the shutters of his room were opened to let in the light; a black Tourmaline stone in his pocket allowed him to feel protected and he started to wear clothing in all colors.

His mother was amazed by the change and once I explained that excessive use of a particular color could have these side-effects, she introduced an abundance of color into her home, improving the life of the whole family.

THE ELEVENTH COLOR—A SENSORY AND EXTRASENSORY PERCEPTION OF THE TRUTH

The eleventh color is that of a sensory and extrasensory perception of the truth. We frequently perceive the truth only to turn our backs on it and take "short cuts," closing our eyes in order to avoid seeing what we don't wish to see. Sometimes we ignore things even when they're under our noses, not wishing to see the truth.

This color relates to the sense of vision. Good sensory vision allows us to experience the practical world and good extrasensory perception allows us to experience the spiritual world. When we have a hard time seeing how things happen around us, we tend to block our vision, whereupon we require glasses... People who wear glasses find it difficult to see the bitter truth and, since there are things that they simply don't wish to see, their sensory perception weakens and the world around them seems blurred.

Extrasensory vision enables us to see the world beyond, to see a human being and recognize their mood; to see the aura around each person, animal or plant; to see a human being in depth and to be able to look at someone and see what is happening inside their body, see their skills, abilities and hidden virtues. Due to blocked sensory and extrasensory perception, problems with sight may develop and a person could suffer from headaches like migraines.

144 | Noah Goldhirsh

1. Red

In the course of their life, those whose eleventh color is red are supposed to learn to believe in themselves and their way of seeing things; to believe in what they see due to sensory and extrasensory perception. They tend to vacillate between wanting to trust what they see and wanting to believe what the people around them say.

They will sometimes completely believe the worldview of those around them and sometimes they will only believe what they themselves can see; they need to achieve balance and see that sometimes we tend to turn our eyes away from the truth when it is too hard or painful. Honest observation helps them learn the lesson of perceiving the truth at all times and it is belief in their ability to see the truth that best helps them to safeguard their own truth.

2. Yellow

Those whose eleventh color is yellow tend to have a very emotional perception of things around them, their own truth and that of others. If they like what they see they will believe in it wholeheartedly; but if what they see is abhorrent to them, they are likely to avoid it and the entire situation on various pretexts. They need to learn to balance their emotional observation, wake up from emotional illusions and see their truth and that of others as it is, warts and all.

Loving their own truth helps them to perceive it and the truth of others around them, and to safeguard it as best they can.

3. Blue

People whose eleventh color is blue perceive truth intuitively. They observe a particular place at the right moment in order to perceive the truth others attempt to hide, and since their intuitive abilities direct them toward the truth even when they don't wish to see it, they will, on occasion, have to learn a painful lesson about truth even if they are trying hard to ignore it. Thanks to their abilities, the truth is revealed to them for better or for worse, even if their eyes are closed. Their strong intuition helps them to see and safeguard their truth; they need to learn to listen to their gut feeling and inner voice in any situation, see the truth fearlessly and act in the best way possible for them.

4. Green

Those whose eleventh color is green see the truth only when they utilize their willpower and are likely to lean toward the perception of others as a result of either diminished willpower, or excessive influence by those around them. They're likely to perceive the truth of others as correct without relating to how they themselves see things and, consequently, to surrender to others and follow them and their perception of the truth. Alternatively, they could stubbornly adhere to their own perception of the truth even if they're wrong, dragging others behind them, without being able to stop.

They need to learn that even if the truth is difficult, they should see it just as it is and by no means ignore it, because only their willpower can allow them to see their truth and so improve and shift it as they wish, thus preserving it.

5. Pink

Those whose eleventh color is pink are creative in how they perceive truth and are likely to "rose tint" an ugly or difficult a truth or, alternatively, "black tint" some other truth. Seeing their truth enables them to be very creative in all areas of life and their important life lesson is to learn to be creative to a degree, not "whitewash" a truth they don't want to see but change it into a truth they do want to see.

They need to learn that if they don't like a certain truth, they must use their creativity to change it and achieve the best possible situation, their creative perception helping them to see their truth and safeguard it as best they can.

6. White

Relationships greatly affect how people whose eleventh color is white see the truth and if they are excessively affected by others' perception of the truth, they are likely to be attracted by someone or some group and unquestioningly "adopt" their truth. In other cases they may insist on adhering to their perception of a truth at all costs, even if their insistence causes them to be alone and alienated from society.

They need to learn to moderate their ways of perceiving their own truth and that of others, to achieve a balance and arrive at their own truth without being overly affected by the way in which others see the truth.

They primarily see the truth when in a relationship and must learn to be able to see their own truth and that of others simultaneously, conducting themselves as best they can both for themselves and for those around them, because people and their relationships with them help them see and best safeguard the truth.

7. Purple

Those whose eleventh color is purple have a high spiritual capacity and are able to see and sense the profound truth intrinsic to them and those around them. Their way of perceiving truth is essentially a spiritual one; since they believe that a lie will harm them and others, they will, on the whole, insist on seeing the truth as it is and act accordingly.

Their extrasensory perception is primarily the result of a previous lifetime's expertise on a subject. They can see even a hard truth from the perspective of time and place, and they walk their spiritual path accordingly in the best way possible.

They must learn to conduct themselves through their spirituality, to see even the most painful truth as a life lesson and try to mend the situation in the best possible way.

8. Orange

Those whose eleventh color is orange learn to see their truth best through studying any field that appeals to them; studying is the most important way of learning how to see their truth and that of others. When they learn to see their truth, they will also learn how best to safeguard it.

If they allow themselves to study, they expand the horizons of their truth, and should they avoid studying—their truth will shrivel up and disappear.

Studying will help the truth to reveal itself and teach them how best to safeguard it.

9. Gray

Those whose eleventh color is gray perceive truth in connection to honor and if they respect both their way of perceiving truth as well as their own truth, they are able to behave accordingly.

If they mock their environment, saying such things as: "Who cares about the truth," "All people are liars," etc., they are likely to get stuck in a never-ending maze of anger and disrespect for their own and others' truth. Since it is very important to them to have their own truth respected, it is particularly important that they learn to respect and balance their way of perceiving their own truth. When they learn to respect their own truth as well as that of the world around them, they are best able to see and safeguard this, acting accordingly.

10. Brown

Those whose eleventh color is brown have a very practical way of seeing their truth and, since they are able to see what they should do in order to live in truth, all that is left for them to do is work hard on how they perceive things and learn to do everything in their power to see the truth and act accordingly and practically.

Any occupation that incorporates their capacity for vision leads them in the right direction, sharpening this capacity for seeing their truth; when they see a harsh, unpleasant truth, they need to know they are able to act in a practical way in order to change it; their practical ability helps them to best see and safeguard their truth.

11. Rose (classic)

Eleventh color rose is the "classic" color of sensory and extrasensory perception and those whose eleventh color is rose see the truth even if others try to hide it. They are blessed with the ability to see the truth inherent in any situation and will mainly learn to develop their own unique ways of seeing, perceiving the truth that is hidden from others' eyes. They speak the truth like the boy in the story: "The emperor has no clothes..." When they speak their truth, listen to them because they see better than everyone else. They see auras and are devotees of the supernatural; they need to learn to develop their ability and use it for their own good and the good of the world, because honed sensory and extrasensory perception enables them to see and best safeguard their truth.

12. Black

Those whose eleventh color is black only see their truth if they withdraw unquestioningly because the truth is hidden inside them, and they need to reflect on it for it to become a conscious insight.

If they see a harsh and ugly truth they cannot make peace with, they tend to withdraw to see what to do, deep thought always leading them toward their truth.

Learning guided visualization and meditation helps them learn to see hidden truth and act to safeguard it in the best way possible.

13. Crystal

Those whose eleventh color is crystal best see their truth when perceiving an issue in all its facets; false or half-hidden situations anger and confuse them.

When open and candid with themselves and their environment, they see their truth best. They always need to insist on seeing the whole picture, the whole truth, acting only when they clearly and comprehensively perceive as many aspects as possible and the truth is transparent and acceptable to them in every sense of the word.

Lucidity and clarity of vision lead them toward their truth, helping them to safeguard it in the best way possible.

A Personal Experience

A 55-year-old woman came to me for therapy. She was worried by experiences of strange sensations. She told me that whenever she met anyone, she'd know all sorts of things about them, although she'd never met them before. She said: "I just take one look—and see everything... I see illnesses, feel I know how to heal them... what should I do?" I explained to her that she actually had a highly developed extrasensory ability. When we did her Wheel of Colors, we saw that her first color was rose, and her eleventh color was purple. I advised her to wear purple clothes, a purple amethyst and to learn healing techniques. This woman did a Reiki training with me and today treats people with great success.

THE TWELFTH COLOR—FINDING OUR CALLING

The twelfth color ends the Wheel of Colors—helping it to start again for, without an ending, there can be no new beginning.

This color shows how we safeguard our truth and connect to tranquility. As this color safeguards truth, it in fact guides us to our true calling, which we reach only at the end of the Wheel, once we have completed all our experiences. When the Wheel turns in an optimal fashion, we are best able to reach our calling and live in harmony with it for the rest of our lives. This color is linked to our sense of hearing; after all, each human being's true calling is to listen to their inner voice and act with it. Our inner voice is really our own and only when we listen to our truth can we act in accordance with it, activating the Wheel once again. This color indicates our true calling and, when combined with the colors 4, 7 and 13, it directs our path in life for, when balanced (color No. 4), we are in the optimal situation of our center (color No. 13). This quartet shows us the true direction of our lives, anything we wish to do always beginning with color No. 1, which is possible if we feel protected by color No. 7. The twelfth color tells us we must listen to our inner voice and act from profound knowledge of our truth in order to live a full, balanced and truly happy life, to walk the paths of our calling and best achieve our life goals.

1. Red

People, whose twelfth color is red, will safeguard their truth and connect with their inner tranquility through their belief. This is the end of the Wheel and their final, true lesson is to learn to believe in themselves and their abilities. Their calling is to do anything they choose based on profound belief—belief in what they do, sharing it with those around them. The ability to believe in themselves will lead them to develop themselves and those around them in the best possible way, fulfilling their calling on earth.

If they believe in themselves and are at peace with their life path, they will be able to reactivate the Wheel, reach color No. 1 from a place of complete belief in their abilities, safeguard their truth, connect with their inner tranquility, help their Life-Wheel to revolve constantly and manifest their calling out of true belief in themselves and others.

2. Yellow

Those whose twelfth color is yellow, safeguard their truth and connect to tranquility from a profound love of themselves, others and their environment. They love only at the end of the Wheel as it takes them considerable time to open their hearts to love. Love will help them manifest their calling, be at peace with their truth and share their love with those around them. Their calling is to love themselves and the world in which they live, acting from love and spreading their love around.

Once they love what they do, they can move to color No. 1 to best activate their Life-Wheel. Love of truth enables them to start everything in life from love, acting confidently in the knowledge that they are loved and loving and able to complete the Wheel and re-start it in the best possible way. When they learn to love themselves and their truth, they will be able to safeguard it and connect with their inner tranquility, ultimately loving the world and every living thing in it.

3. Blue

Those whose twelfth color is blue, safeguard their truth and connect to their tranquility through intuition, which best helps them listen to their inner voice and safeguard their truth. When listening to their inner voice, they are connected to the truth and live their calling in the best possible way. When attentive to their inner voice, they are connected to life's truth and their calling. Sometimes it is difficult for them to connect with their intuition; to them it seems an elusive and unmanageable domain they find hard to define and, since this is the color that completes their Wheel, they understand its full meaning only when they reach the end of the process.

Their calling is to live an intuitive life, preserving their deep inner truth and constantly listening to their inner voice. Once they learn to listen to their intuition and act in accordance with it, they can move to color No. 1, activate their Wheel of Life in the best possible way, living intuitively and harmoniously with themselves and those around them.

4. Green

People whose twelfth color is green, safeguard their truth and connect with tranquility through willpower and their calling is to utilize willpower properly in all areas of their life. Once they decide they wish to live their truth, be attentive to their inner voice and stand up for themselves, they can facilitate the true manifestation of their calling. They need to learn to be strong and adhere to their truth, preserving and protecting it at all costs, for they are capable of doing so, and no-one can do it for them. Once they go inward, preserving their truth, they activate their calling, teach those around them the properties and virtues of willpower, thus activating their first color, starting new projects, every day turning the Wheel of their life in the best possible way.

5. Pink

People whose twelfth color is pink safeguard their truth and connect to their tranquility through creativity, fulfilling it at the end of their Wheel. Creativity implies anything they do by themselves, in their own unique way, connecting them to the truth and to their inner tranquility, helping them to safeguard their life truth and that of others around them. When creating something in their own way, their truth grows, safe-guarded and reinforced; their inner voice echoes in their ears, helping their creativity to find expression in all areas of their life. Their calling is to learn to really create, while paying attention to their inner voice; they will frequently help others find and create their calling in the best possible way.

Creativity helps them to fulfill everything they've learned in the course of the Wheel's cycle; activating the Wheel of Life and re-creating their life constitutes the basis of color No. 1, starting the cycle of the Wheel once again.

6. White

Those whose twelfth color is white, connect with their truth and listen to tranquility through the relationships in their life. Sometimes considerable time passes before they trust themselves, another person, or their responses within relationships. Relationships with people evoke insights about themselves, connect them to their truth and teach them to listen to their inner voice and live accordingly. The relationships in their life enable them to understand what is really important to them as well as the nature of their truth. They learn this at the end of their Wheel, once they have endured a lot and learned all their lessons. Their calling is to achieve good and constructive relationships, learning and teaching those around them how to enjoy a real relational connection, continuing to listen to their truth at all times so that they can start their wheel over again with their color No. 1.

7. Purple

People whose twelfth color is purple, safeguard their truth and connect with their inner tranquility in spiritual ways. When they learn to heal and be healed, feel gratitude for what they have and complete life cycles, they are able to live a life of truth and connect with inner tranquility.

They are natural therapists and must learn to heal themselves of physical and mental pain, completing life cycles in order to progress, taking care of themselves and others through practical, spiritual means.

They need to show gratitude for everything they have, to give thanks for their abilities and the world in which they live in order to connect with their inner tranquility and start their Wheel once again with color No. 1. In most cases, they will choose to act in their own unique, spiritual way and if they do so consistently, they will live their calling through connection to their truth. They need to take care of themselves as they take care of others, completing cycles that are detrimental to them, living a spiritual, powerful life of gratitude.

8. Orange

People whose twelfth color is orange, safeguard their truth and connect with tranquility by learning; in this way they arrive at many insights. They need to learn and teach in order to live a life of truth and connect with their inner tranquility. When at their best, they can learn from anyone, teach and pass on their accumulated experience throughout their Wheel of Life.

Learning will help them progress in life, develop their horizons and enable them to start their Wheel again from color No. 1. They need to learn constantly in order to progress and when they learn to enjoy the learning process itself, safeguard their truth, listen to their inner voice, activating it at all times, they will best fulfill their future.

9. Gray

People whose twelfth color is gray, safeguard their truth, connecting with their inner voice when they respect themselves, their path, their truth, and that of those around them.

Their calling is to respect themselves and the surrounding world and they need to learn and teach that respect and honor constitute true listening, tolerance, acceptance of others and those who are different, attributing importance to all events that take place in the world.

They must learn to honor their inner voice and truth as well as that of those around them in order to reach their color No. 1 and start their Wheel again.

By paying attention to their inner voice and honoring themselves and others, they will best live their calling and fulfill their life.

10. Brown

People whose twelfth color is brown, safeguard their truth, connect with tranquility and manifest their calling when they act and create in a practical fashion.

It takes them time to act as the color of action lies at the end of their Wheel, but when they do take action, they manifest their desires, safeguard their truth in a practical way and connect with their inner voice, which tells them: "Do your best!" Fantasies and empty rhetoric won't take them far; they must take action and be active in order to safeguard their truth, start the Wheel and reach their color No. 1. Their actions and the way in which they take action lead them toward their abilities, helping them to best safeguard their truth and connect with their inner tranquility.

11. Rose

Those whose twelfth color is rose, safeguard their truth and connect with tranquility through their unique vision of themselves and the world around them. Since this color appears at the end of the Wheel, it might take many processes before they are able to activate their unique vision. Their true calling is to see things differently from how they are "usually" seen and "accepted," learn to take a step back in any life situation, observe things differently, see things that are invisible to others and "think outside the box." Their calling is to see and reveal things unnoticed by others and see things in life another way, enabling themselves to activate their color No. 1 and start the Wheel once again in the best possible way.

12. Black (classic)

People whose twelfth color is black, safeguard their truth and connect with tranquility when they go inward, thinking and observing internally.

They gather all their gifts and lessons from the Wheel and connect all the data, their profound thinking coming at the end of the Wheel. Their true calling is to learn and teach how to think and reflect internally in the best, most efficient way, and thinking will lead them onward, open the Wheel before them, carrying them to their color No. 1.

Their calling is to live and act in deep thoughtfulness, listening to their inner voice and that of others, reflecting deeply on things, while connected to their insights and living their truth in the best possible way.

13. Crystal

People, whose twelfth color is crystal, will safeguard their truth and connect to tranquility with clarity and wisdom.

Clarity and the ability to see all sides of a situation arrive at the end of the Wheel once life processes have been explored and examined on all sides. Thus, enlightenment usually comes at the end of the process, clarity accompanying enlightenment.

When they live their truth, they are clear and distinct in thought and speech and able to progress toward color No. 1 on their Wheel.

They can lead other people when they take care to live with clarity and transparency, without half-truths and concealment. Their calling is to be genuine, clear, distinct and honest in all areas of their life. When they set out their goals clearly, they best see a complete, comprehensive picture, while progressing toward their aims, leading others with clarity and integrity.

A Personal Story

A 43-year-old high-tech employee came to me very tired and bored with his work. Despite good relationships with his fellow workers, he felt the time had come to make a dramatic change in his life and "take off."

We did his Wheel of Colors and found that his twelfth color was white. I asked him what he enjoyed doing because it was clear to me that his calling was to work with people. He responded that he most enjoyed guiding and teaching people.

I suggested he study the field of tour guiding and he became a tour guide for overseas tours. When we met again, he smilingly told me: "I used to spend my whole day sitting in front of a computer, 'dying' of fatigue… Today, I walk, guiding for long hours, and I'm full of energy and strength!"

THE LESSONS OF THE WHEEL MIRRORED BY THE HUMAN SENSES: COLORS 8—12 ON THE WHEEL

The events we experience in daily life constitute our life lessons. When we allow ourselves to fully experience events in our lives, and be open to the lessons they bring us, the attendant insights empower us, changing our lives for the better. When we ignore and avoid lessons out of fear or reluctance to change or be changed, our lives become a sequence of monotonous, pointless days. Each lesson we refuse to learn tends to reappear in our lives in different ways, until we are willing to deal with it, learn from it, internalizing what we have learned and acting to improve our personal development. The more we resist learning the lesson, so it becomes a deeper mental and emotional problem which, if it deepens further, ultimately becomes physical in an attempt to make us deal with the lesson and with ourselves.

Any lesson not learned "jams" the Wheel of Truth and the Wheel of our Lives, making it harder for them to revolve.

When the Wheel turns, we progress, even if it leads us to places that are hard to deal with. The cycle of the Wheel leads us to painful insights, helping us surrender in meaningful ways, taking us to a true, constantly changing life, which means a life filled with meaning and satisfaction. A Wheel that stalls, sticks, or stops revolving, physically and mentally "jams" the rest of our lives, halting our spiritual development and preventing us from living a rich, flowing and changing life, filled with meaning and joy.

Repression and denial, internal resistance to seeing the truth before our eyes, or silencing the truth through overeating, watching programs on television or computer, telephone, or laptop, etc., "jams" our Wheel of Life, making it harder for it to revolve and slowing down our progress. When we learn our physical and mental lessons and act according to the insights we've received from them, we can release the Wheel from its sticking place in the mud of life and turn it into a Wheel of insights, progress, joy and success.

Fortunately, we receive many opportunities from the universe to act in a way that benefits us. Our senses always come to our aid, and all that's left is to act fearlessly and in our own best interests.

The lessons of our senses are:

Lesson No. 8: Our most important lesson in this lifetime—the sense of touch.

Lesson No. 9: The lesson of respecting ourselves and others—the sense of taste.

Lesson No. 10: The lesson of knowing the truth and listening to ourselves—the sense of smell.

Lesson No. 11: The lesson of sensory and extrasensory perception —the sense of sight.

Lesson No. 12: The lesson of safeguarding truth and connecting to tranquility—the sense of hearing.

When facing something new in life, we pass through several stages:

First we "feel and sense" our way by varying means in order to explore whether something is good for us and what we want to do in this situation.

Second, we ask ourselves if there's any point in doing it and what we would achieve by doing it.

The "sniffing" stage comes next. We frequently observe "we can smell a rat"; we don't know how to explain why we sense this, but it's a clear sign for us to stop and explore the issue in depth and, if we reach the conclusion that it doesn't suit us, we drop it. In contrast, when an issue seems right or, as we like to say: "I can smell the roses," we feel it suits us and we progress to the next stage.

The next stage concerns in-depth observation of an issue in all its practical and spiritual aspects and, at this stage, we ask ourselves if this issue appeals to us, if there's something suspicious about it, whether it leads us to advance spiritually and practically.

Following these stages, we activate our sense of hearing and ask our inner voice if the issue suits and benefits us. Although we know that the most important thing is to listen to our inner voice, we sometimes tend to pay attention to external voices and attribute importance to what others say...

When we hear that something is suitable for us, we internalize all remaining senses and act as best we can from the learning process, respect for ourselves and others, knowing the truth, perceiving an issue with clarity and listening to our inner voice.

When we act appropriately during all these stages, we are able to achieve our desires, the best results, and enjoy a dynamic Wheel that revolves according to the pace of our lives, leading us to manifest our calling on earth.

PRACTICAL, IN-DEPTH OBSERVATION OF OUR "PAPILLION" LIFE-CONNECTIONS

The connection between opposing segments on the Wheel through its center creates the shape of a bow tie or, as is popularly known, "Papillion." Since this appealed to my students and clients, I have chosen to use it in this book.

The Papillions connect the lessons and the gifts on our Wheel through the Center, each Papillion representing a fixed lesson opposite a fixed gift. The correlation between color meanings and Papillion location meanings gives us a deep and comprehensive behavioral explanation, enabling us to materially explore a person and their behavior. It is advisable to use personal Papillion colors in any situation, particularly if they are difficult or challenging, using clothing items, food, healing stones, etc.

THE CONNECTIONS BETWEEN OPPOSING WHEEL SEGMENTS (PAPILLIONS) AND THEIR MEANINGS

1-13-7
Entry, centering and protection
New beginnings, balance and protection

This Papillion refers to all new beginnings in our lives such as a new project, new job, new relationship, etc. On the one hand, it shows us (color No. 1) the beginning of our path and our ability to start to do new things while, on the other hand (color No. 7), how to feel protected and confident so that we can walk a new path or start something new, because feeling protected gives us the courage required for new beginnings. The two colors meet and connect by means of the Center (color No. 13), enabling us to be centered in our tasks and act in our unique and personal way.

When combined and working in harmony, the colors 1-13-7 show us how to begin a new task, overcome any obstacle, feel protected confident of our ability to live and act beneficially in new situations in our lives.

2-13-8
Relationships
Our most important life lesson

This Papillion refers to relationships in our lives—how they affect us, what we have to learn from them and the direction they send us in. When we're in a relationship (color No. 2), the most important thing is to learn to know the person in front of us; know how to respond and behave in the best way possible for us and for the relationship (color No. 8), always behaving truthfully and in a balanced way (color No.13). These three colors will advance us along our path, enabling us to lovingly accept all the difficult lessons waiting for us in life's relationships, to balance, grow and mature physically and mentally; to learn to behave without resentment and anger, moving forward in the best way for us and those around us.

3-13-9
An honorable way of life

This Papillion relates to the way in which we choose to live our lives in the most honorable and worthy way we, and the world around us, see fit. How we build our lives from the beginning, combining and expanding our abilities (color No. 3), connects with our ability to respect our wishes, our lives and our environment (color No. 9). When we live our unique personal path in a way that is balanced (color No. 13), respecting ourselves and the entire world, our lives are filled with meaning and we conduct ourselves in the best way possible out of interest and enjoyment, affecting the environment's ability to respect us, our wishes and our way of life.

These three colors define the life path we choose to live, honoring ourselves, our choices and our environment.

4-13-10
Self-centering and knowing the truth
This Papillion refers to our ability to center and be truthful with ourselves, live a fully balanced life with ourselves and our environment, always telling the truth, without wasting time on lies and pretense.

When we are focused on ourselves and what is important to us (color No. 4), we connect with our inner voice and listen to it (color No. 10), whereupon we live a life of truth in accordance with our true nature (color No. 13), free of the desire to please others.

These three colors enable us to live a life of truth, listen to our inner voice, and manifest our deepest wishes.

5-13-11
Creativity in the mirror of our world
This Papillion refers to the ability to reflect differently on ourselves and things around us, perceive them as they are in our eyes, and view things differently from the accepted way. Seeing things just as they are, without embellishment, enables us to act differently and creatively in order to achieve our goals. When we feel a rising desire to create (color No. 5), we must open our eyes, able to see things differently from those around us (color No. 11), acting in our own unique way (color No. 13) in order to come up with wonderfully

creative solutions.

These colors enable us to tell ourselves and our environment how things appear to us and act with great creativity to achieve our aims and goals while revealing creativity and resourcefulness at every stage of our journey.

6-13-12
Manifesting our goals

This Papillion relates to our ability to connect with our inner truth, safeguard and share it with the world around us and manifest our calling because, when we're connected to our calling and act accordingly, we share what is most important to us with the world. Sharing our abilities and gifts with the world (color No. 6) leads us to acknowledge and manifest our calling, each of us having a role to play in this universe (color No. 12), and when we listen to our truth and calling, internalize them and act in a way that affects all aspects of our lives (color No. 13), we are able to share them with the universe and fulfill our roles to the best of our ability.

These three colors enable us to listen to our inner truth, choose our life path, and share it with the world around us.

Opposite is an example of a Papillion:

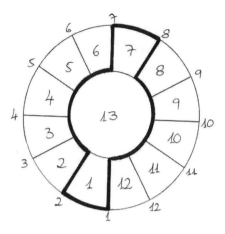

COLOR ASTROLOGY

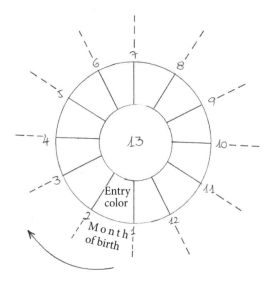

A major part of our observation of the spiritual world through color deals with the field of Color Astrology. Native American astrology has many unique properties based on the observation of Nature, changing seasons, animals and the colors surrounding human beings on all sides. In-depth spiritual learning about the world around us has birthed an incredible, precise form of astrology that deals with our lives mainly through the here and now.

The purpose of Color Astrology is to understand how human beings behave, why they behave in a certain way, and what best helps them manifest their life. Since color is the main subject of my book, I will relate only to the subject of color in astrology and won't go into detail regarding animals. (To deepen knowledge of channeling messages from the world around us, you can read about the meaning of seldom encountered animals on our path in my book: *The Power of Animal Messages*).

In Color Astrology, we divide the year into twelve months according to the usual division of months, January through December, each season characterized by its magnificent natural colors; each month also has its own color, which affects the entire world.

All human beings are affected by the color of the month in which they are born, the color of the month in which they are living at this moment, and by the correlation between these colors and the colors of their Wheel. Astrology combines all meanings of colors, and each month we are affected by two main colors: first by the general color of the month, which affects the entire world and, secondly, by our personal color that relates to a particular month. The combination of the two colors is our lesson for that month and, once the lessons are learned, they become gifts.

Color Astrology constitutes an entire field of reference related to the meaning of events in our lives, both at the moment they take place and retrospectively upon reflection. An analysis of the events and their in-depth understanding are implemented by two techniques, which contribute to identifying the meaning of a color:

1. **Line of Truth** technique
2. **Earth Walk** technique

Full identification consists of all the techniques and enables us to receive a clear, in-depth picture of our past, present and future life.

An examination of people's Wheel of Colors and the connection to their astrology enables us to see where each person is in their life, what they have learned and internalized, what they have yet to learn, and the nature of their calling and how compatible they are with others. An examination of Color Wheel compatibility is usually done according to a significant connection between people, such as a wedding or a work partnership, etc.

Native American Astrology unfolds our life lessons clearly, constituting the most effective way for us to truly understand our personality, insights in relation to our past, and the ability to create a better future. In moments of hardship and loss, we can comprehend where we stand, why things happen, and the direction of the lesson we have experienced in order to act more effectively.

MONTHS OF THE YEAR—THEIR COLORS AND MEANINGS

January—orange

The month of January is known as Snow Moon and is the beginning of the annual Wheel. Its color is orange, the color of learning, for we come into the world in order to learn.

In the month of January, we learn the truth of our lives by means of our relationships with those around us, through the power of love. The color orange is a combination of the color red—belief, and the color yellow—love: We learn best when we love what we learn and love and believe in our teacher.

We encounter many lessons during this month, some of them hard; it is through our life lessons that we learn and progress in the world. We achieve a whole understanding of the month when we know our personal month color and realize on which lesson to focus during the month of January, which opens the New Year, helping us to learn things in depth.

Learning becomes easier when we appreciate it and its contribution to our lives. Without learning, there is no development or progress and when we don't develop or progress, life loses its meaning.

When we open our hearts and allow ourselves to learn, we become proficient and wise, and can best progress and manifest our dreams.

Our lives constitute a series of lessons we must learn and integrate. Our goal is to learn our life lessons as best we can and progress as much as we can physically, mentally and spiritually. Every learned lesson becomes our gift and is a part of our personality for the rest of our life.

February—gray

The month of February is known as Hunger Moon and its color is gray, the color of self-respect and respect for others. During this month we learn about honoring truth and our principles and those of the people around us. The hair of wise elders is gray in color and we must learn to listen to their words, respect ourselves and our human brothers and sisters, the animals, Mother Earth, and the whole universe.

The feeling of respect or honor is a stumbling block in our lives, particularly if we feel we've been disrespected or hurt, or if people haven't shown us the respect we deserve.

When respect prevails among all creatures on our planet, it is possible to live side by side in harmony, but when our relationships are characterized by judgment and lack of respect, it is difficult for us to live harmoniously together, and most people will fight to the death for their honor.

Humanity's lesson is to learn to show respect for a person, their opinions, beliefs and way of life; to honor the animals in our world, and appreciate and respect the planet on which we live, safeguarding the delicate balance of the world around us. It is only when we stop harming those around us that we are able to live in a state of true respect.

When we teach our children the meaning of an honorable life, we enrich ourselves and the entire world, living in a wonderful universe of flowing, harmonious existence and mutual respect.

March—brown

March is known as Crow Moon and is brown in color, the hue related to practicality and connection to earth. This is the month we learn to activate our capacity for learning; to balance and implement what we've learned in every area of our lives in a sound and balanced way. Many of us know the way, but few of us allow ourselves to walk it because many things hamper us: fear, worry, income insecurity, indecisiveness, etc.... We need to learn the truth: it is our thoughts that hold us back and action silences thoughts, proving to them that they're wrong when they wander through our minds, frightening us in every possible way.

Being able to take practical action is the blessed ability to fulfill our life lessons and callings, because any delay in this drags us into an "in between" state, which is destructive for all of us.

Laziness, boredom and freeze are obstacles in our lives and when we do not fulfill ourselves, we feel tired, angry and worried. Balanced action is our life-purpose and when we act from a place of knowing our truth we are filled with interest, energy, hope, vision and flexibility. When we plan our next step, we must remember that planning in itself is a practical step that will transform our deep inner truth into action at the right moment. Proper, balanced action is our calling in life, filling us with meaning, joy, pleasure and real satisfaction.

April—rose

The month of April is known as Grass Moon and is rose in color, the hue related to sensory and extrasensory perception. In this month we observe, see our profound inner truth and that of the world around us.

It is the month of observing ourselves in the mirror with wide-open eyes, seeing ourselves and our lives in a way that is clean and true. This is the time to make an organized list of all the things we want to improve and change and act from a place of sincere and truthful vision.

We tend to walk through the world seeing only what we want to see. We frequently ignore the bitter truth facing us because it is hard to gaze at the truth, change and be changed...

A paraphrased quote from the Buddha says: 'Three things cannot be long hidden: the sun, the moon, and the truth.' We must remember

172 | NOAH GOLDHIRSH

that it is the destiny of truth to be revealed and, ultimately, we will have to see what we are trying so hard to ignore.

Perceiving the truth enables us to be clear and present in every moment of our lives, to live in a state of truth, not on "automatic pilot," and to be at peace with ourselves.

Every human being has a capacity for extrasensory perception. When we allow ourselves to develop this, we are able to see beyond, achieve incredible spiritual teachings and insights in all spheres of our lives, making the desired changes in accordance with our needs and abilities. It is a time to awaken, open our eyes and see the truth within and around us.

May—black

The month of May is known as Planting Moon and is black in color, the hue related to looking inward, meditation and listening to the inner voice. This is the month for hearing our inner truth. This is the month we go inward to examine who we really are, what we want, where we are going and how we feel about ourselves and the world around us. We are inundated with noise on all sides, afraid to close our eyes for a second; and we're distracted by external factors like computers, television and smart phones that have taken over every aspect of our lives.

We don't let ourselves stop, think or gaze inward to see what is happening inside ourselves. We have all sorts of excuses: "No time," "no energy," and so on, and so forth… But actually, we're afraid to take the time to stop and go inward, because we're afraid of what is hiding there in the depths of our souls. Our opinions of ourselves are often determined by external stimuli, according to other people's "likes." Many people silence their inner voices with drugs, alcohol, etc. Anyone who meditates knows that what is found within is completely different from what we think; knowledge, inner peace and quiet are powerful and infinite. Meditation leads us to the deepest, most accurate insights; to the inner quiet we are seeking. This is the time to drop everything for a while, close our eyes, connect with the deepest part of inner knowing and listen to our inner voice that will best show us the right way forward in our lives.

June—red

The month of June is known as Rose Moon and is the color red, the hue related to belief in ourselves and others. The month of June helps us to develop our belief through communication, speaking our truth fearlessly and with gratitude. Speaking the truth is a problem for most of us, mainly because of the most difficult question of all: "What constitutes truth?" We all have our own truth. Every human being sees the truth differently from their peers and even if we listen to someone else's truth, it is not necessarily our truth. How will we know the truth and how will we engage with it? Speaking unembellished truth might attract hurt, anger and infinite quarrels, because your spoken truth might hurt someone else.

Research has shown that most of us use "white lies" on a daily basis, when we want to make people happy or avoid hurting them. When we maintain our inner truth every day, seeing the truth in others increases the good in the world.

When we lie for evil purposes, to steal, hurt or cheat, we increase the evil in the world because by lying, we support and promote evil. Our truth is our inner light and, just as any plant requires light and grows toward it, so truth enables us to develop ourselves, flourish and grow. A lie causes us to fade and wither; just as any plant might wither in darkness, any concealment will cast its heavy shadow on us. The real risk is that someone who constantly lies will degenerate, forgetting the nature of truth. Speaking the truth is humanity's greatest gift and, when truth is spoken generously and lovingly, it helps us grow and flourish, shed the remnants of our past and courageously face the tasks of the future.

July—yellow

The month of July is known as Heat Moon and is the color yellow, the hue related to the unconditional truth of love. It is the month for enhancing our ability to love our truth, and that of others, through the relationships in our lives.

Most of the poetry written in the world is about love and it is love that sets our world in motion.

Our most basic and meaningful love is self-love, but most of us tend to be angry with ourselves, and are frequently full of self-criticism, lacking compassion for our faults and weaknesses. If we don't love ourselves, how can we love others?

If we really and truly love ourselves, we are filled with true insights and can progress without looking back in anger, for we understand that the purpose of any life lesson is to empower us and help us be kinder to ourselves and to those around us.

When we love ourselves, we easily find a place in our hearts for all earth's creatures, accepting them as they are without judgment; we respect them and avoid hurting them.

The more we open to our capacity for loving others, so we develop our ability to love ourselves without judgment; and loving self-acceptance best enables us to learn our life lessons, implementing them with love and joy.

August—blue

The month of August is known as Thunder Moon and is the color blue, the color of intuition. It is the month of giving in the service of truth, the month of learning how to serve people, take care of them and heal them. We all occasionally receive clear messages from our unconscious, and our intuitive knowing of things usually turns out to be right. When we listen to our inner voice, it guides us in difficult moments in the best and wisest way.

This is the time to develop our intuitive abilities and listen to our "gut feelings." Most of us have been raised to act according to our minds, to act logically and according to the available facts, but we know that actually, we often act according to intuition, even when it contradicts the expected.

The development of our capacity for intuition is more available to us today than it ever was in the past, for humanity, once respectful of intuition, has, in recent centuries, venerated the technical and the mechanical but is now returning to our origins, gut feelings, intuition and spiritual knowledge.

It is possible to connect to the inner voice in various ways, such as: meditation, channeling, cards, consulting the I Ching, etc. Trusting and allowing yourself to develop through good communication with your intuition ensures that your life lessons will be properly understood, and you will be synchronized with your feelings and the universe in the best possible way.

September—green

The month of September is known as Hunting Moon and is the color green, the hue related to growth and willpower. This is the month in which we learn to live our truth and safeguard our principles by developing self-esteem and willpower.

We all want health, love, financial abundance, joy and interest in life, security, children, etc. In our childhood we were always told what to do and, in most cases, we weren't allowed to do as we pleased. Most of us have learned to employ strong internal and external resistance, while holding the worldview that it is extremely difficult to achieve what we want on our own. Consequently, most of us employ our willpower when we need to resist something but find it hard to do so in order to achieve what we want.

Successful people in our world have learned to harness their willpower to the achievement of their goals and, since willpower is reinforced by action, they grow and develop all the time. In contrast, people who don't succeed in our world have learned to employ willpower only in the short term, to use money, drugs, alcohol, etc., distortions that paralyze them and their willpower, and they become people who lack true willpower, getting "stuck" in places that are not beneficial for them.

Exerting true willpower comes from an ability to determine what you really want. In order to achieve your goals in life, allow yourself to find a quiet place, without any external disturbance and prepare a list of at least 21 points that detail your goals and the things you wish to achieve in your life.

It is advisable to list all your wishes, even if some things seem impossible to achieve.

This list constitutes a powerful work tool for understanding your true wishes, and it will help you focus, share your positive goals with the universe and support you in employing your willpower and achieving your goals in the best possible way.

The month of September is a month of growth through willpower, which drives our Wheel of Life, determines our dreams and leads us to our goals in the best possible way.

October—pink

The month of October is known as Falling Leaf Moon and is the color pink, the color related to creativity and original activity. In this month we connect to our creativity in order to express our truth through action, since each one of us forms our own unique way of life. The meaning inherent in creativity is unique, original action that finds expression in a thousand ways, the goal of which is to share our abilities and virtues with the world. The palms of our hands are pink, and we create everything with them. We all create in our own personal and original way.

Human creativity has made our world multicolored, fascinating, incredible and unpredictable, for creativity enables us to give flight to our inner meaning. We have come into this world in order to live life in our own unique way and make a mark, each of us forming our own path. The process of creativity empowers and makes us happy and everything we ourselves have created is more valuable than anything we could buy. When we share creative processes with our children from a young age, we enhance their inner strength, teaching them how best to express themselves. Any cookie your children bake with you tastes a thousand times better than one bought in a store. Give flight to your creativity; don't be afraid of criticism; let go of your thoughts; do original things in your own way—and the world will open before you as wonderful and astonishing as ever.

November—white

The month of November is known as Beaver Moon and is the color white, the color related to relationships, attraction and rejection. In this month, we share our profound inner truth with the world. The most important aspect of any relationship is the ability to share our truth, creating a relationship of true reciprocity. If we know that someone hears us, accepts us just as we are, warts and all, we are able to be balanced, secure and happy.

All human beings long for sharing and a sense of belonging; we must learn to create for ourselves the best relationship with the people who are best for us. Good, stable relationships are based on mutual trust, love and acceptance and when we find a person who is truly right for us, we are attracted and drawn to them.

If a relationship is bad for us, there comes a stage when we feel a strong revulsion and don't want to be near someone who harms us. We need to learn to be honest and share the truth even when it is painful; if we feel we cannot be with someone, we must release them lovingly so that they can part from us and go on their way.

The good relationships in our lives support and advance us, whereas bad relationships bring us to a halt, hurting and humiliating us.

Listening to and sharing with people helps them to create the optimal relationship for themselves and those around them, supporting them beneficially over time.

December—purple

The month of December is known as Long Night Moon and is the color purple, the color related to spirituality and gratitude, healing, and the ending and closing of cycles. This is the time we show gratitude for all the good in our lives, reinforcing our healing ability and completing cycles in the various areas of our lives. This is the month when we are aware of the size of the revolving world and its abundant gifts. The annual cycle has come to an end; we reap what we have sown and thank the universe for all its gifts. The ability to say thank you for all that we have is not to be taken lightly; most of us are preoccupied with what we don't have. The good in our lives is taken for granted; we only respect what we have when we might lose it, or are in positions of hardship and distress, such as illness or an accident. Saying "thank you" in advance opens up channels to receive what we want. The ability to say thank you for what we have enables us to see ourselves through the eyes of abundance, instead of through the eyes of wretchedness and lack.

Nothing we have is self-evident and we must learn to acknowledge what exists, knowing how to let go of pain, sorrow and illness, and end each journey we have begun in order to be at peace and happy with ourselves and what we have. We need to be able to end relationships that aren't good for us in order to find better, more suitable ones; leave a job that doesn't suit us to find the job of our dreams; and learn to let go of behavior patterns that are not beneficial, so we can live our life on earth in the best possible way.

LIVING THE MONTHLY CYCLES OF THE YEAR

Each year of our lives is a twelve-month period of physical, mental and emotional learning.

Each month of the year has its own color, which teaches us and the surrounding world a complex and meaningful lesson.

Each of us has a personal Wheel of Colors and when we combine our Wheel with the general monthly Wheel of Colors, we receive a personal lesson together with humanity's general lesson. This combined lesson is the most profound, personal one and is learned each year anew.

When observing our Wheel of Life, we see that certain lessons tend to repeat themselves.

When we allow ourselves to learn the lesson that has appeared in our lives, we develop and progress, but if we resent the lesson it will keep reappearing in our lives until we manage to internalize it.

The true purpose of Color Astrology is to enable us to observe our lives, better understand the past, properly live the present and willingly accept the lessons of the future.

The qualities of our birth month are characteristic of us and how we conduct ourselves in the world, directing us toward the main lesson that accompanies us in all areas of our lives. If we manage to implement the lesson, we are happy and satisfied, and if we fail to implement the lesson, it is difficult for us to be at peace with ourselves and our environment. From one year to the next, we grow and develop with our lessons, thus attributing profound importance to our birthday, which completes the year we have just finished, opening a new year in our lives. Our birthday is the day of our new beginning—the day on which the old lesson of the previous year ends and we have internalized to the best of our ability what we have learned, and the lesson of the new year begins in full force.

The series of months is formed as an inner developmental process that takes us on a new spiritual journey each year, encouraging us to progress and move from one lesson to the next as best we can. We need to learn to work with repeated lessons every year in order to arrive at a profound spiritual understanding of our lives and develop in all spheres.

Each year takes us on a new journey of learning that begins in the month of January. The journey enables us to change ourselves and our lives each month, completing the cycle at the end of the year in the month of December.

THE YEAR'S MONTHLY LESSONS

1. January invites us to join in the most wonderful life adventure of learning, one in which we will learn to live with love and belief.

2. February teaches us to respect ourselves, the universe, our learning process and that of those around us, so that the teaching is real, honorable and profound.

3. March teaches us to act and implement the lesson we have learned. The activity gathers all the lessons we have learned in life, actively employing our spirituality, integrating insights into our personality and turning each lesson into a true life-gift.

4. April teaches us to see ourselves and the consequences of our actions. When we open our eyes and are able to see sincerely and honestly how our actions impact our lives and the lives of those around us, we can improve ourselves and the world around us, living a life of truth while connected to our life lessons and their consequences.

5. May teaches us to go inward and listen to our inner voice. In April we looked outward at the results of our actions, and now we need to look inward, see how we have deeply changed thanks to our life lessons, listening to our inner voice, seeing our inner truth and acting accordingly.

6. June teaches us to speak our inner truth aloud, the truth we admitted to in May, while best enabling ourselves and others to hear it.

Speaking our truth fearlessly is the first stage of true communication. Real communication builds trust in any relationship.

We need to believe in ourselves and our inner voices—so that we can learn to believe in others. The month of June teaches us to speak our truth, believe in ourselves and create good, real relationships with ourselves and those around us.

7. **July** teaches us to really love ourselves and those around us. Love is what motivates our inner and external worlds, and this is what enables us to learn each lesson, progress in our lives and reach any chosen place. Helped by a love of truth we can change our world, hold out a hand to all world creators and live in harmony in the best possible way.

8. **August** teaches us to listen to our intuition and gut feelings and act accordingly.

The desire and the ability to help others are intrinsic to us and we must learn to act and serve those around us truthfully. Intuition is our inner compass, and when we learn to use it in order to take action, to listen to our gut feelings and act accordingly and without fear, it will lead us to our spiritual ability so that we can best take care of ourselves and others.

9. **September** teaches us to employ our willpower and flourish, develop and succeed in every sense of the word. From the moment of our inception we develop and grow, like a germinating seed that makes its way through clods of earth to develop into a huge tree that blossoms and yields fruit.

We learn to make our way through willpower, set out on physical and spiritual journeys and grow to unimaginable heights, attaining the best results.

10. October teaches us to be creative in all spheres of life. Each one of us is different and special, but we all walk the path of life and learn the lessons we encounter on our way. The ability to implement each lesson creatively and uniquely is what unites and empowers us. Creativity fills us with a sense of satisfaction, joy and success, which empowers us with a feeling of self-value; the purpose of our lives is to be creative, unique and original in everything we do on our way.

11. November teaches us about relationships in our lives, showing us how to be sincere and honest and live in healthy relationships with joy and satisfaction in every sense of the word. The important lesson of the month of November is to learn to maintain and foster relationships that are beneficial for us, and to understand which relationships don't benefit us and be able to end them and move on with our lives.

12. December teaches us to connect with our spiritual side, show gratitude for what we have, complete past cycles and heal physically and mentally. This month invokes all the gifts and lessons, concluding the year, enabling us to collect everything we have spread around, reap what we have sown, give thanks for an entire year of lessons, profound insights and mental and physical development, and move on, reinforced, our hands filled with the gifts of the year that has passed, our spirit grateful for everything that has been and willing to go forward toward new beginnings.

THE LINE OF TRUTH

The line of truth is our personality's way of fulfilling our calling on earth and we walk the line from the moment of our birth until we leave this world. When we walk the line of our truth our lives progress and our lessons are learned, and when we diverge from our line of truth our lives get stuck and we feel we aren't developing or progressing.

Each person's line of truth begins in the month of their birth and leads to the month facing them on their Wheel of Colors and months of the year. Those born in:

January walk the line of truth 1-7
February walk the line of truth 2-8
March walk the line of truth 3-9
April walk the line of truth 4-10
May walk the line of truth 5-11
June walk the line of truth 6-12
July walk the line of truth 7-1
August walk the line of truth 8-2
September walk the line of truth 9-3
October walk the line of truth 10-4
November walk the line of truth 11-5
December walk the line of truth 12-6

The meaning of the line of truth changes according to the point of departure and the end point. The purpose of someone born in January is the opposite of the purpose of someone born in the month of July, because the departure point of the former is the final purpose of the latter, who is located at the opposite point. They share the same truth and so experience identical life lessons (love and learning), but their life lessons are essentially different, both in purpose and the way in which they are manifested. Each one of us walks our line of truth back and forth throughout life and our final purpose is to transform the two opposing points into one by learning and internalizing all life lessons.

The Truth Line of Those Born in January

The color orange—their learning—leads them toward the color yellow—unconditional love of truth.

Intrinsic to those born in January is their capacity for in-depth learning, and they learn the issues of their life through love and relationships. Their first tendency is to learn and explore each issue, and only afterwards do they allow themselves to open their hearts and love it. Their purpose is to reach an unconditional love of truth and the ability to trust and love as best and flowingly as they can, the Line of Truth guiding them to learn to open their hearts and live their lives with emotional security.

The Truth Line of Those Born in February

The color gray—their honor/respect—leads them toward the color blue—their intuition.

The honor/respect of those born in the month of February is important to them, and they are supposed to learn about respecting their own truth and principles as well as those of people around them. Their purpose is to learn to listen to their intuition and enhance their ability to serve and honor every human being and living creature on earth. If they learn to live by listening to their inner voice, they are able to walk their Line of Truth with true respect for themselves and those around them, safeguarding the honor of each living creature through understanding, spirituality and true compassion.

The Truth Line of Those Born in March

The color brown—practicality—leads them to the color green—willpower.

Those born in the month of March will learn and know the truth through a balanced life. They tend to be practical, preoccupied with their own truth and that of others and to implement everything they have learned in all spheres of their life in a way that is balanced.

Their practicality must connect with their willpower in order for them to manifest and achieve all they wish in life, and when they learn this lesson and walk the line of their truth, everyone enjoys their quality of practicality because they have a developed sense of justice and will take care of those around them.

The Truth Line of Those Born in April

The color rose—their perception of the extrasensory—leads them toward the color pink—their creativity and originality.

Those born in the month of April are characterized by an ability to see the world differently and unusually. Their capacity for analyzing situations by means of a general perceptiveness that is both sensory and extrasensory, teaches them to connect with their creativity and live an unusually creative and different life. Their Line of Truth leads them to see and do things differently, in a way that is original and creative.

The Truth Line of Those Born in May

The color black—their capacity for looking inward—leads them toward the color white—their relationships with others.

Those born in the month of May tend to be withdrawn and think in order to understand who they really are, what they desire, where they are going and how they really feel about themselves and the world around them. Walking the Line of their Truth helps them learn to share their insights and their inner truth with those around them and to change the world.

The Truth Line of Those Born in June

The color red—believing in themselves—meets the color purple—all gifts, all lessons, end and healing.

Those born in the month of June are supposed to tell their truth fearlessly, constantly, and to develop their belief through communication and gratitude.

They need to learn that when they tell their truth, they are able to complete cycles, heal and heal themselves.

It is very important to them to learn to believe in themselves, to express gratitude for all the good in their lives so they can live the line of their truth in the best possible way.

The Truth Line of Those Born in July

The color yellow—unconditional love—meets the color orange—life lessons and learning truth.

Those born in the month of July are supposed to love and give properly and beneficially for themselves and those around them. They are supposed to learn how to love and give in a balanced way, loving themselves, not only others, and understanding that the universe has one basic rule: energy must be given in exchange for energy.

Mutual giving and receiving is the best way to live in the universe, and the truth line of those born in July leads them to learn the capacity for giving and receiving love in a way that is beneficial and balanced.

The Truth Line of Those Born in August

The color blue—their developed intuition—meets the color gray—respecting themselves and others.

Those born in August are supposed to use their intuition at all times and in all situations so that they can truly serve from a place of real respect, for themselves and those around them.

They are supposed to learn to develop their ability to listen to their inner voice and to be able to connect to their inner healer without calculation in terms of respect, power or taking control of another. Wholehearted giving and service out of respect for themselves and others will lead them along their Line of Truth, helping them to realize their abilities.

The Truth Line of Those Born in September

The color green—their willpower—meets the color brown—their practicality and the connection with the earth and reality.

They have very powerful willpower and must learn to act realistically to achieve and manifest their dreams.

When a new idea occurs to them they must harness it to reality, work hard and manifest it, for their Line of Truth guides them to the ultimate combination created when willpower is connected with the ability to implement. Their calling connects them to infinite action and, when they allow themselves the legitimacy to move from a world of dreams and desires to a world of creativity and reality, they can achieve anything they wish beneficially, enjoying the fruit of their labors.

The Truth Line of Those Born in October

The color pink—their creativity—meets the color rose—their ability to see everything from a different perspective through sensory and extrasensory perception.

Those born in October create their path differently from others. They strive to live life in a way that is original and unique, and their creativity is nurtured by their ability to see reality materially and spiritually.

Their Line of Truth leads them creatively and they must learn to enable themselves to see and invent things without worrying about being unusual, for when they give flight to themselves, they discover there is no limit to their creativity.

The Truth Line of Those Born in November

The color white—relationships in their lives—meets the color black—their tendency to thinking, observation and withdrawing.

The natural ability of those born in November to bond with people around them sometimes overshadows their ability to withdraw inside themselves for deep observation, change and be changed. When in conflict between their inner and outer worlds they tend to be blunt, or withdraw, suddenly disconnecting from people.

They need to learn to be sincere in all their relationships in order to learn about their meaning, understand what motivates them, and learn about the nature of the goal they seek. On their way along the Line of their Truth they discover that they also teach those around them a complex lesson about the importance of relationships as opposed to individuality, thinking and withdrawal.

The Truth Line of Those Born in December

The color purple—their capacity for spirituality, gratitude, healing and closing cycles—meets the color red—their belief in the universe, themselves and those around them.

Those born in December are given multiple gifts and lessons and they tend to be impatient, quick-thinking and preoccupied with many parallel fields. They need to learn to appreciate the gifts they are given, to give thanks for all the good in their lives, to be healed and close cycles in their lives in order to arrive at true belief in themselves and those around them. Those born in December may have strong faith in an idea, religion, etc., hop easily from one subject to another, and any new idea will delight them. When walking their Line of Truth, they believe in themselves and learn how to close life cycles and are able to attain faith and spiritual satisfaction in a beneficial way.

EARTH WALK

The Earth Walk is our path on Earth in this lifetime and it includes the collection of large and small life lessons that we will experience in the course of our lives. Native Americans describe life as a journey, a walk along life's paths on the way to understanding our calling on Earth. Our life paths are constantly changing in accordance with the fabric of our lives. Sometimes we walk such a narrow path it seems we won't be able to take one more step, when suddenly it expands, becoming a beautiful, comfortable, main path that is broad and clear, and life sometimes leads us along a main road that is wide and clear, when suddenly, at the end of it, we see a sign: "Dead End," with several indistinct paths splitting off... Since we are human beings and require a sense of security and stability in life, we tend to be shocked and afraid when we encounter the end of a path. We are frightened by signs telling us "Dead End," "No Way Through," etc., and get angry at life. After all, we have always walked that path, our intentions were good, and it is so hard to change our way! But all our shouts, tears and protestations don't help us. When one path ends, we have to find another way and walk it, for even if we wait and procrastinate, the facts won't change: that path won't take us anywhere, and we have to change direction.

In the course of our lives we encounter people who evoke a shift in us and we change our path as a result of their actions and behavior to us and the environment, and every encounter that brings about change will also change the path we have chosen to walk. A shift in the path we walk usually makes us pause a moment, sometimes instinctively, sometimes calculatedly, and take a step back in order to better observe the situation. Having examined the situation we continue to walk in the direction we have chosen, events and the people we meet frequently making us turn and take a completely different path, and/or joining the people we meet along the paths of our lives. When observing the path we walk in life, we see what the Native Americans call "Earth Walk."

If we wish to know how a particular event has impacted our lives and what we have learned from it, we relate to the Earth Walk on the Wheel of Colors and months of the year.

Finding the Earth Walk
To find the Earth Walk we divide the Wheel like a clock, the month of January being number 1, followed by all the months, in order, up to the month of December, which is number 12 on the Wheel.

In the color of our choice, we mark the number of the month in which the event occurred and that we wish to understand in depth. It is advisable to use different colors for the various events on the Wheel in order to understand each event individually and see the trends in our lives.

A person we meet in the month of November will teach us the lessons for that month (specifically) and the lessons of the month of May (the Line of Truth from November—May). In order to know the nature of the Earth Walk and how the encounter with someone has affected us over the years we must mark the month in which we met, and then "walk" three steps back—counterclockwise—on the Wheel, which means going back three months, and marking it.

We reach the month of February—opposite the month of August, which constitutes additional lessons we have to learn from the encounter with that person. Our purpose in finding the Earth Walk is to attain the insights each month gives us as well as a general insight regarding the situation.

When significant events happen in a certain month year after year, we must understand that this month is supposed to teach us many lessons and pay particular attention to the meaning of the month and its attendant lessons.

On the Earth Walk we relate to the color of the month according to the calendar and the color of our birth month. These connections tell us why we have had certain experiences, clarifying our lessons, our purpose and how best to achieve it. Our life path tends to be long, difficult and not always clear; understanding the lessons of the path gives our lives meaning, helping us to live a life of truth from a place of profound awareness.

PERSONAL AND UNIVERSAL MESSAGES OF THE MONTHS OF THE YEAR IN THE MIRROR OF COLOR

Combining the Universal and the Personal Message with each Month of the Year

Every month of the year has a general meaning and a message related to the entire world as well as a personal message and meaning that relate to us individually.

Combining the universal and the personal meaning is the best way to know and understand what is happening mentally and spiritually with us every month and the implementation of these messages helps us to work with ourselves and those around us, succeeding in drawing the best out of each month.

In order to combine monthly personal and general messages, we must draw the personal Wheel of Colors intertwined with the general Wheel of Months. The best way to unite them is to:

1. Draw your Wheel of Colors on a blank piece of paper, using a pencil or pen to precisely mark and emphasize the segments; make sure the right numbers appear on the segments and color them appropriately.
2. Write your birth month next to segment 1 (located where 6 is on a standard clock); those born in March, for instance, will write down next to their segment No. 1 the month of March; those born in June will write down next to their segment No. 1 the month of June and so on. Color No. 1 is the color of our birth and our beginning, thus we always write our birth month beside it.

3. Continue to write down the consecutive months, for example—
    for those born in March: write born in March; having written
    down March next to segment No. 1, write down beside segment
    No. 2 the month of April; beside segment No. 3 the month of May
    and so on. In this way you will create two intertwined Wheels.

Once we have numbered all the months of the year intertwined with
the numbers of the Wheel, we are ready to read.

Each month now has two colors: your personal color on the
Wheel of Colors and the color of the month according to the general,
monthly Wheel of the year.

The combination of the two colors constitutes your lesson for that
month.

Each month's lesson is repeated every year, and when we learn
to work with our life lessons, we realize that the monthly lesson
progresses and changes from one year to the next according to the
changes that take place in us.

A lesson well learned returns as a gift, a new ability, a way to break
through boundaries and succeed.

Color Astrology reminds us of the month's meaning and calling
but leaves us to find the way to engage, change and best create our
lives. By understanding the months and years of our life we can
prepare for the coming lessons, consider what we wish to do and
flow with the energy of color and time in a way that is best for us and
those around us.

COLOR CARDS

We frequently face complex, harsh and fateful situations and find it difficult to ask the right questions to help us discover and resolve the situation we are in, because every issue in our lives tends to impact others. For example, a person who wants to leave their job because they don't enjoy it must take into account the effect their leaving will have on additional issues in their life, such as money, the people they are supporting, their reputation, their self-esteem, etc. In order to reach a situation in which we can distinguish between the issue we must address and other issues, while taking care of the former, we can and should use color and channeling. The use of Color Cards combines channeling and color techniques in order to gain insights from our infinitely knowledgeable sub-conscious. The method is suitable for anyone who comes to the conclusion that they wish to stop thinking about "What should I do?" and start thinking about "What would be best for me?"

Preparation of a pack of therapeutic color cards

In order to prepare a pack of therapeutic color cards ourselves, we need the following materials:

White card

Scissors

Paintbrush and gouache or acrylic paints, or colored pencils

Ruler and pencil.

A. Draw on the card, with the help of the ruler and pencil, 42 rectangles, each measuring 6 x 9 cm.

B. Cut out the rectangles according to your markings.

C. Color the front of each of the cards you cut out according to the instructions in (D) and leave the other sides white.

D. Using the colors of your choice, paint three cards of each color: Red, Yellow, Blue, Green, Pink, White, Purple, Orange, Gray, Brown, Rose, Black, Crystal and Beige.

E. We can write down the meaning of each color card like this and as illustrated on page 337:

Red = Belief x 3

Yellow = Love x 3

Blue = Intuition x 3

Green = Willpower x 3

Pink = Creativity x 3

White = Relationships x 3

Purple = Healing and gratitude x 3

Orange = Learning x 3

Gray = Respect x 3

Brown = Practicality x 3

Rose = Extrasensory x 3

Black = Mindfulness x 3

Crystal = Clarity x 3

Beige = Taking time for yourself x 3

Diagnosis with the help of Color Cards and the Life-Wheel illustration

Diagnosis takes place sitting down in a comfortable, quiet room with a partly open window. On a table one can place such energetic aides as: a lit candle, a stone, a plant or a vase of flowers.

The client is given a blank, white sheet of paper, A3 or A4, and pencils; prepare additional sheets of paper on one side for drawing or work.

The therapist sits calmly and quietly opposite the client who is invited to work quietly and without stress, at their own pace.

The client is asked to draw a circle.

They are then asked to divide the circle into segments according to the subjects they wish to explore in their life, for example: love, family, friends, making a living, etc.

The client determines the number of segments and subjects.

The client is asked to close their eyes, turn the sheet of paper around, place their hand anywhere they wish on the paper, open their eyes and see which segment their hand is touching.

The subject is written down on a sheet of paper. If the subject's hand lands on two subjects, both must be written down on separate sheets of paper, one for each subject.

The pack of cards is spread out. The client is asked to choose three cards for each subject, according to the following questions:

1. How I used to relate to this subject in the past.
2. How I relate to it in the present.
3. What will help me to resolve the problem and improve my situation in the future.

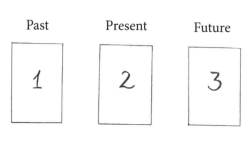

For example: Regarding the issue of "work," my client chose the following cards: Yellow for the past, red for the present, and green for the future.

The meaning of this choice is: Yellow—in the past, he related to his job emotionally, taking everything to heart.

In the present—red—he believes he must examine the issue and his ability, actively improving the situation and believing in his strength and talents.

In the future—green—he must use his willpower to resolve the problem, improve his future, grow and progress in his life.

I suggested my client use the three colors he'd chosen in his clothing and food, emphasizing the use of green to reinforce his willpower and improve his future situation.

It is advisable to encourage the client to note down any insights received in order to continue working and using colors he's chosen in relation to clothing and healing stones, eating healthy food of the right colors and making a note of thoughts, ideas and conclusions in relation to the subject.

CHOICE OF COLOR

Most of us choose colors intuitively and our choices change from one day to the next according to our physical and mental states. Our capacity for choice also tends to be influenced by external factors such as our environment, the people we're with, and so on. Over the years we prefer certain colors to others and we tend to choose them more frequently; and there are colors we don't usually use that will, in certain circumstances, suddenly attract our eye.

When attempting to choose a color for ourselves we tend to be influenced by the accepted fashion and/or the opinions of people around us, since it is usually easier to detect other people's state of mind than to clearly see our own and it is advisable to choose colors energetically in order to avoid external distractions. Choosing a color intuitively is an excellent way to understand which color would be beneficial for us. We need to trust the body's ability to choose the color required for the enhancement and balance of our physical and mental state. It is possible to choose the required color using simple colored cards we make ourselves. When we wish to choose a color for ourselves or for a client, we can use relatively simple cards that relate only to the meanings of colors, which we can prepare with various techniques. The following are several suggestions for using color cards. Any choice you make will be the right one for you.

- Cards made from plastic material known as "Mapal." Prepare cards out of Mapal in every color possible, i.e. at least 13 cards (crystal = transparent). It is advisable to have at least two of every card in the pack. Choosing a card is done with closed eyes. The client spreads out the cards on the table, passing their hand over the cards until they feel a "tug" or "heat" above one of the cards; take the chosen card.

- Cardboard cards, one side of which is blank, the other colored. These cards can be bought from craft stores and are ready-made; one side has a simple illustration that is the same on every card in the pack, and the other side is white. Color in the white side according to the list of colors. It is advisable to have at least two copies of every card in each color. The cards are spread out on the table, their colored side facing downward. The card is chosen intuitively and turned over in order to see the chosen color.

- Blank, smooth cards on both sides with a colored sticker on one side. These blank cards with a uniform color on one side of the card are ready-made and sold in packs at craft stores. To add the required colors, buy stickers in all colors, and stick them on one side of the cards. It is advisable to have at least two copies of every card in each color. Spread out the cards on the table, the side with the uniform color uppermost. Choose a card intuitively and turn it over to see the chosen color.

OUR LIFE CYCLES IN THE MIRROR OF THE PERSONALITY

Diagnosing a person's feelings, standing in the family and in society according to a free sketch of their life cycles

The diagnosis is made according to a free sketch of the life cycles by means of a technique based on the kind of drawing and the meanings inherent in its colors.

Materials:

A4 sheets of paper
Pastel-oil paints, a 24-color kit is advisable.
A table / smooth floor
A quiet undisturbed room

The Diagnostic Process

- The client is given two blank sheets of A4 paper and a box of crayons.
- The client is instructed to draw a circle on the paper in the color of their choice.
- They are instructed to draw a second circle inside the first circle, in the color of their choice.
- They are instructed to draw a third circle inside the second, in the color of their choice.
- The therapist allows the client to draw as they wish at each stage. Some are satisfied with a simple drawing, while others develop the drawing. Any kind of drawing is acceptable.

- The therapist explains the meaning of the circles so that the client can note down explanations on the second sheet of paper.

The Meanings of the Circles

We all live in interwoven circles:

The external circle—the world

This circle indicates how the person perceives the world in which they live.

The second circle—family and friends

This circle shows how the person sees their immediate surroundings, family and friends and relationships with them.

The inner circle—me

This circle shows how the person sees him/herself and responds to the questions Who am I? and What have I come to do in the world?

The size of the circle indicates a person's self-confidence and their place in the world, showing us how they see themselves and their place in the world. Circles that are average in size indicate balance and an attempt to balance physically and spiritually; particularly large circles reflect problems with boundaries and self-definition, while particularly small circles are characteristic of eating disorders.

The colors chosen by the client for each circle they draw indicate their exact state of mind, empowering insights regarding the circles drawn.

The best way to diagnose circles is through observation and sharing.

Allow the client the time they need to develop and cooperate. Explain simply the meaning of the circles and enable the client to note down their insights.

Listen to the client and enable them to participate in the diagnostic process and respond at each and every stage to what they are told.

COLORS AS HEALERS

Colors heal us with their energetic vibrations, and we use light, food, healing stones and clothing of various colors to receive the energy of color. The best, most suitable energy for us is the natural energy that exists in our world.

Healing Light

The most healing energy for our bodies comes from the sun. Our skin absorbs the entire color spectrum from the sun and transfers the energy to the whole body. People who live in places where there is a lack of sunlight tend to suffer from various illnesses.

The use of sun energy contributes extraordinarily to our physical and mental energy and the usual recommendation is to be exposed to sunlight regularly at appropriate times.

In Color Therapy treatments, color radiation techniques can be utilized through sunrays directed at a particular area. For example, when the blood flow to the feet is weak, one can expose the affected feet to the appropriate light.

In Color Therapy, a color torch is used to radiate various colors onto the body. Color radiation is incredibly effective and can be found in the appropriate stores. The recommendation is to use our natural sunlight and if we wish to use a particular color in the treatment, we allow the sun to shine through the desired color, sitting or lying down while the color is transmitted to the area we wish to treat.

Color should be used for a limited time. In most cases we begin by exposing the body to the required color for two or three minutes, judiciously extending the dose as needed. Do not continue to use a color for more than ten minutes; we must pay attention to the body's response to the color radiation and act accordingly. A Color Therapy specialist should be consulted.

HEALING FOODS

Food in its natural colors and textures, without artificial additives, heals and builds our bodies.

When eating food of a certain color, the energy of the color enters our bodies. It is advisable to consume healthy food of all colors daily, emphasizing the colors our bodies most need.

Natural Food Colors:
1. **Red:** Tomatoes, strawberries, raspberries, peppers, cranberries, goji berries, grated raw beets, cooked beets, watermelon, red grapefruit
2. **Yellow:** Lemons, bananas, grapefruit, corn, chickpeas, millet, amaranth
3. **Blue:** Blueberries, water in a blue glass bottle
4. **Green:** Leaves of all kinds, cucumbers, sprouts (green peppers are not ripe and should not be eaten as they are considered toxic), green peas, avocado, mung beans
5. **Pink:** Any food mixed with beet juice, peaches, pink Himalaya salt
6. **White:** Salt, rice milk, almond milk, oat milk, almonds (almonds and beer nuts are brown and white) white beans, onion, garlic, potatoes (brown and white), quinoa, coconut and its products
7. **Purple:** Purple cabbage, eggplant, beetroot, purple carrot, passionfruit (purple + orange), purple onion, purple grapes
8. **Orange:** Sweet potato, pumpkin, carrots, orange lentils, turmeric
9. **Gray:** Gray food is usually not fresh healthy food. Peeled sunflower seeds can be defined as gray, Atlantic salt is also grayish, but apart

from these one should be careful with food that appears gray.

10. **Brown:** Bread, almonds, other nuts, whole flour, Teff flour, brown lentils, chocolate (without added milk), potatoes (brown + white)

11. **Rose:** Pitaya, anything mixed with beet juice

12. **Black:** The color black in foods usually appears in the form of seeds: black wild rice, kalonji, black pepper, black sesame seeds and sunflower seeds

13. **Crystal:** Water—the natural color of water is crystal. By means of water charged with color it is possible and easy to use all colors (see page 228 on charging water with colors).

There are many kinds of food and only a small selection is mentioned in this list. The rule is to carefully and wisely examine the food we put in our bodies.

HEALING STONES

The stones were formed millions of years ago and consist of minerals and natural colors. In Color Therapy, we use only natural stones without color additives.

The stones transmit their color waves and waves of energy from the materials of which they are made. The energy they produce is highly significant, flowing constantly and steadily.

I warmly recommend treatment through healing stones for any situation. Sometimes, the effect of the stones on the body seems rather slow, but they always work and have a beneficial, long-term effect.

They can be used in treatments, placed on the body in areas we want to heal; placed around us to balance energy and prevent radiation harm from electrical appliances; kept in our pockets or worn for a time on the body—necklaces, bracelets and/or rings.

The stones listed here represent only a small number of magnificent authenticated stones. They are sold in the appropriate stores at reasonable prices and are easy to find and use. Many stones are found in nature around us and can be collected and used in various treatments.

You are invited to choose any stone that attracts you and use it to treat yourself or others. The process of choosing stones is important and pleasurable so you should find a store where you can hold stones in your hand and choose them energetically, for everyone is attracted to the stones and colors they particularly need.

The Colors of Healing Stones

1. **Red:** Ruby, Garnet, Red Jasper, Red Coral, Fire Agate.
2. **Yellow:** Citrine, Yellow Calcite, Topaz, Amber.
3. **Blue:** Lapis Lazuli; Sodalite, Aquamarine, Turquoise, Blue Quartz (Blue Aventurine), Blue Lace Agate, Blue Calcite, Labradorite.
4. Green: Emerald, Green Quartz (Green Aventurine), Malachite, Jade, Amazonite, Green Calcite, Moss Agate.
5. **Pink:** Rose Quartz, Pink Tourmaline, Unakite (green and pink), Rhodonite, Rhodochrosite.
6. **White:** Howlite, White Quartz, Pearl, White Jade, river pebbles, White Calcite, Moonstone (the moonstone stone appears in other colors as well), White Coral, Mother-of-Pearl.
7. **Purple:** Amethyst, Sugalite, Fluorite.
8. **Orange:** Carnelian, Orange Calcite, Fire Agate.
9. **Gray:** Snowflake Obsidian (white and gray with black), Tourmaline Quartz, Smokey Quartz, Hematite, stones and rocks in shades of gray from the beach, and mountain streams.
10. **Brown:** Various kinds of Jasper, Brown Calcite, Tiger's Eye, Petrified Wood.
11. **Rose:** Rhodonite, Rhodochrosite.
12. **Black:** Black Tourmaline, Black Onyx, Porous Black Lava, Obsidian (shiny black lava).

13. **Crystal:** Transparent Quartz, Optical Calcite, every rainbow that appears in natural stone, Rainbow Moonstone.

THE USE OF COLORED FABRICS
IN TREATMENT

In Color Therapy we use colorful cotton and silk fabrics as an effective therapeutic tool. Real silk from China is a fabric that has a beneficial effect on the body; however, its production process is cruel, causing suffering and death to living creatures. I don't recommend materials made in this way when it is possible to use other materials in a way that is easy and cheap. Cotton fabric is well suited to our bodies and in Color Therapy I recommend the use of 100% cotton fabrics, particularly organic cotton, in the colors required for the treatment of various areas.

Placing fabric of a certain color on the body transmits and streams its color into the body, thus it is advisable to prepare in advance squares of fabric in various colors (the size of the palm) for use in energetic treatments. During the treatment, we see which colors the body needs, choose the squares of appropriate colors and place them on the body in the appropriate places and on the chakras. For longer treatments, it is advisable to use scarves of various colors and wind them around the treated area.

For example:
Winding a turquoise scarf around the neck soothes a sore throat and hoarseness.

Winding an orange scarf around the area of the womb and sexual organs eases menstrual pain.

Winding a scarf with the colors green, purple and orange around the back, eases backache, strained muscles, etc.

A Personal Experience

Over the years I have frequently been invited to lecture about the use of colors in physical and mental treatments and, at each lecture, people tend to ask me for practical "tips." I advise girls and women who suffer from menstrual pain to be examined by a gynecologist and, if everything is in order and there is no hidden problem, to place a warm orange towel or an orange scarf around the belly and lower back when suffering from menstrual pain. The results are impressive. In the months following the lecture, several women always call to thank me for the tip that made a difference in their lives.

When we wish to start a new project we can wear a garment in our No. 1 color and if we wish to enhance action related to our calling, we add a garment in our No. 12 color, and so on.

The technique of deliberately wearing clothes in the colors of our choice makes us aware of each step we take, helping us to manage and improve our lives in all spheres.

COLORFUL CLOTHING

The colors of the clothing we wear transmit their color wavelength, affecting our bodies that are built to absorb light and color vibrations. It is advisable to wear clothing of all colors, changing the colors we wear according to need, and pay attention to the various sensations evoked when we wear different colors. We should choose the colors of the clothes we wear according to what we feel and be aware of our sensations on a daily basis.

The simplest way to use color on various occasions is to wear clothing that matches the colors of our personal Wheel of Colors, for example: People whose beginning color (color No. 1 on the Wheel) is blue, should wear something blue with every new beginning, to ensure success and productivity.

People whose balancing color is pink (color No. 4 on the Wheel) should wear something pink when they're ill, for this is the color that will bring them balance and best help them heal. If people are feeling threatened and unconfident, they should wear something in their protection color (color No. 7 on their Wheel). The color considered best for all situations is color No. 13 on your personal Wheel, but if your color 13 is gray or black, two colors that tend to be problematic when over-used, use the color crystal (which contains black and gray), and you will thus be able to use all the colors your body needs while emphasizing your main color.

For maximum use of color, it is possible to wear either clothing or stones in the colors we consciously need on any particular day. For example: If we have an important exam and wish to be focused, we can wear clothing in our colors No. 13 + No. 4 and if we feel we need protection during the exam, we can add something in our color No. 7.

THE CHAKRAS

What Chakras Mean and How they Heal

The chakras are energy centers located in the body and that stream energy into and out of the body in the form of a spiral. Chakra is a Sanskrit word meaning "wheel." Each chakra is responsible for introducing and extracting energy from specific areas of the body, and the chakras work together synchronically to disperse energy through the body in a balanced way. There are thousands of chakras and they serve as key areas for energetic treatments of our body.

In Color Therapy we focus on seven basic, familiar chakras and I will add several additional important chakras.

The seven basic chakras are:

The Root Chakra—First Chakra

The color of the Root Chakra is red, and it is located between the anus and the genitals.

The Root Chakra belongs to the Earth Element and is connected to the energies of survival, to earth, food, sexuality, sound health and making a good living.

This chakra is the beginning and the basis for all energetic movement from the earth to the heavens. It encourages us to act, streaming earth energy into our body, allowing us to combine our body and spirituality in a practical way. This chakra is particularly significant for new beginnings, when we want the foundation to be stable and well-grounded in the earth. A disrupted flow of energy in the Root Chakra might cause a sense of physical and mental weakness, a lack of joy and desire to live, a tendency to over-weight, hemorrhoids, constipation, eating disorders such as anorexia or bulimia, fear of new things, inability to ground oneself and a general tendency to illness.

When the Root Chakra is balanced, the person is active, healthy, energetic and filled with a passion for life.

We should take care not to over-use the color red. If a client suffers from high blood pressure, they should avoid using the color red or use it judiciously. Treatment should be undertaken mainly through the soles of the feet.

Red underwear contributes to a beneficial flow of energy in the Root Chakra.

People who suffer from cold feet can wear red socks to stimulate the blood flow.

The Root Chakra is best activated and balanced by the use of red stones, such as Ruby, Garnet, Red Jasper and Red Coral.

A balanced use of red contributes to the basic health and sound activation of the Root Chakra.

The Family Chakra—The Second Chakra

The color of the Family Chakra is orange, and it is located between the navel and the genitals, about three fingers' width under the navel.

The Family Chakra belongs to the Water Element and relates to sexuality and emotions, particularly related to family. This Chakra increases its activity during adolescence, and the color orange encourages and stimulates proper hormonal development. When the Family Chakra is balanced it opens and streams intuitive and extrasensory powers, which is where the term "gut feeling" derives from.

When the energy flow of the Family Chakra is disrupted, it could cause problems in kidney functioning, the bladder, and blood circulation, the menstrual cycle and ovulation, problems with sperm production, impotence or premature ejaculation in men and an inability to reach orgasm among women. Problems with the functioning of the Family Chakra also relate to fear, anxiety and skin problems and, in severe cases, even mental instability and insensitivity.

The Family Chakra is balanced and activated best by orange stones, such as Orange Calcite, Carnelian and Sun-stone.

Orange is the color of life, a color antidepressant that evokes joy and deep meaning in our lives. The Family Chakra streams energy-of-life into our bodies, helping us to live a balanced, happy life, enjoying the functioning of our bodies in the best possible way.

Family Chakra treatment with the support of the color orange helps to soothe lower back pain.

Men who suffer from prostate problems should wear orange underwear that cover the location of the Family Chakra.

Women who suffer from menstrual pain should wear orange underwear and/or place orange fabric or a warmed orange towel on the area of the Family Chakra. Treatment with the color orange in this area will also ease heavy bleeding during menopause and a variety of hormonal problems.

Treating the Family Chakra with the color orange improves the body's energy flow, balances the functioning of the reproductive organs and urinary system and supports our physical and mental stability.

The Solar Plexus Chakra—The Third Chakra

The color of the Solar Plexus Chakra is yellow, and it's located in the center of the body below the ribs, in a direct line beneath the Heart Chakra.

The Solar Plexus Chakra belongs to the sun and the element of fire; it has special significance because it is here that the energy rising from the earth meets the energy descending from the heavens. When these energies meet and merge in a balanced way, we are at our best.

The Solar Plexus Chakra streams sun energy into the body, which affects our will, vitality and energy.

If the energy flow of the Solar Plexus Chakra is disrupted it might cause digestive problems, tiredness and exhaustion, lack of self-esteem, severe mood swings and a tendency to depression, nervous breakdowns and terminal illness.

A balanced Chakra supports living a satisfying and enjoyable mental and physical life; fresh ideas emerge, one's willpower is activated; one feels full of life, active, creative and illuminating the world. This chakra is best activated by yellow stones, such as: Citrine, Yellow Calcite and Amber.

Treating the Solar Plexus Chakra with the color yellow stimulates and encourages us to act and create in all areas of our lives, helping us to fulfill ourselves in any area we choose.

The Heart Chakra—The Fourth Chakra

The colors of the Heart Chakra are pink and green, and it is located in the middle of the chest, at the meeting between the fourth and fifth ribs. Its classic color is green but when we add the color pink to the color green, the two colors act together beneficially, wonderfully improving the functioning of the Chakra. The Heart Chakra belongs to the Air Element and is connected to love, encouraging us to open our hearts, love ourselves and those around us, surrendering our attachment to objects. Love activates our world and is our most powerful motivating force, the most healing force in the universe.

Disruption of the Heart Chakra energy flow might cause feelings of sadness, loneliness and depression, mental and physical vulnerability, chronic illness and dependency on others.

The Heart Chakra is best activated by combining green and pink stones, such as: Rose Quartz and Green Aventurine (together) Rhodonite, Rhodochrosite, Emerald and Moonstone.

Treating the Heart Chakra with the colors green and pink balances us emotionally, calming us, healing past emotional wounds and helping us to love, feel loved, be at peace with ourselves and live in balanced, loving and respectful relationships with those around us.

The Throat Chakra—The Fifth Chakra

The color of the Throat Chakra is blue; located at the center of the neck, it engages with the voice, communication, expression and creativity, encouraging us to talk, speak and share what is in our hearts with our fellow men and women. The Throat Chakra belongs to the energy of the voice and relates to freedom of expression and the ability to influence others verbally.

Disruption of the Throat Chakra's energy flow might cause problems with the thyroid, a stiff and painful neck, inability to communicate properly and repeated throat infections.

The Throat Chakra is best activated by blue stones, such as: Turquoise, Aquamarine, Lapis Lazuli and Sodalite.

Treating the Throat Chakra with the color blue streams energy, allowing one to speak and express oneself.

The Throat Chakra streams a person's energy into the universe through the energy of the voice; the ability to express one's true feelings is an enormous and needed gift. Throughout our lives we try to improve our capacity for expression and when the Throat Chakra is at its best, our capacity for expression is activated and we are in harmony with the voice of the universe.

The Chakra of the Third Eye—The Sixth Chakra

The color of the Chakra of the Third Eye is purple; located in the forehead, midway between the eyebrows, it relates to extrasensory perception, intuition, imagination and visual channeling.

Disruption of the energy of the Third Eye Chakra might cause headaches, migraines, tiredness and irritability, sinus problems, nightmares, insomnia, emotional stress and allergic reactions.

The Chakra of the Third Eye belongs to the energy of light, opening our consciousness to the beauty and complexity of the world and seeing the beauty in the souls of creatures on Earth.

The use of extrasensory vision is an innate ability that is enhanced over time by practice, but unfortunately, it is possible to block it almost completely by negating and scorning its power.

Infants and children easily see energetic fields and the auras of people around them but depend on affirmation from their parents concerning how they see the world around them. Parents who tell their children they are "imagining things" or "that doesn't exist" when they mention things that "aren't logical," such as the colors of the auras they see around people, are actually blocking their children's extrasensory vision and preventing them from using their spiritual abilities.

The Chakra of the Third Eye is best activated by purple stones such as Amethyst and Sugalite.

Treating the Third Eye by using the color purple allows us to release our thoughts and connect to our spiritual powers, perceive auras, see and receive spiritual messages and open up to universal light in all its colors.

The Crown Chakra—The Seventh Chakra

The color of the Crown Chakra is crystal; it is situated at the center of the top of the head where a monarch's crown is placed.

The Crown Chakra connects us to the heavens, spirituality, cosmic knowledge and infinite wisdom.

Disruption of the Crown Chakra's energy flow might cause a person to suffer from confusion, excessive intellectualization, fanaticism and obsessive thinking or, alternatively, depression, apathy and reluctance to think.

It is through the Crown Chakra that we receive all our spiritual and channeled knowledge. In people who channel, one can see a "channeling pipe" that brings the energy from the universe to the Crown Chakra.

The Crown Chakra is best activated by Transparent Quartz, Optical Calcite and by a combination of a number of stones, such as: Transparent Quartz, Labradorite, Amethyst, Aquamarine and Turquoise, which help channel and convey information from the Crown Chakra to the Throat Chakra, speak and convey all information received.

Treating the Crown Chakra with Crystal enables universal energy to reach us and balance our entire body physically and mentally. The Crown Chakra provides us with infinite knowledge from the Source, a spiritual connection with helping spirits and light entities, profound insights and spiritual learning that comes directly from the Source. When the Crown Chakra is balanced and working well, it helps our spiritual health and takes care of our mental clarity. Allow the energy to reach you, always invite goodness, communicate only with light entities, and all the information and energy from the universe will come to you.

CHAKRAS RELATED TO PHYSICAL AND MENTAL BALANCE

Our entire body is served by a wise system that streams energy through energetic channels lined with thousands of chakras. The following are a number of important, additional chakras that should be treated in order to ensure physical and mental balance:

- Mid-Chest Chakra (between the Heart Chakra and the Throat Chakra)
- Palm Chakras (center of the palm and the back of the hand)
- Joint Chakras (shoulders, elbows, hips and knees)
- Feet Chakras (center of sole and top of foot)
- Finger- and Toe-Tip Chakras (at the tip of each finger and toe)
- Liver Chakra (above the liver)

These chakras help direct the energy flow and, in the course of a Color Therapy treatment, we place stones or fabric squares on them to transmit additional colors to heal and balance the body.

Mid-Chest Chakra

The Mid-Chest Chakra lies between the Throat Chakra and the Heart Chakra and opens our hearts and eases our breathing. In Color Therapy we treat the Mid-Chest Chakra with stones in all shades of pink, such as Rhodonite, *Rhodochrosite*, Rose Quartz and various pink-shaded fabrics.

Palm Chakras

The Palm Chakras lie at the center of the palm and the back of the hand and are connected by a broad, particularly powerful energy conduit. The Palm Chakras are highly active in most people. They actively stream the energy into and from the body, allowing us to use our energy in every creative process, such as work, cooking, treating ourselves and others, sculpting, playing an instrument, drawing, etc. It is advisable to pay attention to any rings or bracelets we may be wearing because they change the flow of energy. We can wear bracelets made from healing stones intended for a specific purpose, such as: A bracelet made from stones according to the therapist's personal Wheel of Colors; a bracelet of stones according to the Native American Wheel of Months; a bracelet of stones for treating current physical and or mental problems, etc.

The Palm Chakras are most powerful when we treat and stream energy via energy healing techniques, such as Reiki, Healing, etc.

In energetic healing, I ask the client to intuitively choose two stones, one for the right hand and one for the left, and to hold them for the duration of the treatment.

The stones impact the process of streaming energy into and out of the body, helping the client to stream their own energy and feel they are an active part of the therapeutic process. The Palm Chakras balance and enhance active and creative processes, therapy, giving and receiving. All colors of the rainbow suit them and transparent quartz, the color crystal, works well, perfectly activating them.

Joint Chakras: shoulders, elbows, hips, knees
Shoulder Chakras

The area of the shoulders and neck is the "area of responsibility" and it is frequently stiff, painful and "locked" because most of us feel we are carrying a heavy burden on our shoulders. During energetic treatment of the shoulder area, I place transparent quartz generator crystals with the point in the direction of the joint, streaming into it all the colors of the rainbow. The recommended color for the shoulder area is green, supported and enhanced by purple. Adding fabrics and/or green and purple healing stones balances the energy in that area, allowing the client to heal and remove the burden from their shoulders.

Elbow Chakras

The Elbow Chakras act in synchrony with the Shoulder Chakras, balancing the energy flow to the Palm Chakras; their importance lies in their role as an energetic "transition station."

Most of us have a tendency to "lock our elbows" and when the transition station of the elbows is rigid and "locked," the energy flow to the hands and upper body slows down.

During treatment, the client's hands are relaxed along the sides of their body, the backs of their hands on the treatment table, palms upward and open, the stones they've chosen lying inside the palms. Placed on the table, as close as possible to the client's body, is a transparent quartz generator that faces the elbow; small purple, green and orange stones are placed inside the elbow, making sure to avoid burdening the veins. You can use more than one generator, arranging them in a circle with their sharp end directed at the elbow and/or shoulder. Treating with the help of the color orange (Orange Calcite, Carnelian), works wonders when adding the colors purple, green and crystal.

When treating frozen shoulder, you can add the color red (Ruby, Garnet, Red Jaspar). When treating tennis elbow, you can add Green Jade.

Hip Joint Chakras

The Hip Joint Chakras balance our posture and stream energy from the center of our body to our feet. It is difficult to place stones on these Chakras, so we place the stones on the table, alongside the client's body, as close as possible to the Chakras. The recommended colors for treatment are: crystal, orange, brown, green and purple and, in acute cases, you can add the color red. Effective treatment of these Chakras will do wonders for the client's posture and the directions they will take in their life.

Knee Chakras

The knees bear the weight of our upper body and the Knee Chakras are responsible for the energy flow from the Hip Joint Chakras to the soles of the feet.

The energy of the Knee Chakras is directed toward mental and physical progress. People suffering from knee problems and pain and who have difficulty with mobility, often tell us they are experiencing a spiritual block related to some issue in their spiritual and emotional lives, or that they are having difficulty progressing in life, and we must help them to realize that it is actually the spiritual block that is causing the physical one.

I treat these Chakras with brown stones and, especially, Tiger's Eye, in order to provide a practical outlet for the stuck energy and enable the client to take a courageous step forward.

For comprehensive treatment of the Knee Chakras it is advisable to use combinations of the colors brown, green and orange, placing healing stones and fabrics in these colors on and around the knees. It is also advisable to place a transparent quartz crystal on each Knee Chakra to reinforce and hasten the action of the stones.

Feet Chakras

The Feet Chakras are located in the center of the back of the foot and in the center of the sole of the foot and, like the palms, are connected by a conduit. The Feet Chakras are responsible for the flow of energy to and from the earth and for the connection with reality; they are affiliated with physical and mental stability and processes of progress and/or setbacks in life. When there is a good connection with earth energy and the flow is good and balanced, physical and mental progress is made and one can achieve one's life goals. When the flow of energy in the feet Chakras is unbalanced, there is increased hesitation and it is difficult to decide where to go and what to do. In times of difficulty in choosing a path of progress in life, people tend to trip, sprain an ankle, etc., because the energy flow is disrupted and the body is trying to signal that there is a serious problem related to choosing a direction in life.

It is very comfortable treating the Feet Chakras when a client is seated. When treating the Feet Chakras, we create a circle of stones close to each other and the client sits inside it. All kinds of stones can be used, and, in the circle, it is also advisable to include stones we've found, collected or brought from the beach, the mountains or our natural environment.

The client sits inside the circle, placing their feet on a stone/ stones (please choose small, smooth and comfortable stones for this purpose); gently set the stone/stones we have selected on the back of the feet without applying pressure. We must take care to use only small stones and avoid the use of heavy stones or applying physical or mechanical pressure to the foot. In the case of a break or sprain, we place another circle of stones around the bandaged foot or cast; it is desirable to use a necklace of natural stones, which are easily bought from the appropriate stores. A necklace of natural stones is suitable because it forms a circle that doesn't open and is pleasurable to work with. The recommended, appropriate stones for this treatment are Calcite stones for treating bones, muscles and tendons and the recommended colors for treatment are: brown, golden-brown, yellow, orange and green.

Sitting inside a circle of stones helps many situations and the colors must be adapted to the client's needs. In cases of fear and anxiety, difficulty making a decision, or connecting with tough issues, we can add Black Tourmaline, Quartz Tourmaline or Black Onyx.

One can sit inside a circle of stones and/or put one's feet inside the circle of stones even while reading a book or watching television. The energetic effect of the circle of stones increases in time, balancing the body's energy.

Fingertip and Toe Chakras of the Hands and Feet
Fingertip Chakras

Fingertip Chakras are highly sensitive to touch and we feel and examine things with them. Energetically speaking they look like laser beams coming out of the tips of our fingers. When we work with the energy of beneficial materials, like fruit and vegetables, the energy flows best. The energy of natural things, such as water, stones, earth and sand, drains unnecessary energy from the body, cleansing and balancing the Chakras and refining our energetic sensations.

A simple way to constantly impact the Chakras is by wearing rings and bracelets made of various materials. According to Chinese Medicine, gold reinforces energy, silver disperses it, and healing stones work with our energy to balance it, so it is advisable to choose jewelry that combines gold and silver with healing stones in various colors according to the client's needs. Women who paint their fingernails stream the energy of the color they have chosen into their bodies.

Toe-tip Chakras

The Chakras in the tips of our toes are highly sensitive, acting as laser beams, shining and "feeling" the energy as we walk forward. To balance the energy flow, it is advisable to walk barefoot on earth, sand and grass, and paddle in water, etc. The Chakras at the tips of our toes are beautifully activated when sitting inside a circle of stones. Women who paint their toenails stream the energy of the color they have chosen into their bodies.

The Liver Chakra

The Liver Chakra is located above the liver and closely attached to it; all our anger, outbursts and the process of cleansing physical and mental poisons that enter the body pass through this Chakra. In energetic healing, light, small stones in the colors green, purple, orange and pink are placed on the Liver Chakra for maximum cleansing of the liver and, for deeper healing, it is advisable to add Transparent Quartz (crystal).

When working with the Liver Chakra, we should add a cleansing process with a change in eating habits, green shakes, etc.

Treating the Chakras balances and reinforces the energy flow in the body. Listen to your intuition and, in every therapeutic process, add stones and colors to the treatment in accordance with your senses and the state of the client.

When our Chakras are balanced, the energy flow in the body finds balance and facilitates the opening and healing of blocked areas. A sound, long-term energy flow leads to physical and mental health and a life of satisfaction and joy.

MAKING HEALING BRACELETS

Wearing a healing bracelet of stones is a wonderful way to receive the energy of natural color and energetic balance in a way that is easy, available and quick (see illustration on page 344).

Types of Healing Bracelet
- Bracelets according to the personal Wheel of Colors
- Bracelets according to the months of the year
- Bracelets for specific purposes—eating disorders, fertility issues, etc.

All bracelets are made only with natural, non-dyed stones and it is advisable to string them on nylon fishing line.

Making a bracelet according to the personal Wheel of Colors
Stones are threaded according to the client's personal Wheel of Colors. The stones are threaded in the following order: 13-1-13 - 2-13-3, and so on, in this way the number 13 is in contact with all the colors.

Making a bracelet according to the months of the year
The stones are threaded according to the classic order, transparent quartz (crystal) serving as No. 13, that is: crystal-red—crystal-yellow—crystal-blue, etc.

Making bracelets for specific purposes
When making a bracelet for a specific purpose, we must relate to:

- The client's Wheel of Colors (for instance: their protection color, balancing color, etc.).
- The energetic qualities of the healing stones (for instance: stones for fertility, stones for serenity, etc.).

EXAMPLES

A fertility bracelet

The recommended stones for a bracelet intended to help treat fertility issues are: Rose Quartz, Jade, Rhodonite, Rhodochrosite, Ruby, Garnet, Rainbow Moonstone and Carnelian. It is advisable to add the client's stone No. 4 and if we don't know it, we can add Transparent Quartz.

A bracelet for eating disorders

The recommended stones for a bracelet intended to help treat eating disorders are: Apatite, Jade, Rose Quartz, Rhodonite, Rhodochrosite, Rainbow Moonstone, Brown Jaspar, Red Jaspar, Blue Calcite and Turquoise. It is advisable to add the client's stone No. 4 and, if we don't know it, we can add Transparent Quartz.

A protection stone

The recommended stones for protection are: Tourmaline Quartz, Black Tourmaline, Obsidian, Onyx and Petrified Wood. It is advisable to add the client's stone No. 7 and if we don't know it, we can add Transparent Quartz.

A bracelet for treating nausea + nausea when traveling

The recommended stones for treating nausea are: Malachite, Rainbow Moonstone, Aquamarine, Rose Quartz, Green Aventurine,

Jade, Brown Jaspar and Carnelian. It is advisable to add the client's stone No. 4 and, if we don't know it, we can add Transparent Quartz.

A Personal Experience

A client of mine underwent difficult surgery. I arrived at the hospital after the surgery and brought him a red coral bracelet. My client immediately put it on and kept it on his wrist the whole time.

The hospital medical staff were surprised at the rapid recovery of his incisions and, at my next visit to the hospital, one of the nurses said to me: "All of us, doctors and nurses, are astonished. We have never seen such quick recovery. The incisions healed within two days and look as if he underwent surgery two weeks ago!"

COLOR-CHARGED WATER

The use of water for healing is particularly noticeable in Homeopathy and Bach Flower Remedies, treatment methods that consist of water-based remedies charged with the energy of various substances. Multiple studies have shown that water is easily affected by any energy and has a capacity for holding and retaining a concrete energetic memory of any substance so, when water is charged with the energies of various substances, we can use that water for healing. I use Bach Flower Remedies in my treatments and have taught this practice since the eighties; thanks to the combination of color energy and flower energy, I have had wonderful results, as my clients and students can testify.

The energy of the color has an astonishing effect on the water and the technique of charging water with various colors is simple and incredibly easy.

- When wishing to charge water with a particular color, we choose an open glass container, such as: a bottle, glass, jar or jug in the desired color.
- Pour tap water into the glass container (check to see if you can drink your local tap water).
- Place the glass container of water in sunlight. You can cover the container to ensure clean water.
- Leave the colored container of water in the sunlight for 2-12 hours.
- If we keep the color-charged water in the fridge, its energetic quality is preserved.

When my students prepare colored water at home, they are always pleasantly surprised by the results, for each color has a different effect on the energy of the water and its taste.

It is possible to charge water with color by means of healing stones in the following way:

- Fill a glass container with water and place a stone of the desired color inside it. Only natural, non-dyed stones that don't disintegrate should be selected for charging.
- Leave the stone in the glass container of water for 2-12 hours and, in some cases, you can leave the stone in the water for much longer.
- After charging, remove the stone from the container, drink the water and enjoy its wonderful energy.
- Try and enjoy!

COLOR SPIRALS

Color Therapy treats body and mind through a combination of energetic, verbal and physical therapy. All the therapeutic techniques work well together, creating a healing sequence.

My favorite energetic therapy technique is known as "color spirals." The spiral is the most energetic form in nature and using it together with various colors enables us to give an excellent treatment. This technique combines intention, guided visualization, energy bubbles, colors and the dispersal of energy through the Palm Chakras and the Third Eye Chakra.

In this technique we use mainly the color gold in combination with healing colors, but we do not use gray or black. I have used this technique for many years, teaching my students to treat themselves and their clients.

Therapy by means of Color Spirals

It is advisable to treat clients in a quiet room with an open window, meditational music, plants, stones and lit candles.

The client lies down, or sits, and closes their eyes. The treatment starts with the energetic bubble process explained on page 318:

- We bring our awareness to our intention, envelope ourselves in a gold bubble and fill ourselves with light.
- We surround the client with a gold bubble and fill them with light.
- We join the two bubbles by means of a delicate gold conduit that connects the bubbles in the area of the Heart Chakra.

Once we've completed the energetic bubble process, we energetically check the state of the client.

Placing our palms at aura height, about ten centimeters above the client's body, we disperse the needed color to all areas of the client's body through our palms and third eye.

Choosing for the client and dispersing color is done according to the state of the client's body, which we see, and the colors of the Chakras. The process continues for several minutes, depending on the client's need.

In places where we see the client needs more energy, we imagine a turning spiral of color, for instance, a pink spiral. We choose the client's most significant color as the first, basic and primary color of the spiral. Around the first color we add the second, one that seems suitable for integration into the treatment at that point, making sure that the spiral continues to turn all the time.

In order to enhance the energy of the color, I suggest adding gold edges to the spiral as the third color. For instance, excellent spirals for treatment are: Pink—green—gold, purple—green—gold, orange—green—gold, purple—pink—gold.

When the spiral we imagine is turning with the colors we have chosen, we project it gently above the place where the client most needs it. We place our palms above the client's body, infusing the spiral with energy and "intending" the flow of color to the client in the best possible way. Please avoid accelerating the process because each person has their own energetic pace. This treatment wonderfully heals and stimulates the client's energy.

Recommendations for Color Spirals According to the Chakras

Crown: Crystal—purple—gold.
Third eye: Purple—crystal—gold.

Throat: Blue—purple—gold.
Heart: Pink—green—gold, or green—pink—gold.
Solar plexus: Yellow—green—gold, or yellow—purple—gold.
Family: Orange—pink—gold, or orange—green—gold.
Root: Red—orange—gold, or red—pink—gold.

You can integrate various colors depending on what you see and understand. You can use only one or two colors or add colors to the spiral. Experience of many years has taught me that the number three is the ideal number for working with human energy.

Optimal Color Integration

Pink—green—gold: For balance and healing the Heart Chakra and for general healing.

Pink—purple—gold: For healing emotional problems, for closing cycles, for partings.

Pink—orange—gold: For balancing and healing reproductive organs, for reproductive problems and childbirth.

Green—pink—gold: For balancing and healing the Heart Chakra and for general healing.

Green—purple—gold: For general balance, helps to heal and end illness, excellent for treating chronic illness.

Green—orange—gold: For general balance and healing.

Crystal—purple—gold: For balance and healing after a parting, for spiritual channeling.

Crystal—blue—gold: For balancing and healing the Throat Chakra, for clear and resonant speech.

Crystal—pink—gold: For emotional balance and healing, helps to open the heart.

Blue—purple—gold: For balancing and healing the throat, for true expression, for recovering from a parting.

Blue crystal—gold: For general balance and healing of throat and respiratory problems.

Purple—green—gold: For general balance and healing, for parting from mental and physical behavioral patterns.

Purple—crystal—gold: For general balance and healing, for chronic illness.

Purple—blue—gold: For balance and healing of the throat; encourages verbal expression.

Purple—pink—gold: For emotional balance and healing and for recovery after painful separations.

Purple—orange—gold: For balancing and healing reproductive organs.

Purple—yellow—gold: For balancing and healing operational power.

Purple—red—gold: For balancing and healing sexual organs and sexual desire, and for delayed birth.

Purple—brown—gold: For balance and grounding.

DIAGNOSIS BY DRAWING PALMS

Each person has their own unique fingerprint and way of expressing him/herself in every area of life. The source of our innate creativity lies in the unconscious and when we are connected to our unconscious, we can best understand and implement things for ourselves and those around us. Over twenty years ago, I developed this method of drawing the palms as a diagnostic tool, when I discovered that free, intuitive drawing is a good way to access the unconscious. People who paint tend to feel freer, more sincere and to give expression to the self. Most people only paint in childhood, and the ability to paint is considered by most to be the field of talented professionals. When I ask adults to draw during a diagnosis, they tend to say: "I don't know how to draw," "Nonsense, I'm not a kid in kindergarten anymore," and so on. These defensive reactions show that most people aren't enabled to be creative or connect creatively to their unconscious.

Deep within us lies our inner child who loves to create, dare and experiment, but most of us tend to shackle the inner child in chains of "maturity" and "wisdom." Opening the door to the inner child is a shift that enables us to examine our lives with fresh eyes and advance toward goals we were previously afraid to verbalize, for our inner child is daring, takes risks, knows it all and is full of mischief and play. Color Therapy through drawing helps us open our eyes to new possibilities and enjoy the creative process.

The materials for drawing the palms are prepared in advance:

- A set of 24 quality oil pastels.
- Blank A4 or A3 paper.

- A wide, comfortable table that provides a good space for creativity or, alternatively, a comfortable floor to lie on.
- Moist wipes for those who wish to clean their hands at the end of the drawing process.

The diagnostic process yields wonderful results when carried out in a quiet, supportive environment. Comments stop and "jam" the incredible process in which our inner child engages and begins to have fun, so we should quietly observe the nuances of the process and avoid commenting during the drawing.

While drawing, the "self" emerges and, in order to allow the mind to flow best in time and space, we let the process take its course without any kind of comment, apart from positive reinforcement when a client finds it difficult, criticizes him/herself, or wants to throw up their hands and give up. In this process, we begin to work with a pre-agreed system and specific outlines—continuing more and more freely until the client feels they have completed the process. Clear instructions at the beginning help people enter a process with confidence; we all need pre-set boundaries and the confidence provided by instructions in places we don't know.

The drawing process starts with basic facilitation in three stages. It is important to wait until the end of each stage before facilitating the next:

1. Place your palms on a white sheet of paper.
2. Using pastel crayons, mark the outline of the left hand with the right hand, and the outline of right hand with the left hand.
3. Color the palms of your hands drawn on the sheet of paper in any way or color you choose. I usually say: "You have plenty of time, let yourselves enjoy the process and take pleasure in the drawing!"

Part of the diagnosis results from observing clients while they draw and color. We understand the things that are most important to the person by the order in which they choose the colors and, by the way in which they place their palms on the paper and color them; we understand the messages from the soul.

Indicators of the Accurate Diagnosis of a Drawing

- The way in which hands are laid on the paper
- Choice of color/colors for the outline (boundaries)
- Choice of colors for painting the palms
- Manner of drawing and the different ways of painting
- Finding hidden symbols hidden in the painting
- Finding "fragments," signs of pain, etc
- Diagnosis according to the division of right and left sides
- Diagnosis according to the division of the paper into areas
- Diagnosis according to parts of the body represented in the palm.

The diagnosis takes place in conversation with the client so that we can arrive at the deeper layers of their personality.

It is important to encourage the client to ask questions, give them detailed answers and explanations, and discuss possible solutions to problems that arise during the diagnosis.

Diagnosis according to the palms of the hands refers to a person's present state, but it is possible to see past events, as well as the hidden potential of the future. We can use this as an initial diagnostic tool as well as a supportive diagnostic tool in the therapeutic process, which helps us to clearly see the state of the client and where they stand in terms of the process. With repeated diagnoses, it is advisable to choose colors with closed eyes to ensure diagnostic accuracy, as, once they have experienced diagnosis, it is difficult for people to ignore the knowledge they have gained.

Ways of Laying Hands on the Paper

When using A4 or A3 size paper, we can see that people place their hands on the paper in different ways. The most common way is hand beside hand. Since the right hand and the left hand each play a different role and the diagnosis of each hand is different, it is important to observe which of the hands is drawn higher on the paper, for this hand represents the more significant and dominant side in the client's life at the present moment, which is the side that wishes to break out. For right-handed people, the right hand signifies the conscious, rational and active side, whereas the left hand signifies the unconscious, spirituality and hidden desires of the heart. For left-handed people, the left hand signifies the conscious side, rationality and action, while the right hand signifies the, unconscious, spirituality and hidden desires of the heart.

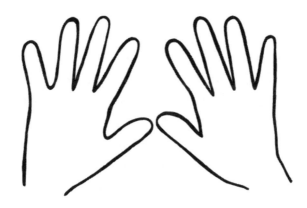

WAYS OF LAYING HANDS ON
THE DRAWING PAPER

Kissing Hands

In a drawing of a pair of hands laid harmoniously one beside the other, almost at the same height, thumbs touching or almost touching, the palms look as if the thumbs are kissing, or like a pair of kissing doves. This drawing is characteristic of someone who strives for balance in their personal life, attempting to infuse their environment with harmony, and they will appear among people who are presently at a harmonious and balanced stage of their lives. In order to see a person's state clearly, we must pay attention to additional signs, such as the colors they choose, the way they paint, etc.

Hands Crossed

This is a drawing in which one hand looks as if it is on top of or partly covering the other hand. A drawing like this indicates that one side of the body is trying to hold back the other. We need to find out which the person's dominant side is in order to know whether their conscious side is trying to hamper the unconscious, causing the person to continue the path allocated to them without changing him/herself or his/her life, or whether the unconscious is trying to tell the person: "Hey, stop! See what you're doing and where you're going; check: Is this really beneficial for you?"

Opposing Hands

A drawing in which each hand is placed in a different direction, mostly in the opposite direction of the other hand. Opposing hands indicate a situation in which the person is standing at a crossroads and is having difficulty choosing their path. This drawing appears when people are at a stage of significant change in their lives, seeking a new way, and having difficulty choosing what they should do regarding an important field in their lives.

Drawing the Same Hand Twice

A drawing in which the same hand appears twice, is usually a double drawing of the non-dominant hand. In most cases, the client won't notice that they've drawn the same hand twice, and when shown the duplication, will usually say things like: "I can't draw with my left hand, so I drew my left hand twice with my right hand." Since the non-dominant hand is connected to the unconscious, the duplication of this hand indicates a need for spiritual change and/or the need for radical change. A drawing like this shows that the client is not implementing the change they wish to make, because the "action hand" was not attached to the picture.

It is rare for the client to draw their dominant hand twice. In such a case, this refers to a situation in which the client does all they can and more in the practical sphere, virtually ignoring the unconscious, the spiritual and the emotional realms.

Although a drawing like this seems to people to be an innocent mistake, it actually reveals the here and now state of a person, their hidden feelings and secret intentions.

A Third Hand that Appears in the Drawing

This is a very rare drawing that mostly appears when a parent's child preoccupies their thoughts, or when someone feels control of their life isn't entirely in their own hands but in the hands of someone else.

A Painting of Only One Hand

This is a drawing by someone who physically has two hands but has chosen to draw only one hand. Someone who chooses to draw just one hand is hiding part of their true self and is, in fact, telling you: "I'm unwilling to open my heart to you. I'm willing to show you only one aspect of myself." This kind of drawing may appear when a diagnosis takes place in a group, not individually, and it indicates that the person is afraid to reveal their true nature, because it is very different from what they outwardly present. The drawing of only one hand by someone with physically one hand doesn't indicate anything apart from the physical lack of one hand.

A Missing Part of the Drawing of a Hand

Who is the person with such a large hand that it can't be crammed onto an A3 sheet of paper?

I personally have not encountered such a size, but there are people whose palms will exceed the boundaries of the sheet of paper and the drawing will emerge with some part missing. A drawing like this is characteristic of someone who strives to "break out" of the framework of their life and into other places, but can't see a way out without harming him/herself or others. Most people would say: "I didn't have enough space on the paper," but the real feeling is one of a strong desire to cross boundaries and a need to break out, despite the fear of being hurt.

Drawing the Outlines of the Palm

The way in which the outlines of the palms are drawn indicates how people take care of themselves and maintain the boundary between themselves and the people in their lives. Interpersonal boundaries are necessary both for the person him/herself and for those around them because they form a clear, whole "self."

A clear outline drawn around the palm indicates the clear

boundaries the person sets for those around them. A fine, broken or invisible outline shows that it is either hard for the person to set clear boundaries or that they are completely lacking in the person's life. An emphasized or very thick outline shows that the person doesn't want others to interfere in their life or invade their privacy.

The colors of the outlines indicate the kinds of boundary people set between themselves and those around them.

THE COLORS OF OUTLINES

Red Outline

Trust determines the kind of boundary a person sets. Someone who draws a red outline will allow anyone they trust to approach them but will distance and protect him/herself from people they don't trust.

Yellow Outline

Someone who draws a yellow outline tends to set different boundaries for people they love than for other people.

Love dissolves boundaries with lightning speed and it is mostly difficult for this person to set boundaries for those they love.

Blue Outline

Someone who draws a blue outline is attentive to their awareness and sets boundaries according to their senses and messages they receive intuitively.

Green Outline

Drawing a green outline is characteristic of stubborn people who set various boundaries solely according to their wishes, who will insist on their boundaries and guard them with an eagle eye to make sure no-one crosses them.

A green outline is also indicative of people who wish to set boundaries and are attempting to develop this ability.

Pink Outline

Drawing a pink outline is characteristic of creative people who change both themselves and their boundaries when necessary; they may not always be consistent, but they are always unique and surprising.

White Outline

Someone who draws a white outline is greatly influenced by other people, their actions and things they say. This is the boundary of someone who tends to listen more to the opinions of others than to their own wishes and personal needs.

Purple Outline

A purple outline is a spiritual one, healing and enabling one to "close" unclear, unresolved situations by setting a simple, clear boundary that is effective for both parties.

Orange Outline

People who draw orange outlines are constantly learning and changing their boundaries according to what they have learned, and their boundaries will change depending on the way they perceive someone and on what they have learned about their own needs.

Gray Outline

Someone who draws a gray outline sets boundaries depending on their self-respect and respect for others, changing them according to the way in which their own and others' boundaries are respected.

Brown Outline

Brown outlines are common to people who are clear and very practical, and who tend to determine practical, consistent and clear boundaries in harmony with situation, place and time.

Rose Outline

A rose outline is typical of someone who determines a boundary according to their perception, who changes their boundaries mainly according to sensory and extrasensory perceptions of a situation.

Black Outline

Someone who draws a black outline sets boundaries that depend on deep observation, depending on their thoughts and needs, mostly as a result of what they have learned and integrated from previous events in their life.

Crystal Outline

An outline drawn in all the colors is typical of someone who attempts to set different boundaries with clarity and transparency, but who is often forced to set different boundaries for different people and change them according to the situation.

Beige Outline

This is an outline drawn by people who are "thin-skinned" and who tend to be easily hurt. They have difficulty standing up for themselves; it is particularly hard for them to set boundaries and they tend to allow others to easily "cross" their boundaries.

Silver or Gold-Colored Outline

A drawing with a silver or gold outline is typical of people who are worried about the issue of money in their lives, who tend to change their boundaries according to their economic situation.

THE WAY IN WHICH PALMS ARE DRAWN

Fine, Almost Invisible Outlines

Very fine, almost invisible outlines indicate a lack of boundaries between a person and his environment. Someone who suffers from a lack of boundaries tends to be easily hurt and feel tired and exploited.

Clear Outlines

Palms that are clearly outlined indicate a capacity for self-esteem without any need to diminish oneself in front of others, and for setting clear boundaries in most aspects of life.

Fragmented and/or Broken Outlines

Fragmented and/or broken outlines indicate someone who has trouble setting secure boundaries in their life. This person tends to set boundaries that could disintegrate and break, creating a picture of inconsistency, reaching situations of confusion, and misunderstanding, anger and frustration.

Emphasized, Very Thick Outlines

Emphasized outlines state: "Up to this point. This is my limit, and no-one crosses it. That's it." Those who draw this kind of boundary may be stubborn and consistent, fiercely guarding their personal boundaries; alternatively people who are concerned about their privacy set very thick boundaries and hide behind them in case their vulnerability is discovered.

Double Outlines

Double outlines appear with people who are hiding something in their lives, lying about a particular issue, concealing their identity or trying to mislead and, in some cases, double boundaries will appear with people who are mentally ill.

We need to be careful when diagnosing double boundaries because someone whose secrets and concealments are "exposed" might be hurt or do harm, or simply sever all connection.

Zigzag Outlines

This outline is characteristic of people who find it hard to explain their boundaries clearly. When zigzag boundaries are "thorny" and sharp, the person tends to outbursts of anger and rage and, if they feel their boundaries aren't being respected, could act out in a way that is frightening.

Invisible Outlines

Invisible outlines are typical of people who tend to be extremely sensitive, vulnerable and shy, and who have difficulty setting and maintaining boundaries between themselves and others.

————	Thin Line
··············	"Invisible" Line
▬▬▬▬	Clear Line
▬ ·▬· ▬	Broken Line
▰▰▰▰	Thick, Bold Line
══════	Double Line
〜〜〜	"Zig Zag" Line
⋀⋀⋀⋀	Thorns

THE WAY IN WHICH A PAINTING IS MADE

The way in which a painting is made changes according to the state of the client at the time they make the painting. Each person paints in their own way, but there are several "classic" ways of painting that are typical of the way in which most people paint (see pages 340-343).

Painting transverse lines with a clear and accentuated transition from one line to another

Painting transverse lines with clear transitions is known as "painting stairs," which is typical of someone who tends to progress in stages, like climbing stairs, preferring to progress sensibly from one stage to another in order to achieve their goals.

Transverse lines with blurred, or no, transitions between them

Painting transverse lines with a blurred transition is typical of someone who wants to progress speedily in a particular field of their life, although they know it's preferable to progress in stages. This manner of painting also indicates that at this stage in their life, their actual progress is fast, and they feel less of a need to "climb steps" in a cautious and calculated manner.

"Smeared" painting with the side of the chalk

Painting with the smearing technique is typical of someone who is attempting to do a lot and so acts transversely, intuitively and all-inclusively. "Smearing" of color with the fingers indicates a need and/or an attempt to blur boundaries and transitions, presenting the picture of a situation that is harmonious and flowing, facilitating a transition from one stage to the next easily and without transition stress. Occasionally, this painting technique indicates the concealment of certain feelings and/or the blurring of the truth and changes according to the person's needs.

Sloppy painting

A painting of several sloppy lines of color or a scribble just to "get it done" is typical of someone who doesn't wish to cooperate and reveal things to us that may be too personal, or someone who is impatient and wishes to complete the painting quickly.

A painting that is detailed and invested in gives us information about the person and helps us to diagnose them precisely and well; thus, a detailed analysis of a painting of the palms actually depends on the painter. When a diagnosis is individual, I explain that it is desirable to add more details to the painting in order to receive accurate information. When the painting is done in group work, most people try to add more details and colors after hearing the meanings for people who invested more in their paintings.

Painting vertical lines

Painting with vertical lines indicates a person who is progressing in their life or in a particular subject and, the more vigorous the lines, the more vigorous the breakthrough.

A clear and accentuated transition between the lines

Painting in such a way that one can see a clear transition between the lines is typical of a person who is progressing in several areas of their life and can see each of them separately, while understanding the whole picture. When this is done in the form of a rainbow, it indicates a person who is striving for the ability to observe and act in a way that is comprehensive, transparent and "crystal clear."

A blurred transition or smooth painting without transitions

A form of painting in which transitions between colors are blurred or invisible indicates a need for smooth, unhampered progress and/ or progress in several areas that are hard to distinguish between.

Messy painting

"Messy" painting, mostly in the form of outward facing "arrows", is typical of someone who tends to progress at all costs, even at the expense of others and, sometimes, even hurting those around them.

Integrative painting—horizontal and vertical lines

This form of painting represents the need to progress in a gradual and informed fashion and the desire to succeed as swiftly and beneficially as possible. Most people integrate horizontal and vertical lines into their painting, and the more noticeable technique in the picture is the way in which they live their personal life.

"Forceful" painting without spaces, achieved by pressing the colored chalk into the paper

This type of painting indicates someone who is preoccupied with their life, attempting to be unaffected by other people and relationships in their life. When the painting is precise and within the lines, it shows difficulty exceeding thought boundaries and the person's need to go into a subject in depth and do real and serious inner work.

The painter sometimes feels that they have no "space to breathe" but, nonetheless, they make every effort, continuing to progress with all their might.

"Soft" painting is done by pressing the chalk gently into the page. The colors of the painting seem delicate and

pastel, and there may be white lines between the chosen colors.

This type of painting shows the person's need for people and relationships in their life and is characteristic of someone who tries to consider people and avoid unnecessary arguments. This person gives others a substantial place in their life and their opinions may affect the person's personal wishes and progress in life.

Painting outside the drawn lines

In this kind of painting, the color that exceeds the lines of the painting of the palm appears in the form of a mountain, a hill, an arrow or "sting."

Physically speaking, this type of painting indicates the precise places that are painful and/or problematic in the person's body. Mentally speaking, it indicates the person's need to break through familiar boundaries and do things differently. This painting may also be an indication of a person's tendency to physical or verbal outbursts of anger.

Accurate painting without deviating from the drawn lines

This type of painting shows a need for perfection, a tendency to meticulousness and difficulty crossing existing boundaries and accepted conventions, and it indicates a person's desire to present a "perfect picture" of him/herself in the eyes of those around them and a need for positive reinforcement from their environment.

Painting "loops" in a repeated pattern (for instance: painting an infinite loop) that appears in a particular place or in the entire painting.

This type of painting indicates that the brain of the painter is concerned about some issue that is preoccupying them. The person examines and re-examines the problem; the issue constantly preoccupies them, and they return to it without any apparent benefit. The problem can be identified depending on its place in the painting of loops in the picture, helping the person to resolve it.

Painting in circles

This type of painting is similar to painting in "loops," but indicates a circular, more comprehensive perception of the problem. The person revolves in "circles" in an attempt to resolve their problems, but they are able to see all sides of the problem and believe that ultimately the solution will be found.

A formal painting—shapes like a square, a circle, triangle, etc, indicating a particular, current issue arising in the person's life

Square

A painting of a square indicates preoccupation with the issue of life's frameworks.

Circle

The painting of a circle indicates preoccupation with the issue of perfection, a capacity for circular vision, and/or an issue that preoccupies a person in several life directions.

Triangle

The painting of a triangle is characteristic of preoccupation with an issue that tends to be troublesome, prickly and painful. The triangle has the shape of an arrow, and someone who draws a triangle knows there is a charged issue in their life that might eventually explode, thus it would be worthwhile to take care of it as soon as possible.

An artistic painting

An artistic painting integrates formal elements in an ordinary painting such as a picture of flowers, an eye, hand, tree, etc. When encountering someone who integrates creative drawings into the painting of their palms, it is advisable to talk to them about their creative, artistic abilities, encourage them to learn and develop as they see fit, emphasizing that the creativity expressed in the painting could indicate incredible artistry waiting for an opportunity to reveal itself and come out into the world.

CHOOSING THE COLORS FOR PAINTING A PICTURE OF THE PALMS

The primary diagnosis of the painting of the palms is carried out according to the colors chosen and their place in the painting. Each color chosen indicates a person's nature and/or a certain way of behaving and, in order to make an accurate diagnosis, we must remember each color's meaning, diagnosing it according to its location in the painting of the palms, and notice where it appears in the person's personal Wheel of Colors. When we are unable to include the Wheel of Colors, we must combine all the information we see in the painting of the palms and diagnose accordingly, but it is advisable to tell the client that combining the diagnosis with the painting of the palms and their personal Wheel of Colors leads to deeper insights for the client and the capacity for deeper and more meaningful healing. Indigenous Native Americans maintain that every color has a positive meaning, and they focus on the positive qualities of a color and its healing capacity. When diagnosing the painting of the palms, we focus on positive and constructive messages that match the chosen color, emphasizing the things that advance a person and contribute to their life and spiritual development.

DIAGNOSING COLORS AND THEIR MEANINGS ACCORDING TO THE PAINTING OF THE PALMS

Red—belief

The color red in the painting represents the issue of belief in a person's life. Each of us lives life in our own way, according to our beliefs. The color red is the color of belief and that of the blood that flows in our veins, and just as without blood in our veins we have no life, it is also impossible to live without belief in ourselves and in the world around us. Belief is fundamental to human life and, although our way of belief might be different, each one of us needs some sort of belief.

Yellow—love

The color yellow in a painting represents the subject of love in a person's life. We all strive to live, love and be loved. The color yellow is the color of the sun—symbolizing the love of truth, because the sun sustains our world, gives us life, light and warmth—and asks for nothing in return.

Blue—intuition

The color blue in a painting represents a person's intuition, helping us to understand how best to activate it. The color blue, the color of water, nourishes us and our world, healing us. Water constitutes about 70% of our body; the human embryo lives in amniotic fluid in the womb for the nine months of pregnancy; and most of the Earth's surface is covered in water. Water is our first, instinctive nature, connecting us to inner, intuitive knowing.

Green—willpower, growth and thriving

The color green in a painting represents willpower and human determination. The color green is the color of plants and trees in our world, and all plants have the capacity for survival and self-adaptation to the environment in order to exist in the various areas of the world. Every tiny seed that germinates and grows into a tree shows us willpower at its best, teaching us that we can achieve any goal we choose when we use our willpower and wisdom.

Pink—creativity

The color pink in a painting represents human creativity as pink is the color of our palms, with which we create the basic things in life. Each human being creates their life in a unique way, creativity encouraging us to progress and leading us to new insights, making things in our own way, every day creating our personal world anew.

White—relationships

The color white in a painting represents human relationships, showing the nature of existing relationships and how they affect human beings. The color white refers to magnetism (the strong attraction to a particular person) or revulsion the (reluctance to approach another person), and and our ability to communicate with people and form blessed and sustaining relationships that are mutually beneficial to all parties.

Purple—spirituality, prayer, gratitude and closing cycles

The color purple is the most spiritual color and, in a painting, it represents those spiritual areas that affect our lives, our need to part from things that aren't good for us and the desire to close cycles with people, illness and life problems.

The color purple represents our desire to heal from the wounds of the past, to be at peace with ourselves, showing gratitude for the good things that exist in our lives.

Orange—learning

The color orange represents the process of human learning in life. Learning is the most important thing in our lives, for without it we could not progress, improve or understand. The most beneficial learning takes place when we believe in the subject and love the person teaching us, for the color orange consists of two colors: red—the color of belief, and yellow—the color of love.

Gray—respect or honor

The color gray in a painting represents the issue of respect or honor in human life. The color gray is the color of wise elders' hair, the people who are blessed with long life, those who have gained the respect of their tribe. Throughout our lives we guard our dignity, and the older we become, the more we know, the more we respect ourselves and are respected in the world. The best way to live is to respect the world, those around us, the Earth on which we live, the trees, plants and all creatures and, most of all, to live with self-respect and respect for our inner world.

Brown—practicality

The color brown in a painting represents the ability to be practical and functional on earth. It is the color of the Earth that provides us with all we need, enabling us to live on it in the best way possible, creating the reality of our lives. The earth doesn't dream; it is practical, alive, constantly functional and creative. Brown refers to the practical side of life, showing us how to act and how to undertake real action, building all areas of our lives.

Rose—sensory and extrasensory perception

The color rose in a painting represents the human capacity for sensory and extrasensory vision, the ability to see things differently, think "outside the box," see things from angles that aren't always accepted and act in a way that is original and unique. The color rose encourages us to open our eyes and observe ourselves and the world around us differently.

Black—meditation and introspection

The color black in a painting represents the way a person thinks and their ability to go inward and observe themselves. Native Americans consider the color black to be the most spiritual because true spirituality is the capacity for seeing yourself and being in deep and constant connection with your soul, beyond all the external "performances." The color black enables us to go inside ourselves, find our true meaning and remain connected to the real inner self.

Crystal—transparency and clarity

The color crystal in a painting represents the human capacity for seeing things clearly, in a way that is all-encompassing and objective, for speaking clearly and comprehensibly, making decisions based on all the data and acting in the best possible way. The color crystal consists of the whole color spectrum, helping us to combine rational and emotional thought, examine an issue in all its aspects and act beneficially with clarity and transparency.

SYMBOLS DRAWN OR CREATED IN A PAINTING

In the process of painting a picture of the palms of the hands, some people choose to draw symbols and/or pictures inside and around the palms of the hands. Pictures and symbols frequently "form" on the sheet of paper, and we only notice them after the painting is completed. It has been our role to discover and diagnose pictures and symbols that were not consciously or deliberately drawn, but stem from the painter's unconscious. Each symbol or picture has its own individual meaning and it is always advisable to ask clients what these pictures mean and understand together with the client why they appear in the drawing of the palms.

Flowers

Someone who draws one or more flowers reflects a period of creativity, flourishing and developing in their life. Drawings of flowers indicate a person's creative ability, and the more complex and optimistic the flowers—so the person flourishes and develops on deeper levels. A drawing of a simple flower with four uncomplicated petals indicates flourishing and creativity; the drawing of a flower that consists of rows of petals indicates flourishing and profound inner development; and a drawing of several flowers together indicates that the person is flourishing and developing in several areas of their life.

Sun

In most cases, the drawing of a sun represents optimism, enlightenment, spiritual belief and the ability to look on the bright

260 | NOAH GOLDHIRSH

side of things. The color of the sun in a painting represents a person's current situation—for instance: A blue sun represents a current use of intuition. The use of the colors black, red or gray in a painting of the sun could reflect a physical or mental problem. The painting of a black sun represents a state of sadness, mourning or despair and, occasionally, indicates illness in the area in which it was drawn; the painting of a red sun might indicate an acute physical problem in the area in which it was drawn; and the drawing of a gray sun could indicate depression, physical and mental exhaustion or chronic illness.

Eye

The drawing of an eye represents the power of observation and capacity for seeing through the third eye, indicating an attraction to mysticism and a capacity for dreaming and seeing things from a spiritual perspective. Most eye colors in paintings are connected to a person's current state, but the drawing of black, red and gray eyes could describe illness, inexplicable fears, worries and excessive concerns and, in the case of multiple eyes in a drawing, even a sense of persecution. When diagnosing adolescents, we must be careful because they tend to draw multiple eyes, feeling that the entire world is constantly looking at them. For example, when adolescents draw a weeping eye with falling tears, we should accept this as a declaration about their emotional state and an opening for a conversation that will enable them to open their hearts and share their feelings with us.

Hand

The drawing of an additional hand has several meanings and it is advisable for us to discuss this with the client. The hand represents action and implementation, and so an additional hand in the painting could indicate that the client is dissatisfied with what they are doing in their daily life. A painting of an additional hand might indicate a client who is greatly influenced by someone, giving that person too much control over their life. An additional hand painted red, black or gray might represent illness and/or a deep physical or mental problem. We should be alert to this situation, particularly in children's paintings, where an extra hand could indicate child abuse.

Tree

The drawing of a tree signifies family, widespread action, massive growth and an ability to engage in several areas at once. Budding trees full of leaves and/or flowers and/or fruit, represent a situation that is positive, optimistic, flowing and advancing. Trees in the fall or tree stumps—represent a state of mourning, the loss of someone important in their life and a sense of failure. The drawing of a tree in colors of red, black and/or gray might represent a problematic state, illness, lack and profound sadness.

House

The painting of a house represents the desire for security, stability, a sense of belonging, family and support. The painting of a secure house indicates a situation in which a client is seeking stability and security and/or making a considerable change in life, body, residence and/or workplace. The painting of a broken home, one that is bleak and devastated, refers to something broken in the client's life and a sensation of instability, loss and devastation. Children whose parents are divorced, or in the process of getting divorced, tend to draw two houses—situating themselves in the middle, between the houses, which is in fact a description of the situation they are in.

A drawing of animals

Each animal drawn has meaning. In order to achieve the whole picture it is advisable to ask the client what the animal they have drawn signifies to them, explaining to them the meaning of their choice in spiritual terms and exploring how it is reflected in their actual life.

Dog
A dog represents true love, loyalty, protection and security.

Cat
A cat signifies the search for self, focus on the self, and preoccupation with the issues of sex and cleanliness.

Bird
A bird represents the need for freedom, the desire to spread one's wings and fly, and the need to break down frameworks.

Hare
A hare represents hidden and open fears, the need for a supportive group, preoccupation with sex and caring for the young.

Snake
A snake signifies a deep and meaningful change in life, mysticism, healing and recovery from illness.

Hedgehog
A hedgehog represents innocence and vulnerability that is hidden in seclusion and spikey behavior toward the external environment.

Tortoise
A tortoise represents a situation in which things progress slowly, a sense of carrying the whole world on your back and the need for seclusion in a place that is safe and protected.

Tiger

A tiger represents power, strength, daring, courage and the capacity for waiting patiently and acting at the right moment.

Lion

A lion represents power, courage, leadership and the ability to lead others along the right path.

Dolphin

A dolphin represents a strong desire to live freely, with pleasure and fun, engaged in love and living in harmony with the environment. However, a painting of a dolphin might also indicate respiratory problems.

Fish

A fish represents the issue of money and fertility and is also a symbol of economic abundance, fertility and success.

Kangaroo

A kangaroo represents concern for someone we are afraid for and "carry in our pocket"; also the ability to survive any situation and hop high in order to escape a distressing situation.

Bird's nest with chicks

A bird's nest with chicks in it represents the need to take care of children, family and/or people who are helpless and dependent on us.

Butterfly

A butterfly represents the need to develop in stages, break out of frameworks, spread beautiful wings, fulfill ourselves, and live a life of liberty filled with beauty, lightness and joy.

264 | Noah Goldhirsh

Horse

A horse represents the need to leave a place that closes us in, to gallop strongly onward and progress swiftly, but it also represents a tendency to carry others on our back.

Squirrel

A squirrel represents a strong need to horde things of all kinds: knowledge, property, money, etc.

Spider

A spider represents the capacity for planning our lives and actions, acting at the right moment.

Ant

An ant represents the need for hard work and patience in a given situation, while knowing that we are stronger than we look and, with the help of the right people, we are capable of doing it all.

These are the animals most people tend to draw and if other animals appear, we can read about them in a book I wrote specifically about the animals we meet on the path: *"The Power of Animal Messages* (2nd edition)."

Nails

Clients sometimes draw nails on the fingers of the palms. For people who draw nails it is particularly important how others see them at that moment, what they say about them, etc. The way nails are drawn indicates the way in which they behave externally and how they wish people to see them—for instance: Someone who draws nails and on each one paints a smiling smiley face is attempting to be perceived by those around them as someone who smiles, loves people, is optimistic and always happy.

In contrast, a woman who draws long, red, pointed nails is conveying: "Beware, I'm bigger than you think and could scratch you if I think you might hurt me." Painting the hint of a nail indicates that how the world perceives the client is important to them, but they tend to be subtle and gentle, and it is sometimes hard to guess exactly what the client wants. Someone who paints each nail a different color tends to transmit very different messages to different people and is perceived by others as someone with "multiple faces."

One or several rings and/or one or more bracelets

A painting of a ring symbolizes an existing relationship and/or a need for relationship. Someone who emphasizes a ring in a painting of their hand indicates a current emphasis on a particular relationship in their life (for example: a wedding ring). If several rings are drawn, this refers to a current preoccupation with several relationships in their life.

A painting of a bracelet on the person's wrist indicates a relationship, but it tends to reflect the sense of someone whose hands are tied—whether this relates to a current issue, or one from the past, which is affecting the person to this day. If several bracelets are drawn, this refers to several issues that "tie the person's hands."

A halo around the palms of the hands

The painting of a halo around the palms and in the background of the sheet of paper indicates the person's spirituality and a high ability to treat others and send energy to those around them.

Background painting

Someone who paints a background for the palms of their hands is showing us that they are striving to be part of a whole and are strongly connected to their environment. A background painting that "swallows" up the palms of the hands indicates that the person is trying not to be prominent in their environment.

UNCONSCIOUS SYMBOLS

Unconscious symbols are visible to the eye only when the painting is finished and, in most cases, the therapist, is an objective observer of the painting, notices them and points them out to the client. When we show the person what appears in their painting, they are usually surprised, because they didn't consciously intend to draw these.

Pregnant women always draw various shapes of an embryo in the center of the hand (the area of the belly and womb) and one can see this even before the woman is aware that she is pregnant. One of my students drew this form and after I showed it to her, she was examined and joyfully discovered that she was finally pregnant. In the unconscious painting of an embryo and surrounding area, women tend to paint their dreams, expectations and/or fears about the pregnancy and the birth.

Physical problems are always reflected in a painting of the area where the problem is located—for example: Problems in the belly are symbolized by a different way of painting the belly area in the palm of the hand. Physical problems are usually symbolized by painting "spikes" and/or "incisions and fragments" in the problem area and in the choice of colors, such as red or black in a certain area.

Worries and emotional issues are reflected in the painting in the form of loops, suggested question marks, "x's," blurred spikes and vague fragments in the painting of the palm of the hands.

Painting the shape of bars indicates a sense of being closed in, hardship, suffocation, being reluctantly in a place the painter has difficulty leaving, either physically or emotionally.

The painting of a net indicates someone who feels trapped in some life situation and profound, ongoing suffering that is hard for the person to escape because of the thought and/or the fact that it is hard for them to change the existing situation. When I see paintings of nets and bars, I advise my client to get professional emotional help.

The appearance of "fragments" and "incisions" in the painting:

People usually attribute fragments appearing in the picture to the state of the color, a fold in the sheet of paper and/or the state of the table. Fragments and incisions in a painting always indicate an acute problem in the area in which it appears on the hand, and should be taken care of, even if it appears to be "just" a fold in the paper.

A painting of the finger tips where the painting is incomplete, color "escaping" from the outlines of the fingers, or the shape of a thorn at the fingertip, may indicate problems such as headaches (chronic or acute), situations of constant thinking and/or sinus or eye problems.

A painting of a "burst" boundary—where the painting of the palm outline is cut off and/or broken—there is a physical or mental problem. For instance: a line cut off in the pelvic area indicates a problem with posture, joints, etc.

DIAGNOSIS ACCORDING TO DIFFERENCES BETWEEN THE RIGHT AND LEFT SIDES

Diagnosis according to a painting of the palms of the hands relies to a large extent on varying attitudes to the right and left sides, the right-hand palm and the left-hand palm. The first question we have to ask the client who comes for a diagnosis is which is their dominant side, and the diagnosis will be carried out accordingly. The division into two sides relates to the conscious and the unconscious and both sides of the body.

Division of Sides in People Whose Right Side is Dominant

Right side

The right side for right-handed people teaches us about their action and implementation processes. This is the side of the conscious and the rational, which refers to the way in which people implement things, how they think in practical terms, and their conscious actions. The right side is the one that is visible to the personality, the one that ostensibly controls us, the side that is familiar to us. The right side enables us to see where the client stands at the moment in terms of their capacity for action and implementation, what their priorities are, their habits and their overt life ambitions.

Left side

The left side for right-handed people teaches us about their unconscious, their emotional and spiritual realm, spiritual and intuitive abilities, and their secret aspirations. The emotional side is mostly the uncontrolled side that people try to ignore and occasionally manage to silence for a while. It is the side that leads people to spiritual development, learning and practical spiritual progress. The left side enables us to see the importance of spirituality and emotion in the life of a person at a given moment, reflecting emotional and spiritual changes that take place. A person's unconscious priorities frequently differ from those of their conscious, and we see this in the diagnosis.

Division of Sides in People Whose Left Side is Dominant

For left-handed people the definitions are the opposite: The left side is the conscious, dominant and practical side and the right side is the unconscious, emotional and spiritual side.

Left side

For left-handed people, the left side teaches us about their action and implementation processes, for this is the aware, rational side that speaks to the way in which people implement things, their way of thinking, and their conscious actions. The left side is the one that is visible to the personality, the one that ostensibly controls people, the side that is familiar to them. The left side enables us to see where they stand at the moment in terms of their capacity for action and implementation, what their priorities are, their habits and their overt life ambitions.

Right side

The right side for left-handed people teaches us about their unconscious, their emotional and spiritual realm, spiritual and intuitive abilities, and their secret aspirations. The emotional side is mostly the uncontrolled side that people try to ignore and occasionally manage to silence for a while. It is the side that leads people to spiritual development, learning and practical spiritual progress. The right side enables us to see the importance of spirituality and emotion in the life of a person at a given moment, reflecting emotional and spiritual changes that take place. A person's unconscious priorities frequently differ from those of their conscious, and we see this in the diagnosis.

The lower part of the palm that connects to the wrist represents the groin and genitals.

DIAGNOSIS BY DIVIDING THE PAPER INTO AREAS

The sheet of drawing paper represents the client's world and environment and its division differs for right-handed and left-handed people. In order to create a precise division of the paper and accurately diagnose the situation, it is advisable to fold the sheet of paper after painting, according to the desired division.

We first divide the paper into two equal halves—the top half and the bottom half of the paper.

The bottom half of the paper represents the earth and current reality, the practical aspect, the ability to implement and the earth connection in the person's life at the time of the diagnosis, which is also connected to the person's past.

The top half of the drawing paper represents the sky, dreaming, a person's desires and aspirations and their connection to spirituality at the time of the diagnosis, which is also connected to a person's future.

Again, we fold the paper into two equal halves—the right-hand side and the left-hand side. We diagnose the right-hand side and the left-hand side according to the client's dominant side, which shows their practical and emotional state.

Diagnosis for people whose right hand is dominant

For right-handed people, the right side of the paper represents the conscious side, logic, and their practical and operative side in life, and the left side of the paper represents the unconscious, emotion, dreaming, hidden desires and spirituality in their life.

Diagnosis for people whose left hand is dominant

For left-handed people, the left side of the paper represents the conscious side, logic, and their practical and operative side in life, and the right side of the paper represents their unconscious, emotion, dreaming, hidden desires and spirituality in their life.

DIAGNOSIS ACCORDING TO BODY PARTS REPRESENTED IN THE PALM OF THE HAND

The PALM MAP (see opposite) can help us discover a problem with an organ in the body when we see a certain color or marking drawn in the area associated with this organ.

Colors that appear in the drawing of the palms may indicate a physical or mental problem are:

red	gray
black	muddy brown-greenish

Markings in the drawing that may indicate a problem are (as shown opposite) forms of:

thorn	sticks
cuts	strings
tears	

and circles, dots and points that were not drawn intentionally by the patient.

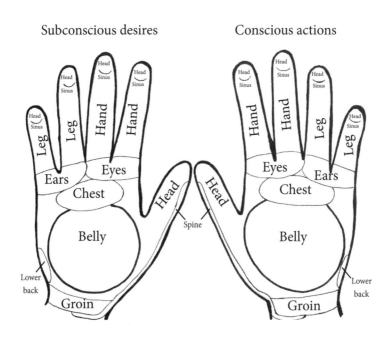

Subconscious desires   Conscious actions

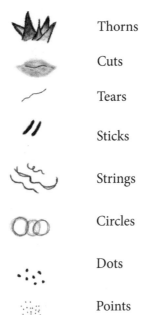

Thorns	
Cuts	
Tears	
Sticks	
Strings	
Circles	
Dots	
Points	

What The Palms Of The Hands Represent

All parts of the body are represented in the palm of the hand and the whole palm reflects the physical and mental state of the body.

A complete diagnosis is made according to the location of the painting's details and the location of the organs in the palm of the hand.

When a part of the palm is missing from the painting, we understand that the client is attempting to ignore a part of their life and/or some part of their body. In many cases, we see that a painting of the palm appears to be "cut off" where the heel of the thumb meets the hand and/or isn't rounded at the edge of it and/or the connection to the wrist and/or the forearm is not drawn. A painting of a "severed" palm is typical of people who live in the here and now, attempting to forget their past and ignore it, or they simply prefer to look to the future and not deal with the past. In contrast, people who paint a palm that is connected to the forearm are currently mentally or actively preoccupied with their past (evoking memories of the past, going through a process of reconstructing past lives, etc.).

The thumb represents the area of the head and neck, reflecting the way in which people think and the physical state of the head and neck.

The next two fingers—the index and middle fingers—represent the way we do things. Our hands reflect what we want to do at a given moment and show us whether we feel deep inside that we should be doing something else and how we want to take action.

The next two fingers—the ring finger and little finger or "pinky"—represent our legs, reflecting where we wish to go right now, whether we feel we're being led against our will, or that we are standing at a crossroads and must choose the best path for ourselves.

The tips of all the fingers represent the head, reflecting problems with sight, headaches, sinuses and a tendency to migraines.

The center of the palm represents our belly, reflecting physical problems, trapped emotions and "keeping things inside us." Since the center of the palm reflects our "soft belly," we should take whatever we see seriously.

Both sides of the palm represent the vertebrae of the backbone, the back, and the hip joints.

WHEEL OF COLORS DIAGNOSIS ACCORDING TO THE CLIENT'S CURRENT PAINTING

A client's Wheel of Colors diagnosis is made in two parallel ways: First, we diagnose according to the colors chosen for the Wheel segments. This choice is made once and goes unchanged in a person's lifetime, as it perfectly represents them and their fundamental nature. Second, we diagnose according to the way in which the client draws and paints the Wheel. The manner of drawing and painting the Wheel changes in the course of a lifetime, and how it is drawn and painted reflects the client's state at the time of the painting, their mood, and worldview of their body, and their place in life in relation to the world around them. It is important that the client draws the Wheel without aid so that we make the most precise and correct diagnosis.

How the Wheel is drawn

A very large Wheel
The drawing of a very large Wheel reflects someone who is preoccupied with internal and external processes of growth and flourishing in their life at the time the Wheel is painted.

A medium-sized Wheel
The painting of a medium-sized Wheel is typical of most people, reflecting a life situation and personal processes that are consistent with the environment.

A small Wheel

The painting of a small Wheel reflects someone who fears making large changes in life, mostly because they are afraid of the reactions of other people.

A minute or miniature Wheel

The painting of a minute or miniature Wheel reflects someone with very low self-esteem and who may have an eating disorder.

A Drawing of the Circumference of the Wheel

The drawing of the circumference of the Wheel (done freely by hand without the help of a compass, plate, etc.) reflects the location of physical problems in the human body. The Wheel is divided according to the organs of the human body and when we see a bulge, curvature or disconnection in a particular area of the Wheel, we examine the corresponding area in the human body, knowing there is some problem.

Drawing the Segments of the Wheel

When someone draws one segment that seems larger than the other segments of the Wheel, it means that this segment takes up a larger place in their life. Most people will draw one or more segments on the Wheel that appear larger than others or, alternatively, they'll emphasize certain segments in their painting.

Painting the Segments on the Wheel

The way in which each segment is painted reflects the current state of the client in the area represented by this segment and we will integrate the diagnosis of how it is painted with the meaning of the color that appears in the segment.

THE MAN AND THE TREE

Color Diagnosis via Paintings of Trees

The technique of diagnosing via paintings of trees is an excellent way to diagnose the current physical and mental state of a person and understand their relationships with their family, friends and the world around them. Over the years I have refined and improved this technique, which is easy to do, enabling us to make an immediate diagnosis at any hour or in any place.

For the diagnosis according to the painting of a tree we use simple tools:

- A blank white sheet of paper (size A4 or A3)
- A pack of oil pastels (24 or 36 colors)

It is advisable to sit with the client in as quiet and calm a place as possible for the duration of the diagnosis. When working with a group it is better to seat participants at a distance from each other, for many adults and children tend to be affected by what is around them, look at the tree their neighbor is painting and "copy" details from it, or add things that weren't in their original painting.

Diagnosis via the painting of a tree is made according to six basic components:

1. Diagnosis according to the classic meaning of the colors used to paint the tree
2. Diagnosis according to the technique of painting the tree
3. Diagnosis according to division of the paper
4. Diagnosis according to symbols that appear in the painting

5. Diagnosis according to the type of tree painted
6. Diagnosis according to the division of the tree into areas

Methods of diagnosis in 1-4, which deal with the classic meaning of the colors used to paint the tree, the technique of painting the tree, the way in which the paper is divided into areas, the way the paper is folded, and the symbols that appear in the painting—are identical to the diagnostic methods I use for painting the palms of the hands, which are extensively detailed on pages 234-277. Certain symbols that appear in a painting of a tree are particularly characteristic of paintings of trees, and I will relate to these extensively later on. Naturally, the two methods are similar in many ways, diagnostic methods according to the kind of tree painted, and dividing the tree into areas (as specified in sections 5 and 6) constitute the main difference in the method of diagnosis according to painting trees. I developed these parallel methods because offering a number of diagnostic techniques enables us to give both therapists and clients multiple and fresh ways of observing their situations without feeling bored, and avoiding repetition of old and familiar things in the course of the treatment.

DIAGNOSIS ACCORDING TO THE TYPE OF TREE PAINTED

Most people draw the "classic" trees shown in the list of painted trees attached at the end of the chapter (pages 295-300).

When you encounter a tree that is drawn in an unusual way, ask the client what they meant in their painting, making use of the list of explanations for the types of trees listed in the dictionary for tree paintings, and listen to your intuition.

The Meanings of the Types of Tree Painted

1. A painting of trees with exposed roots

A painting of any tree with exposed roots that appear in the earth and/or above it indicates a life change in the client. This painting may reflect the client's desire to make a change in their life, change location (physically and/or mentally) and move somewhere else. The Sages said that Man is like a tree in a field—and that uprooting oneself is not easy for anyone.

We all discover that it is difficult to pull up roots from the earth in which they are planted, and even if a change is made willingly and happily we discover that during a move our roots are exposed and we feel sensitive, exposed, easily hurt and at risk. A painting of a tree with exposed roots may also indicate that a person has difficulty putting down roots where they are and connecting to their present environment.

2. Drawing of a tree with a curved trunk

A painting of a tree with a curved trunk first of all indicates a client's physical problem in the area of the back, neck and/or hips, and an accurate diagnosis of the location of the problem is made according to where the curvature is painted in the tree trunk. Alternatively, a painting of a curved tree trunk may indicate that a client feels they are "bowed" or "twisted" by the will of others in certain circumstances, either because of their personality or as a result of traumatic events.

3. Drawing of a tree with a huge top and a tiny trunk

A drawing of a tree with a large and multi-branched top and a relatively small trunk (the difference in size must be accurately measured, and diagnosed only *after* measurement) indicates a person who primarily tends to use their head, particularly respects the thinking part of him/herself and tends not to pay attention to their body. This painting indicates someone who is sunk in a multitude of thoughts, engaged in intellectual issues and tends to ignore the needs of the body. The human being's intellectual and spiritual abilities are considerable and it is important to encourage a connection with the physical aspect and take care of the body, for instance: to exercise and/or practice yoga consistently, in order to balance the spiritual and physical aspects in life and manifest abilities in the best possible way.

4. Drawing of a tree with a small top and a large trunk

A drawing of a tree with a large, thick trunk (particularly a trunk with a triangular shape) and a small top, indicates someone who stresses the importance of the needs of the body and is less engaged in mental, spiritual and emotional issues. A painting of a triangular tree trunk is typical of people who engage in body building, consistently exercising and developing muscles, lifting weights, running, etc.

It is advisable to encourage people to combine thinking and

spirituality in their lives in addition to physical occupations, in order to fulfill all their skills and attain harmony between body and mind.

5. The drawing of a tree that looks like a lollypop

The painting of a tree that looks like a lollypop is typical of children and childish, immature thinking. This kind of drawing shows a tendency to observe things in a general way, indicating difficulty paying attention to small details in any given situation.

6. The drawing of a cypress tree with a top that points upward

The painting of a cypress tree the top of which is sharp and pointing upward toward the sky, indicates someone who is ambitious and goal-oriented and who does all they can to achieve and fulfill what they want. This is someone who will achieve their goals at all costs while ignoring physical and mental difficulties and, occasionally, even without taking other people into consideration.

7. The drawing of a tree that splits into several tops

The drawing of a tree that splits into several tops is typical of someone who hasn't yet separated from mother and/or father figures in their life.

This person is physically and/or emotionally dependent on their parents or close family, preferring to be attached to them. It is difficult for them to separate, think and act independently, as they need physical, emotional and psychological support from the important figures in their life. When a young child draws a tree like this, the drawing is logical and age appropriate. When an adult or old person draws such a tree, they should be referred to a therapist who can work with them on building an independent image of themselves and reinforcing their capacity for true independence.

8. Drawing of a tree that has been chopped down

The drawing of a tree that has been chopped down indicates mourning, profound sadness and a sense that "life is over." A drawing like this is typical of people who have experienced deep loss and are currently in a period of mourning. Someone who draws a severed tree feels his world has collapsed, the tree is cut down—and he doesn't know how to go on with his life. People will sometimes draw a small blooming branch emerging from the tree trunk. This branch represents a new beginning, indicating an ability to rise, overcome difficulties—and start to grow again.

9. The drawing of a tree trunk with ingrained, longitudinal lines

The drawing of a tree trunk with ingrained, longitudinal lines indicates physical and mental difficulties. Someone who draws such a tree has suffered for some time but tends not to reveal his suffering to others. These lines are known as "support lines" and they indicate a person's need for encouragement and support from his environment, and a current sense of suffering, pain and lack of support.

10. The drawing of a tree with crisscross lines ingrained in its trunk

The drawing of a tree with crisscross lines ingrained in its trunk indicates a person's real hardship, pain and ongoing suffering. The lines create a sort of fence or bars, indicating a sense of prison, someone who is imprisoned in a particular situation and has difficulty getting out of it; a sense of physical and mental suffering from which the person doesn't know how to escape. When you encounter someone who draws such a tree—it is advisable to refer him for supportive professional therapy as soon as possible.

11. The drawing of a tree with several tops that emerge one out of another

The drawing of a treetop that contains one or more treetops within it indicates someone who presents an external image that is completely different from what is happening in their heart, out of fear, distress or any other reason.

This pretense is frequently accompanied by "white lies," stories disconnected from reality, and deception. If the outline of the treetop is very strongly painted and emphasized, the person is feeling they must protect him/herself, their thoughts, wishes and ideas—in case they are hurt, and so they don't reveal what is in their mind and heart. It is advisable to refer this person for therapy that will enable them to release him/herself from their fears, to be sincere and authentic with him/herself and their surroundings and speak openly and honestly.

12. The drawing of a tree whose trunk is drawn as one trunk within another

The drawing of one trunk within another indicates a dietary process and a "shrinking" of the person's body. The person feels the boundaries of their body are shrinking and, within the thick trunk a thinner one is revealed. It is crucial to ask the person about their diet discipline, for many people take extreme steps, undertaking a "punishing" diet. It is extremely important to pay attention to children's drawings, particularly during adolescence. In certain cases, a drawing like this indicates an eating disorder like anorexia or bulimia.

13. A drawing of a tree at the bottom of which are grass, flowers, etc.

The drawing of a tree at the bottom of which are earth, grass, flowers, etc., indicates the person's strong connection to the Earth. This painting also shows the importance of the past in the person's life as well as their connection to the place from which they came and where they are today. When flowers are drawn at the bottom of the tree, the person feels their ability to bloom and grow in the environment they live in. This drawing indicates the person's sense of foundation and their physical and mental stability.

14. The drawing of a tree with part of its top "severed" and missing

A drawing of a tree where part of its top is severed and missing indicates a physical injury to the head and/or mental disability. This drawing appears among people with head injuries and among children and people who are intellectually challenged.

15. The drawing of a tree with equally proportionate trunk and top

The drawing of a tree with equally proportionate trunk and top indicates someone who pays attention both to their body and their mind, successfully combining an intellectual life with the needs of the body. We strive to reach a physical, spiritual and mental balance—and the drawing of a tree like this indicates a successful combination of body and mind in a beneficial and balanced way.

16. The drawing of a tree with flowers at the top

The painting of a tree with flowers at the top indicates someone who enjoys a state of spiritual and mental blooming, feeling him/ herself to be in a state of progress and flourishing in their life. It is an optimistic painting and, even if the person who painted it is, at the time, in a difficult or complicated situation, they know they will manage to overcome all difficulties in their life.

17. A drawing of a tree with fruit at the top (apples, oranges, etc.)

The drawing of a tree with fruit at the top indicates someone who sees the fruit of their labors and can enjoy the results of their efforts. People who draw fruit on the tree are in a practical and fruitful period of their life. It is an optimistic picture that indicates coming to terms with life processes, spiritual maturity and belief in the ability to reach a time that is physically and mentally nurturing and beneficial.

18. Drawing of a tree with the sun shining on it from the top, left side of the paper

How we diagnose this picture changes according to the dominant side of the person who has drawn it.

For right-handed people, a sun drawn on the left side of the paper represents a sense of confidence in the deep, inner knowledge that someone is guarding and protecting them and those they love.

For left-handed people, a sun drawn on the left side of the paper represents a sense of physical and practical confidence in the belief and knowledge that someone is guarding and protecting their actions and helping them to arrive at the desired results.

19. Drawing of a tree with the sun shining on it from the top, right side of the paper

How we diagnose this picture changes according to the dominant side of the person who has drawn it. For right-handed people, a sun drawn on the right side of the paper represents a sense of physical and practical confidence in the belief and knowledge that someone is guarding and protecting their actions and helping them to arrive at the desired results.

For left-handed people, a sun drawn on the right side of the paper represents a sense of confidence in the deep, inner knowledge that someone is guarding and protecting them and those they love.

20. When a picture of a treetop "bursts" off the sheet of paper, the person who has drawn it will usually say they didn't have enough space on the paper for the whole tree

The drawing of a treetop that bursts out of the boundaries of the paper indicates someone with a mind of their own who "thinks outside the box," whose thoughts burst through existing boundaries. This painting indicates that multiple plans are running through the person's mind, and they "break" conventions and burst beyond the accepted domains. A person like this prefers to act according to their wishes and won't like accepting the authority of others or their direction, even if it is for the person's own good.

21. Drawing of a tree whose top is mostly off the sheet of paper

The drawing of a tree whose top is mostly off the paper indicates someone who is independent, has a mind of their own (similar to drawing No. 20), a soloist on the level of the soul, preferring to think and do things on their own, and who keeps most of their thoughts and ideas to him/herself. This painting indicates someone who lives an entire life in their mind, frequently "taking flight in their thoughts" and they tend to be idealistic, spiritual and very curious, hovering between various worlds.

22. Drawing of a palm tree (date palm)

A drawing of a palm tree whose fronds droop downward on both sides indicates someone who has to choose between two or more things, and feels overtired from deliberations and the need to choose. This picture also appears for people who feel they give with all their heart to those around them and are physically and mentally tired.

23. Drawing of a tree with exposed branches, which appears in two forms

1. A drawing of a tree with exposed, bare, leafless branches: drawing of a tree in the fall, its branches bare and leafless, indicates that the person who has drawn the picture feels they are in the autumn of their life, everything is at an end and nothing new is growing yet. This drawing is typical of situations of parting, loneliness and depression.

2. A drawing of a tree whose branches are visible, with leaves growing on them: A drawing of a tree whose branches are visible with leaves growing on them indicates that the person who has painted it feels that the growth and prosperity in their life have to do with many people, particularly people who are close to them. The branches growing out of the tree trunk symbolize the people who are particularly close to and courageously connected to the person and are usually associated with their family members. This is a classic painting of a tree and many will paint one like it although, of course, each painting is different according to the personality of the person who has painted it.

24. Drawing of a tree whose lower branches are trailing downward

The drawing of a tree some of whose lower branches are trailing downward indicates the tiredness of the person who has painted it. When the trailing branches appear on the feeling side, they indicate that the person is tired and emotionally and mentally exhausted. When the branches trailing downward appear on the side of implementation, they indicate that the person who has drawn the picture is physically tired, which could be work- or project-related or the result of insufficient sleep. In most cases, the picture reflects the current tiredness of the person, but could sometimes indicate an ongoing fatigue.

25. The drawing of a whole picture, for instance, of a tree with a swing hanging from its branches, grass and flowers at the bottom of it while, above it, birds fly

A drawing of a whole picture, including multiple details, indicates the ability of the person who drew it to see the whole picture of their life, and the scrupulously detailed background indicates the great importance of their environment to them.

Each detail on the sheet of paper has a meaning of its own, for instance: The drawing of a swing shows a situation that is "fluctuating" and unstable on the side it is drawn; a drawing of birds indicates a need for freedom and the desire to "spread their wings" on the side it is drawn; and a drawing of clouds in the sky indicates doubts and a lack of clarity in the person's life on the side it is drawn. Each detail must be related to separately, according to its meaning and the side on which it is drawn.

26. Drawing of a tree planted in a hole in the ground

A drawing of a tree planted in a hole in the ground shows that the person who drew it feels alienated from their environment and planted in one that is alien to them. People tend to draw pictures like this after they've moved apartments or countries or jobs. This drawing sometimes illustrates a person who senses loneliness or feels alien and has difficulty integrating into the company where they work or in their environment.

27. Drawing of a tree completely surrounded by a circle or ring

A drawing of a tree completely surrounded by a circle indicates that the person who has drawn it feels, either temporarily or permanently, utterly disconnected from their environment. This seclusion from their surroundings sometimes stems from a person's fears and a deep need for protection, and it can appear after a bad injury, trauma, or tragedy.

28. Drawing of a very tiny tree in one corner of the paper

The sheet of paper represents the world and environment of the person who has drawn it and the tree represents the person. When a tree is drawn especially small, it indicates that the person who has drawn it feels small, meaningless and without any means of influence in the world. If the tree is drawn in the area of the earth on the paper, it means that the person feels earth-bound and cannot connect with their spirituality. If the tree is drawn in the area of the sky on the paper, it means the person is "floating" and it is difficult for them to connect with reality. The drawing of an especially tiny tree sometimes indicates eating disorders such as anorexia.

29. A drawing of a tree with one or two birds sitting at the top

A drawing of a tree with a bird sitting at the top indicates that the person who has drawn it wishes to be free.

A bird drawn on the emotional side of the tree indicates the person's need for emotional freedom and a release from conventions; and a bird drawn on the practical side of the tree indicates the person's need for release from work and practical tasks.

30. Drawing of a bird pecking or nesting in a tree trunk

These pictures indicate a problem or illness that troubles the person who has drawn it. A bird pecking at the trunk indicates the stage a person begins to be aware of the problem and is troubled by it. The bird nesting in the tree indicates the stage at which the person feels the problem has become part of them and is hard to get rid of.

31. Drawing of a nest of chicks in the treetop

The drawing of a nest of chicks in a treetop indicates that the person who has drawn this picture feels they are obligated to take care of someone dependent upon them, their young children for instance, and they are greatly preoccupied by the thought.

32. Drawing of a tree with a hollow or "eye" in the trunk

Any drawing or image on the tree trunk indicates a physical problem in the body of the person who has drawn the picture; this should be attended to and the person should be referred for medical examination and advice.

If the drawing of the hollow or the eye in the tree has a heart shape, we must pay attention to the emotional vulnerability of the person who has drawn the picture and find out if they are suffering from a painful separation.

33. Drawing of a tree with a dead branch in its trunk

The drawing of a dead branch in the trunk of a tree represents a loss suffered at a young age by the person who has drawn the picture, the implications of which affect them to the present day.

294 | Noah Goldhirsh

DIAGNOSIS ACCORDING TO THE DIVISION OF THE TREE INTO AREAS

A painting of the tree is divided into three main parts: Roots, trunk and treetop.

1. The treetop represents the head of the person painting the tree, and the center of the treetop represents their close family.
2. The tree trunk represents the body of the person painting the tree and, within the drawing of the trunk, there is a further division into areas, according to the locations of body organs.
3. The roots of the tree represent the legs of the person painting the tree and their physical and energetic connections to where they currently are in life.

For right-handed people, the right-hand side of the tree represents logic and practicality and the left side represents emotion and the unconscious.

For left-handed people, the right side of the tree represents emotion and the unconscious, and the left side represents logic and practicality.

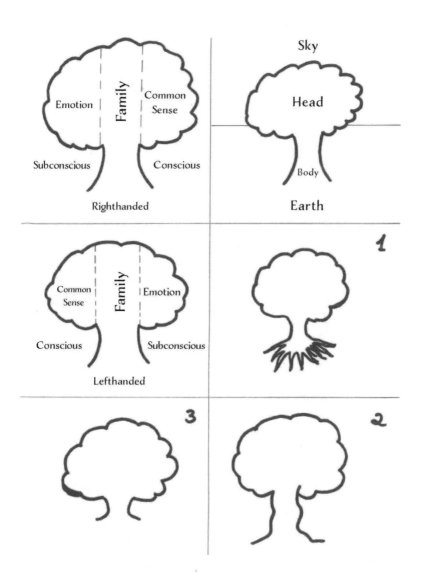

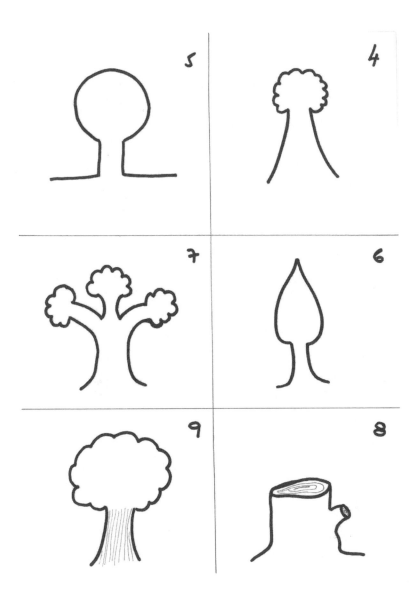

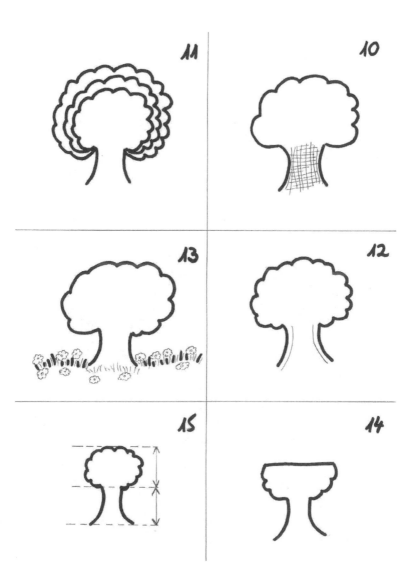

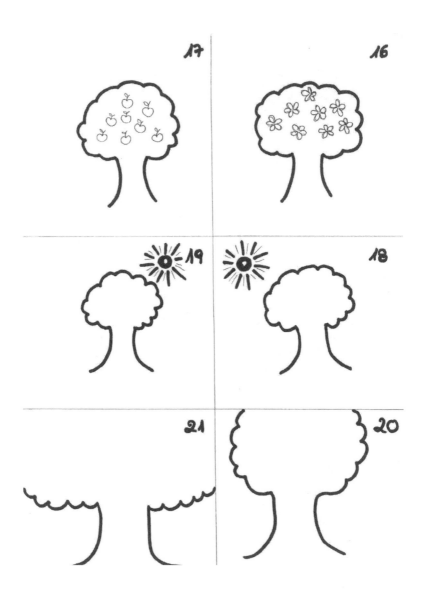

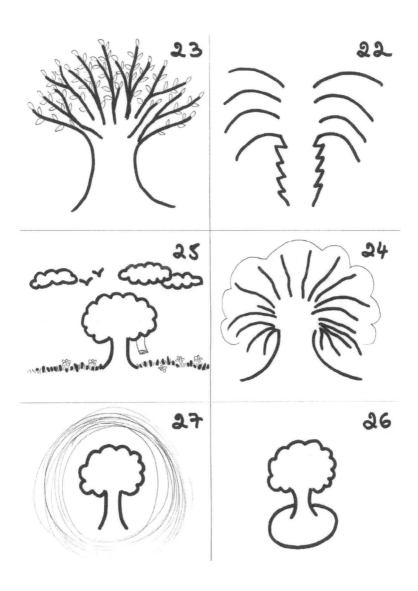

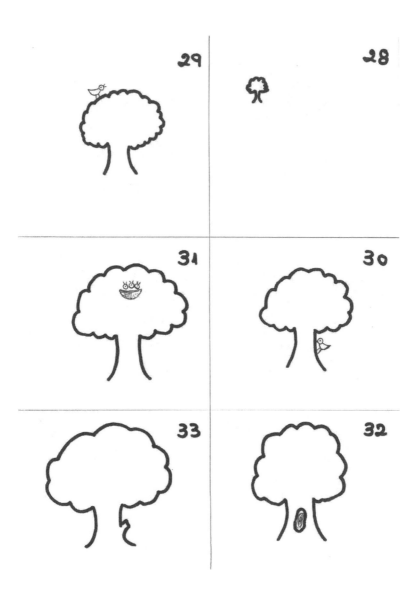

THE DEDICATING OF CANDLES

Throughout history we have lit fires that rise up—flames and smoke carrying our prayers and requests to the sky.

Dedicating candles to a particular purpose is a Native American technique that enables us to ask clearly for anything we wish, acting energetically to achieve it. Lighting fire activates the request and when a candle is lit—the request is granted.

This technique of dedicating candles to a purpose has nothing to do with religion. All we need to do is use our intention for good, working in a beneficial, positive way with light entities in order for our requests to manifest. When our intention is good, our requests are granted, manifesting for our higher good. If we use the technique wrongly, wishing someone harm—the request returns like a boomerang to the applicant and injures them, for the Law of Karma is always activated against anyone who intends harm and hurts, or wishes to hurt others and, as our forefathers have already said:

"Whoever digs a pit—will fall in."

Each candle is intended for one request. If we wish to make several requests, we must prepare a separate candle for each one in advance.

It is very important to define the request clearly and succinctly. We can write down our request so that we repeat it accurately, without stumbling, because in the process of charging the candle, we repeat our request ten times.

Defining the request takes place in the form of prior gratitude—for instance, if we wish to receive a particular job, we say: "I am grateful for getting the job at… as soon as possible and in the best way possible for my own good and that of all parties involved."

An important part in the process of dedicating a candle is known as energetic charging, in the course of which we disperse strong, concentrated energy through our hands. Energetic charging is performed by combining spiritual intention with physical action and in various healing processes any object can be energetically charged (a stone, a bracelet, a chain, etc.) in order to send concentrated energy for healing and protection. Energy sent in this way remains for a time inside the object we have charged, affecting anyone who touches or uses it.

In the process of charging the candle we focus on directing energy to our hands, think good thoughts about the subject of our request, speak our request and "send" the energy from the palms of our hands to the candle.

It is crucial to focus on our purpose and send our request to the universe as clearly as possible. In most cases, we feel a warmth or energetic tingling in the palms of our hands during the charging process, but sometimes (mainly when we are stressed for some reason) the sensation is vaguer. Don't worry, your strong intention is what determines the outcome. Let your intention come from the heart; make your request, combining it with the technique detailed later.

THE COLORS OF CANDLES FOR REQUESTS

Red
A red candle is suitable for protection and is also used for urgent and/or important requests.

Yellow
A yellow candle is suitable for requesting success in tests of all kinds.

Blue
A blue candle is suitable for requesting the development of intuition and channeling, enhancing our capacity for compassion, caring and understanding.

Green
A green candle is suitable when requesting success in any new step we take, or any new projects and economic success.

Pink
A pink candle is effective for requesting a good and successful relationship.

White
A white candle is effective for all kinds of requests since the color white includes all colors.

Purple
A purple candle is effective when requesting recovery, gratitude for what is or closing cycles, and is particularly suitable when requesting

abundance and economic security.

Orange

An orange candle is effective when requesting joy, a good connection among people and raising energy.

Silver

A silver candle is effective for all types of request. It is advisable to dedicate and charge silver candles when the moon is full, because the color silver is connected to the moon and will imbue requests with all the power of the full moon.

Gold

A gold candle is effective for all requests; its use best ensures the manifestation of the request. It is advisable to dedicate and charge gold candles at sunrise or midday because these are the hours when the sun is at the height of its power. The color gold is connected to the sun and will imbue requests with the full power of the sun.

Brown

A brown candle is effective when requesting grounding, balance and a connection to reality.

Rose

A rose-colored candle is effective when requesting the capacity for extrasensory perception, increasing the use of the third eye and seeing beyond the issue at hand.

Black

We do not use black candles for dedication because many cultures contextually relate them to evil.

Crystal

A glass container filled with oil and a wick serves as the color crystal. This color is suitable for making all types of request but it is very difficult to charge the container. The use of the color crystal is especially effective for ambiguous situations that are hard to navigate, because this color helps us to clarify situations and act in the best possible way.

The technique for dedicating candles requires us to prepare in advance:

- A calm quiet place where we are not interrupted.
- An unused candle with a color that is suitable for the request.
- A specific request that is formulated precisely and succinctly.
- Long matchsticks.

How to dedicate a candle:

Before dedicating the candle, we ask for the protection and help of all light entities, saying:

I am grateful to be surrounded only by light entities who guard, protect and help me.

We sit comfortably and place the candle on a table or flat surface in front of us. If we wish to dedicate several candles, we place all the candles for dedication in a safe place to one side, focusing each time on dedicating one candle at a time. The candle is divided into three parts:

1. The bottom part
2. The top part
3. The wick

- Hold the candle in the non-dominant hand, turning the bottom part upward; "wrap" the bottom part of the candle in the dominant hand and slowly turn it clockwise with the non-dominant hand.

Through both palms of the hands, stream your intention into the candle, speaking the request aloud or silently, three times in succession, charging the candle with the request.

- Turn the candle, holding it in the non-dominant hand, the top part turned upward, "wrapping" the top part with the dominant hand and slowly turning it clockwise with the dominant hand. Through both palms of the hands, stream your intention into the candle, speaking the request aloud or silently, three times in succession, charging the candle with your request.

- Place the candle on the table or a flat surface, light a match, saying aloud or silently: "I dedicate you to…" repeating your request. Light the candle.

- Place both palms at a safe height above the candle flame, bringing your awareness powerfully to your intention and speaking your request aloud or silently three times in succession.

- Place the candle at home or at work in an energetic place where you can see it. When the candle is lit your request begins to work. If you wish to leave the room or home for an extended time, say to the candle: "Thank you for bringing your light to the purpose for which I dedicated you" and snuff it out.

Do not leave a lit candle unattended

- When you return to the place with the candle and wish to re-activate the request, light the candle, saying: "Thank you for bringing your light to the purpose for which I dedicated you."

Once our request is fulfilled with the help of the candle, it has in fact completed its function and can be buried in the ground, melted in a fire, or buried in the garbage.

If a dedicated candle burns down before our request is fulfilled, we bury the remains in the earth or garbage and dedicate another candle to our request.

Each candle is dedicated to only one purpose.

We can dedicate several different candles one after another to various purposes in order to help us manifest our dreams. We frequently feel tired after charging several candles because this is not a simple process and it requires a lot energetically.

Once all the candles we wished to dedicate have been charged and dedicated in the best possible way, we can light several dedicated candles at the same time, while making sure there is a safe space between each candle.

The request often manifests quickly but occasionally it will take time for it to do so. When we wish to make a short-term request—for instance, requesting success in a particular test—we dedicate a small candle.

When we wish to make a long-term request—for instance, a request for a good, ongoing relationship—we choose to dedicate a large candle.

For permanent requests—for instance, a request for security and protection—we choose a large candle and renew it whenever it burns out.

You can keep the dedicated candles wherever you please and light them regularly.

Explain clearly to anyone who wishes to light charged candles instead of you that only you may touch these candles and only you may light them.

If you are not at home and want someone else to light the candle for you (for instance, if you have an exam and want a candle to be lit for your success) ask someone to light the candle and transmit your intention from a distance.

A lit candle must not be left unattended in any situation!!!

308 | NOAH GOLDHIRSH

THANK YOU

The Power of Gratitude in Advance
and Good Intentions

Words that sound so simple and routine, **"Thank you very much"**, are actually magical words—wonderful, strong, beneficial and infinitely powerful words. Our ability to say "thank you very much" in gratitude to the universe best allows us to receive what we ask for. Most of us are accustomed to saying "thank you" only after receiving what we have requested because we've been taught to adhere to a material, not a spiritual, concept according to which acceptance precedes gratitude.

It is a cosmic truth that giving opens the way to giving; acceptance opens the way to acceptance; and gratitude in advance opens the way to giving and receiving.

When we show gratitude in advance for something we want, we actually invite it into our lives, enabling it to manifest and reach us.

Showing gratitude in advance enables us to transform our desire into reality in all areas of life.

When I encountered the Native American way of thinking for the first time, I fell in love with the concept of "saying thank you in advance," which breaks the convention of saying thank you at the end of a process. People used to say to me: "Wait, don't be so quick to thank me...wait until something happens..." But I happily and lovingly adopted the spiritual custom of saying thank you in advance, before receiving what I asked for. How wonderful to discover that we live in a world where showing gratitude for everything is allowed and desirable—before, during and afterwards!

Time is only an illusion of the logical, thinking part of us. Time does not exist. Actually, the only thing that does exist is the present moment.

The past does not exist; it is past and done with. The future does not exist; it has not yet appeared. Only the present moment really exists in life.

At this very moment we determine everything—who we really are; what we want; what we request for ourselves and for others.

Saying "thank you very much" is an expression of gratitude to the universe in which we live and make a living, and it treasures within all the abundance and goodness that exists inside us and within our surroundings.

Ask yourself: What am I requesting for myself? What do I want?

Make a list of at least 21 things you want and request for yourself.

It is hard to make this list, because we are accustomed to focusing on what we don't want. We find it hard to define what we really want in life and it is difficult for us to believe that everything exists within and is available to us.

In the course of our lives we experience rejection, dissatisfaction and disappointment. Our thoughts tend to be critical, angry and negative, and negative thinking tends to stick, becoming a habit that is hard to change. As a result of our way of thinking, accepted behavior and education in most of the world, most people have a hard time believing in and trusting their inner strength, spiritual power and ability to fulfill themselves, manifest their desires and receive their heart's desire.

We can, from this moment onward, decide to practice a positive way of thinking that will enable us to invite satisfaction, success and good, wonderful things into our lives—turning this into a new and excellent habit that will benefit us in any situation. Positive thinking and gratitude in advance for the granting of our requests requires mental practice and overcoming years of skepticism, but the rewards are immense!

Working with gratitude to the universe and saying "thank you very much" in advance is very simple.

Define a simple sentence, request or purpose in a few words, formulate the sentence accurately and speak it aloud or in your heart—for instance, we don't say "Thank you very much for not disqualifying me from the race," but: "I'm very grateful for being able to run the best race possible."

We make our request and show gratitude, as if our request has already been granted. We must remember that time is just an illusion, and when we use the past tense to speak of something we want in the future, as if it were already ours, we change time—what we asked for becomes ours, and the future becomes the present.

When asking for something, we must be sure the sentence consists of three main parts:

1. We start the sentence with the words: "Thank you very much for/ I am very grateful for…"
2. We define our request in positive language.
3. We end the sentence with the words: "for the good of all related parties."

Part A: Gratitude in advance attracts what we request into the here and now. When we speak in the past tense about something we want in the future, as if we have already received it, we transform the energy of the future in accordance with our request.

Part B: Defining our request in positive language ensures that it will be kindly received. Evil, hurtful requests badly hurt the applicant and their karma, and any use of negative language, negative requests or negative intentions should be avoided at all costs.

Part C: When we ask for something for the good of all related parties, we are in fact asking for ourselves and for a group of people, and the power of intention of group requests is a most powerful force.

For example: when you ask to succeed in an exam for the benefit of all related parties, the intention is that your success in the exam will gladden and empower you as well as your parents, friends and teachers, and the request is transformed from a personal request, affecting only you, to one whose fulfillment will gladden and empower many people.

When our request for ourselves is in fact the heart's desire of many people related to us, innate to the request is also the power of their intention, which helps the request to manifest in the best possible way.

At the end of the request it is possible and desirable to express gratitude once again to the universe, spirit guides and all light entities.

Aided by intention and gratitude in advance, it is possible to make "small" requests—for instance, finding a parking place, succeeding in a test—as well as "big" requests, such as for health, economic abundance, etc.

When we make our request like this, frequently and regularly, for things we truly want, with real respect, our request can manifest in the best possible way. When a request does not manifest as we wish, although we have made frequent requests, we must understand that it will manifest differently and in a way that better suits us and our karma.

PROTECTION AND RELEASE RITUALS

Protection

At some point, we all experience a sense of fear, anxiety and insecurity, sensations that also exist while we try to deny them. These sensations frequently prevent us from manifesting our abilities, from daring to break through boundaries and act differently from what is accepted.

There are multiple kinds of energy in our world: some are pleasant and advance us; others stop us.

We are all energetic entities, and we sense energies of all kinds. Some of us sense energy and respond powerfully to it and some sense it to a lesser extent, but all of us have the capacity to sense and work with energy.

We need to remember that fear is a type of energy, but we don't have to explore this energy for a long time.

At any given moment we can convert the energy of fear into that of confidence and power.

When we feel confident and protected, we can sense, act and progress in the best possible way.

Energetic protection provides us with the best possible environment, significantly diminishing our fears and anxieties, and enhancing our strength.

There are multiple physical and mental protection techniques for us and our environment; each person can choose the technique that suits them.

I believe that only light can disperse darkness. The protections I work with are the protections of light energy and light entities, which point to light and goodness in the universe.

Over the years I have become aware of the power and practicality of two powerful energetic protections:

A. A Native American protection technique, where we declare ourselves to be a light entity, defining the kind of energy streamed through us. The sentence used by Native Americans is:

I am a being of light and goodness
Only light and goodness can come to me
Only light and goodness can flow through me
And only light and goodness will exist here

This protection technique illuminates us, defining our choice of the energy of love and light.

B. A protection technique that precisely defines the meaning of the protection we request. This technique has proved to be the best and most effective one and thousands of people use it with great success.

In order to be well protected we express gratitude aloud and/or silently for the protection we are requesting around us:

* Thank you for surrounding me only with light entities that guard, protect and help me.
** Thank you for surrounding us only with light entities that guard, protect and help us.
*** Thank you for surrounding me and all of us only with light entities that guard, protect and help me and all of us.

The first protective sentence helps the applicant at any hour and in any situation. It invites light entities to surround the applicant, and this protection is recommended in any situation in which the applicant senses fear, loneliness or the need for additional protection around them. We use the first protection sentence in any situation, whenever we wish, and without limitation. The next two protection sentences help us to ask the light entities for help and they define the protections that we request around ourselves, those we love and anyone who chooses to come to us.

When someone requests protection <u>for themselves alone</u>—they need only say the <u>first sentence</u>. The sentence can be said several times as needed.

When someone requests protection <u>for themselves and whoever is with them</u>—family members, friends, clients, etc.—<u>all three sentences must be spoken consecutively</u>. The sentences can be said several times as needed.

The most important energetic law related to protection states that the sentences must only be said for someone we know for certain has chosen light and light entities, and not for people who don't know who they are or what they have chosen.

My basic assumption is that if someone comes to me as a friend, a family member or a client, they have chosen to come to be in relationship with light entities, and so I may say the three sentences and include them in the protection of the light entities. In contrast, when I meet people by chance—for instance, when I am among strangers, traveling by train with them—I don't have the right to say the sentences about or for them, for they have the right to choose to be with whom they wish, and cannot be forced to work with light entities. Thus, in this case, when traveling, we ask for the protection of light entities only for ourselves. When traveling with friends, family and so on, we may ask the light entities for protection for ourselves and for them, but not for anyone else on the train, etc.

What is the difference between light and dark entities in our world?

Light entities do not make us do anything.

The right to choose is the most sacred right in the universe. We always have a choice.

Dark entities maneuver people, impose, force or make them

act according to the will of the dark entity—by using force, fear or physical and/or mental coercion. Dark entities take away people's right to free choice.

Light entities always give us free choice, even when we make a choice that isn't good for us.

Our right to choose is fixed, eternal and limitless and cannot be taken away from us. We have the right to choose, to make a mistake, and we have the right to fix our mistakes!!!

Free choice is the way of light in the world, and anyone who forces us to do things against our will—imposing things on us that negate our choice—is walking the path of the dark entities.

When we ask the light entities to surround and protect us, we are choosing light. Our personal choice can be changed at any given moment, and so, at each and every moment, we must clarify for ourselves: where do we stand, who are we and what do we want to be.

We can ask the light entities to be with us, protect us and help us in any situation in life; when things are difficult for us, we can ask them aloud or silently for help. It works to the same extent.

We can write down the first sentence on a small piece of paper and put it in our pocket, or bag, etc.

For children who feel they need protection, who fear exams, who have trouble falling asleep at night, and so on—we can write down the sentence for them to put in their pocket, school bag and/or under their pillow. It's important to explain the sentence to children. You will be amazed at how quickly they remember it by heart and how natural and right it seems to them.

It is advisable to request protection in a place where the window is open (or outside, in the open air), putting your hands together in front of the heart center and asking either aloud or silently. Placing our hands together near the Heart Chakra joins the right and left sides together, balancing us and improving our physical and mental state. This is the most fundamental protection and it can be used anywhere, at any time, in any language, without limitation. It is advisable for the applicant to say it in their mother tongue.

PROTECTION THROUGH COLOR

A protective energetic bubble

If we wish to protect ourselves more actively, we can use a technique that combines protective energy with healing colors and universal energy.

The technique is known as a "protective energetic bubble" or a "protection bubble."

Every human being can learn to create a protective, energetic bubble in a process that is partially conscious and partially intuitive, and, over time, every human being learns to activate an energetic bubble in the way most effective for them.

Creating an energetic bubble can be done standing up, sitting down or lying down, as you wish. It is usually more comfortable for beginners to create a protective energetic bubble sitting down and, after practice, it is possible to create the protective bubble easily and quickly in any position.

Creating a protective bubble (sitting down)

It is best to sit somewhere as quiet as possible, near an open window, or outside in nature. If we are working in a room, we can light a candle nearby.

- We ask for the protection of the light entities (*I am grateful for having only light entities around me who look after me, protect and help me*).

- Closing our eyes, we ask universal energy for a huge energy bubble the color of sunlight, a transparent, crystal, gold color, requesting that this become the most suitable, beneficial energy, specifically for us and all our needs.

- Choose how you wish to enter the bubble: It is possible to "open a door" in the bubble and go inside; "wear" the bubble, or simply to allow the bubble to surround us on all sides.

- We breathe the golden light of the bubble into our body, filling it with energy from head to toe, in the following way:

o Breathe the golden energy in through the nose, streaming it into the head, from there to the neck, shoulders, arms and hands, chest and back, belly, sexual organs and buttocks, and from there to the legs and the tips of the toes. Allow the energy to fill the entire body, feeling how each place it reaches is cleansed of tension, stress and pain, filling up with energy that is soothing, healing, pleasant, warm, gold and illuminated.

o Imagine a transparent pipe from the opening to the vagina (for women) or from the point between the testicles and the rectum (for men) into the earth below. Pour into the transparent pipe and the earth below all your fears, anger, pressures and worries accumulated by the body. All these unhealthy energies are really organic compost for the earth and our energetic waste is converted into the clean, pure, holding energy of Mother Earth.

o Imagine another transparent pipe, parallel to the first one, coming out of the earth and entering the body.

o Through this pipe flows good earth energy that is powerful, healing, balancing and reinforcing, rising from the Earth and into the body. Earth energy heals the body, balancing us and reinforcing our ability to implement what we want. Both pipes act simultaneously: One pipe removes the excess energy we have accumulated, pouring it into the earth, while the parallel pipe streams good new energy from the Earth into the body.

Inside the energy bubble we are in, two energies flow together: the energy of the sky—heavenly energy that flows into the body from the Crown Chakra—and earth energy, which flows into the body through the Root Chakra.

When these two energies are properly combined, they balance, reinforce and heal the body.

When we are inside an energy bubble, we are protected body and soul, cleansed from all excess energy, receiving new, pure energy from the universe, growing stronger and healing.

After devoting time to the practice of the energy bubble, most people prefer to absorb golden universal energy directly from the crown chakra instead of streaming it through the nose.

Make the energy bubble for balance and protection any way you wish; any technique you choose will be beneficial for you.

We choose the color for the energy protection bubble according to the type of protection we need. The recommended colors for protection are:

- Color No. 7 according to your personal Wheel of Colors.
- The color red—for the strongest temporary protection.
- The color white—for spiritual protection.
- The color gold—for universal protection.
- The color green—for strong protection, particularly recommended for the protection of plants and trees from pests.

To accurately create particularly strong protection, it is possible and even desirable to combine several colors in the bubble, the combinations determined by the personal Wheel of Colors and the personal need when creating the protection bubble.

We can combine the colors parallel to each other, or use the layer technique, setting the colors in layers, one color surrounding the body, placing it on top of the next color, enveloping the first color.

The most powerful protection is created by using the color red. Red protection is considered the strongest protection of all and is recommended only for times of real and concrete danger, as a covering for the gold energy bubble, leaving it only for a brief time.

In times of real and concrete danger, we invite the gold energy bubble and once we are protected inside it, we "wrap" the outside of the bubble in the color red:

We imagine a strong red enveloping the entire bubble from the outside, which constitutes a barrier that prevents anything from reaching or hurting us.

It is very important to remember: Do not leave the red envelope around you for longer than a quarter of an hour!

Only use the color red in an emergency and remove the red envelope around the gold energy bubble immediately after you leave the place of danger.

It is possible to envelop the gold bubble in other colors, for additional purposes:

- For powerful spiritual protection—envelop the gold bubble in strong, shining, blinding, white light
- For plants and trees—envelop the plant in a golden bubble, then surround it with the color green. The colors can be "mixed" together in the bubble
- For relaxing—we can wrap the golden bubble in the color pink, for pink relaxes people physically and mentally. The color pink can be left on the bubble for long periods of time, for a pink envelope is effective for difficult meetings and conversations, and so on. The color pink will ease the atmosphere during the conversation, making it more comfortable, calmer, and moderate, helping to reach agreements in a good spirit.

CREATING A QUICK ENERGY BUBBLE
FOR PROTECTION

This technique can be done standing up, sitting down or lying down. It is advisable to be in as quiet a place as possible, with an open window, or outside in nature.

Request protection from the light entities.

Imagine you are a transparent jar in human form, the opening to the jar is the head, the crown chakra, and from below, imagine two pipes connected between the legs and going into and from the earth.

We insert ourselves into the energy bubble of golden light we have requested.

Stream the energy and light from the bubble into the body from the top downward to the tips of the fingers and toes.

Stream two types of energy together through the pipes: through one pipe, stream all the excess energy from the body into the earth below, and through the other pipe, stream wonderful earth energy into the body.

We can use the golden bubble or wrap the bubble in the colors of our choice.

The energy bubble for protection is valid for an hour, after which it begins to dissolve. It can be renewed if we wish. It can be renewed many times over, depending on our wishes and needs.

The energy bubble is wonderful for illness, helping to accelerate the body's natural recovery process, especially in conjunction with the colors of a person's personal Wheel of Colors.

Once we practice and become experienced in creating an energy bubble, the process only takes a few minutes.

PROTECTION BUBBLES FOR OBJECTS, PLANTS AND ANIMALS

A protection bubble for objects

When we wish to energetically look after property and/or protect some object, such as a bag we leave on the beach, a car, and so on, we must first create a transparent golden energy bubble to protect ourselves. Once we are protected, we invite a red protection bubble, wrap the object we wish to protect in the red bubble, connecting three red "anchors" from the bubble in the earth beneath.

It is possible to enhance the protection, repeating the process three times in succession.

Obviously, we must all take the necessary precautions, avoid relying solely on the red protection, using it only as an energetic addition to keeping our possessions safe. It is extremely important to remember that when we return to the object, we must "dissolve" the bubble around it before using it again.

A protection bubble for animals

If we wish to safeguard and protect an animal, we can make an energetic protection bubble for it exactly as we do for ourselves, our family, friends and clients.

The process of creating an energetic protection bubble for an animal is simple and easy:

1. Create an energetic protection bubble for ourselves.
2. Envelop the animal in an energetic protection bubble the color of transparent gold.

THE POWER OF COLORS | 325

3. Imagine two pipes between the sexual organs of the animal and the earth, one pipe leading into the Earth and the other leaving it. The process of streaming the energy inside the energetic protection bubble around the animal is activated in the same way as it is around human beings and, ultimately, the animal will be protected within an energetic gold bubble.

4. In the case of concrete danger—for example, if your dog passes a large dog that might attack him—immediately envelop your dog's gold bubble in red energy, making sure to "dissolve" the red energy once you are out of danger.

A protection bubble for plants and trees

If we wish to safeguard and protect a tree and/or a plant, we can do so easily and simply. An energetic bubble process is very helpful for healing and strengthening trees and plants when they're damaged and weak. Envelop the tree or plant you wish to treat in an energetic bubble the color of gold, or green, or an energetic bubble combining both these colors.

Leave the bubble in place; it will dissolve of its own accord. Treating plants and trees that are sick, weak, etc., with the help of an energetic protection bubble yields incredible results, but the process must be repeated frequently, and remember that the healing process can take a long time.

326 | NOAH GOLDHIRSH

RELEASE RITUALS

Our lives consist of relationships we have with various people at different times.

Every relationship comes to teach us a lesson of some kind; in most relationships, we learn several related lessons; the purpose of these relationships in our lives is to teach us to change and move on. Some continue throughout childhood; some continue into maturity; and some last for just five minutes… We all have relationships in our lives where the lesson is complete, but we don't know how to end the relationship.

Each relationship consists of at least two people who are energetically attached in a way that is hard to sever.

The energetic connections that bind us are actually strands of energy, each strand constructed out of a different energy: the energy of love, or hatred, sadness, anger, pain, etc.

When a relationship comes to an end, it is usually hard for us to end it in a good way: A fine thread of energy is left between people, binding them to each other. This energetic thread makes us think of the person from time to time, even when the connection is long over. Sometimes, this thread tangles with our lives uninvited, like a shoelace that comes untied and trails along the floor—and that we occasionally trip over. Anger and pain can bind us to people beyond time and space and, unfortunately, most of us find it very difficult to release ourselves from past events and people who were once in our lives.

Release rituals are intended to liberate the person from unresolved connections that disrupt their life. A Release Ritual can help someone end an old relationship from which they can't disconnect, release themselves from relationships today that aren't good for them, and even release relationships with people who have died, leaving us with a sense of pain and loss. We frequently repress the wounds of the past, although we know that the wounds created are not healed by repression. A Release Ritual enables us to cleanse past wounds and heal.

Release Rituals can help us part from people who harm us; end relationships that hurt us; release ourselves from previous relationships that stop us from moving on in our present lives; "cleanse" what is troubling us and part from the pain and wrongs done to us; part from old anger and unfinished business accompanying us. A Release Ritual can help us to move on, progress and create our present and future lives in the best possible way, without the burden of the past on our shoulders.

The Release Ritual has three main effects:

1. The release of unfinished business
2. The release of automatic reactions in the present
3. Release and the ability to take beneficial action in the future

The Release Ritual helps release physical and mental illness and various kinds of addictions (addiction to compulsive eating, addiction to smoking cigarettes, etc.).

We often need more than one Release Ritual to release a group, person, habit or illness.

It is advisable to repeat each Release Ritual at least three times; we can do so as many times as we wish.

Most people fear doing a Release Ritual at first because fear of releasing the familiar and the known is very strong, and fear of loneliness is the greatest existential fear of all. We need to remember that the Release Ritual frees our lives from those for whom it is time to go, enabling us to continue our path in the best possible way.

328 | Noah Goldhirsh

After doing the Release Ritual, we may expect the following results:

- The person/group/illness we have released will completely vanish from our lives
- The person/group will remain in our lives, but our relationship will be cleansed and improve
- The illness or habit will gradually fade until it disappears

Some of the people we have released will attempt to get in touch immediately after the Release Ritual, for, although they don't know we have released them, they sense it energetically and one way or another, they will try to maintain the relationship with us. Remember that renewing the relationship or not is always our choice to make and we have the right to disconnect from those we believe are not good for us.

Carrying out the Release Ritual is rather like stopping a rope-pulling contest where two parties are each holding the end of a rope and pulling with all their might. Each party is sure they are in the right, saying: "I'm right. The other party must apologize and/or change."

Both sides could continue the argument forever, each one pulling their side of the rope... but the moment one of the parties lets go of the rope, the other party has nothing to hold onto. The rope is useless. It is no longer attached to the other party. The release is effective for both parties, even if it is difficult for one of the parties to admit it.

When releasing someone who has died, the person releasing them is energetically relieved because they enable themselves to continue their life without constantly thinking about the deceased. Consequently, the soul of the deceased is also relieved because it can move on, fulfilling its missions in the world beyond.

The Release Ritual is very important and is enormously helpful in cases of sexual abuse, rape, etc., after which the victim is left attached to the abuser by a terrible thread of fear, hatred and pain.

The Release Ritual facilitates a release of trapped emotions and helps the victim return to life.

A NATIVE AMERICAN RELEASE RITUAL

This ritual is enacted only in daylight, outside the home, and it is advisable to carry it out under a tree.

A large tree should be chosen, somewhere private and as secluded as possible, near a pool (sea, river, lake, etc.), or standing under a tree on the top of a mountain overlooking the sea.

In the event there is no tree nearby, the Release Ritual can be carried out on the seashore, near the water.

A bottle of water should be prepared in advance and placed nearby. We can release:

- Someone who is in our life
- Someone we have parted from
- Someone who has died
- A group of people
- A habit we wish to stop
- An illness from which we wish to recover
- Anything that impedes us and hampers our lives

Standing at ease, we imagine as clearly as we can the person, group of people, or the habit or illness we wish to release. We raise the palms of our hands in the air, holding them out in the following way:

Right-handed people: The palm of the right hand turned downward, the palm of the left hand turned upward (right—roof, left—vessel).

Left-handed people: The left hand turned downward, the right palm turned upward (left—roof, right—vessel).

We imagine we are holding hands (virtually only!) with whoever or whatever we wish to release, observing energetically what we wish to release, speaking the entire Release Ritual aloud.

332 | Noah Goldhirsh

THE NATIVE AMERICAN RELEASE RITUAL FORMULA

_____(Full name) _____(person's affiliation with me) I ask your forgiveness for everything that has happened between us in this life or any other.

_____(Full name)_____(affiliation) I forgive you for everything that has happened between us in this life or any other.

_____(Full name) _____(affiliation) I forgive myself for everything that has happened between us in this life or any other.

_____(Full name) _____(affiliation) I release you with love!

At the end of the ritual, after speaking the four sentences, shake your hands in the air and wash them with the water from the bottle. If you are near the sea, you can wash your hands in seawater.

The energetic meaning of the ritual is determined by the name we say at the beginning of each release sentence.

When wishing to release someone specific, we say clearly at the beginning of each sentence the full name and their affiliation to us, for example: "Reuven Levy, my father." If we don't know the person's name, we describe them and their affiliation as accurately as possible, for example: "The commander of the camp, where I served in the army."

When wishing to release a group of some kind, we speak the name of the group and its affiliation with us—for example: "All the children in my class in primary school," "All the people who served in the army with me," etc.

When wishing to release an illness, we speak the name of the illness, affiliating it with us, for example: "My headache"...

When wishing to release a habit, for example, overeating, we say: "My overeating"... When wishing to release an addiction, for example, addiction to cigarettes, we say: "cigarettes (the brand)... that I smoke"...

It is crucial to state clearly who and what we are releasing, so that the release will be energetically clear, speaking loudly and clearly so that we can hear ourselves.

The Release Ritual consists only of beneficial words and the release works both in terms of relationships in this lifetime and in previous lifetimes.

Make sure to release only when you wish to, and only if you have decided to and are sure of your actions!

Curiously enough, the release works even if you don't mean what you say—that is, you can recite the Release Ritual even if you are angry at the person/illness/addiction, etc. and don't really forgive them.

If it is very hard and you don't feel you are completely liberated, repeat the Release Ritual three times over until you feel relieved (that is: a whole Release Ritual—washing of hands; a whole Release Ritual —washing of hands; a whole Release Ritual—washing of hands and end).

The Native American Release Ritual is intended to liberate us from all the factors within and outside ourselves that brought us to the relationship, harmed our energy and caused a problem or our illness.

When we release a bad memory we have kept in our hearts for years, insults hurled at us and that have remained alive inside us, past mistakes and hard experiences—we release ourselves in the best possible way in order to live, cleansed and energetic, in the present. There is no need to drag the past behind us; with the help of the Release Ritual it is possible to leave the past behind, for ourselves and others, the situations we were in, learn from the past, move on authentically to healing and change, reminding ourselves that we are different today than in the past.

Releasing the past and giving up thoughts of wrongs done to us are extremely important, for in this way we give up many of the thoughts that distract our minds and disturb our lives. After a Release Ritual, many of our thoughts become irrelevant and disappear. With the aid of the Release Ritual, we can let go of the past, move on as we wish, without the heavy weight we have carried in our hearts and minds, free to recreate ourselves and our futures.

With the aid of the Release Ritual, we relinquish our anger and the desire for revenge—for when we forgive ourselves and others, we have no further need for anger, revenge and loss of energy invested in various strange thoughts and plans for revenge.

The Release Ritual enables us to part from thoughts of anger, deprivation, insult, sorrow and pain, and recover from sensations of worthlessness, loneliness and helplessness. When we are freed from all the negative energy that we have carried with us over the years, we can live our lives in love and joy, completing the journey of our lives in the best possible way.

THE END ... AND A NEW BEGINNING

Many people come to me to learn how to change their life for the better. We all reach significant crossroads in our lives where we ask ourselves: "What should I do? Which direction should I take? Who will help me find the real answer?" All the answers are within us.

I teach people to look inward and find the answers to their questions in stillness.

The best way to find answers to our questions is to close our eyes and, in deep mindfulness, gaze inward.

Allow yourself to listen to your inner voice and grow.

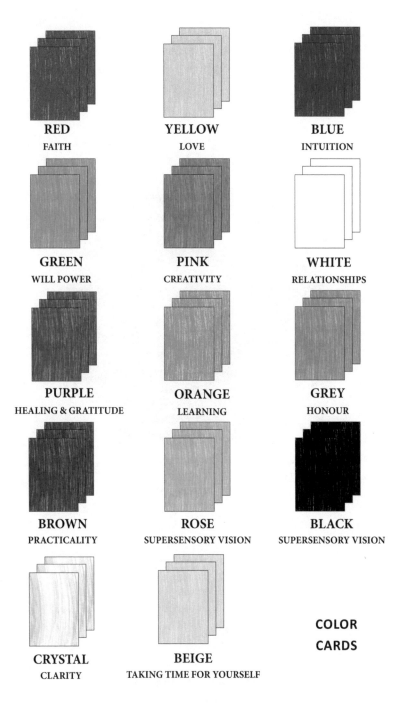

| **RED** | **YELLOW** | **BLUE** |
| FAITH | LOVE | INTUITION |

| **GREEN** | **PINK** | **WHITE** |
| WILL POWER | CREATIVITY | RELATIONSHIPS |

| **PURPLE** | **ORANGE** | **GREY** |
| HEALING & GRATITUDE | LEARNING | HONOUR |

| **BROWN** | **ROSE** | **BLACK** |
| PRACTICALITY | SUPERSENSORY VISION | SUPERSENSORY VISION |

| **CRYSTAL** | **BEIGE** | |
| CLARITY | TAKING TIME FOR YOURSELF | |

**COLOR
CARDS**

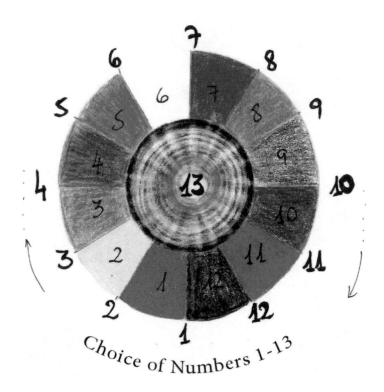

Choice of Numbers 1-13

THE CLASSIC WHEEL

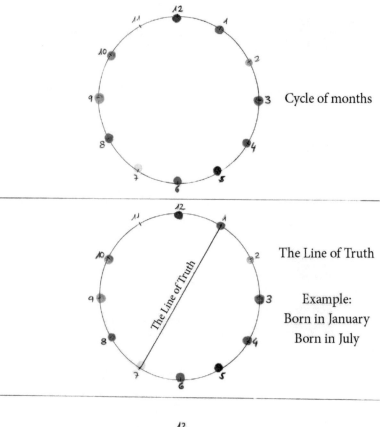

Cycle of months

The Line of Truth

Example:
Born in January
Born in July

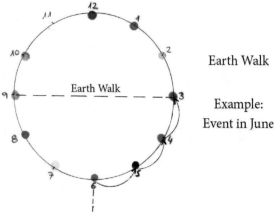

Earth Walk

Example:
Event in June

ASTROLOGY IN COLORS

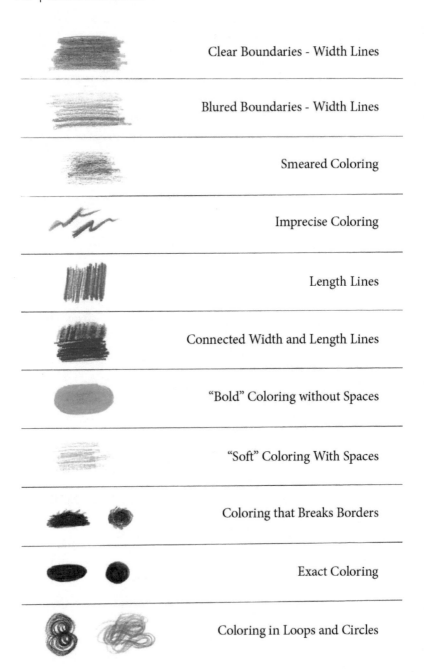

Clear Boundaries - Width Lines

Blured Boundaries - Width Lines

Smeared Coloring

Imprecise Coloring

Length Lines

Connected Width and Length Lines

"Bold" Coloring without Spaces

"Soft" Coloring With Spaces

Coloring that Breaks Borders

Exact Coloring

Coloring in Loops and Circles

WAYS OF COLORING

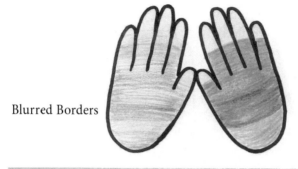

"Kissing" Hands

Width Lines
Clear Borders

Blurred Borders

Hand on Hand

Smeared Coloring

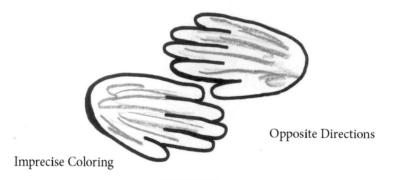

Opposite Directions

Imprecise Coloring

HAND DRAWING

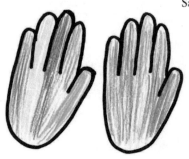

"Rainbow"

Same Hand Twice

Length Lines

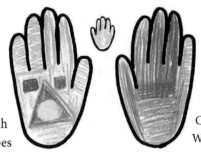

Drawing with
Specific Shapes

Third Hand

Combination Coloring
Width and Length Lines

One Hand

"Bold" Coloring
No Spaces

HAND DRAWING

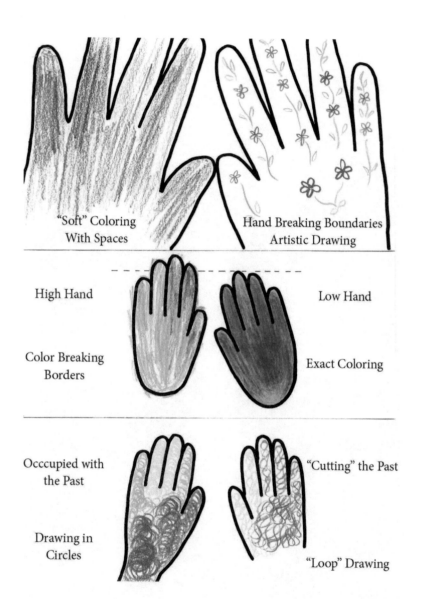

"Soft" Coloring
With Spaces

Hand Breaking Boundaries
Artistic Drawing

High Hand

Low Hand

Color Breaking
Borders

Exact Coloring

Occcupied with
the Past

"Cutting" the Past

Drawing in
Circles

"Loop" Drawing

HAND DRAWING

HEALING BRACELETS